The Long Shadow of Lincoln's Gettysburg Address

The Long Shadow of Lincoln's Gettysburg Address

Jared Peatman

For Bob and Carey,

With thanks for the friendship and best wishes for the future.

Jared Peatman

Southern Illinois University Press
Carbondale

16 15 14 13   4 3 2 1

Library of Congress Cataloging-in-Publication Data
Peatman, Jared.
The long shadow of Lincoln's Gettysburg Address /
Jared Peatman.
    pages cm
Includes bibliographical references and index.
    ISBN 978-0-8093-3310-3 (cloth : alk. paper)
    ISBN 0-8093-3310-4 (cloth : alk. paper)
    ISBN 978-0-8093-3311-0 (ebook)
    ISBN 0-8093-3311-2 (ebook)
1. Lincoln, Abraham, 1809–1865. Gettysburg
address. 2. Lincoln, Abraham, 1809–1865—Oratory.
I. Title.
E475.55.P34 2013
973.7092—dc23   2013011015

For my family

Thy name shall be Abraham, for a father
of many nations have I made thee.

—Genesis 17:5

Contents

Figures

Acknowledgments

I spent over ten years working on this project, off and on, and thus owe debts of sincere gratitude to a significant number of people without whom I never could have brought this book to fruition. I began the project in 2001 as an undergraduate in one of Gabor Boritt's Lincoln seminars, and he has encouraged this book's progress over the last decade. At Virginia Tech, my committee of James I. Robertson Jr., William C. Davis, Kathleen Jones, Neil Shumsky, and Peter Wallenstein helped sharpen my loose collection of ideas into a presentable thesis on Southern responses to the Gettysburg Address. Additionally, Dan Thorp, Rob Stephens, Justin Nystrom, and Jack Atkins offered both help and encouragement. At Texas A&M University, April Hatfield graciously agreed to serve as my chair despite her busy schedule and differing research interests. Julia Kirk Blackwelder, Cynthia Bouton, Peter Hugill, Andrew Kirkendall, and Harold Livesay rounded out the committee and provided an amazing breadth of knowledge. I am honored that such an illustrious bunch of scholars would spend so much of their time helping with my project. Additionally, Walter Kamphoefner championed my work from the beginning though not formally serving on the committee.

My graduate career would not have been possible without substantial financial support. At Virginia Tech, I am honored to have received support from the history department, as well as the Frank S. Roop Memorial Scholarship and a Virginia Tech Graduate Research Development Program grant. At Texas A&M, funding came from the history department, Melbern G. Glasscock Center for the Humanities, Cushing Library, College of Liberal Arts, and the Office of Graduate Studies. Additionally, a Gilder Lehrman Institute Short Term Fellowship in 2009 provided for a week's research in New York. Lastly, I thank the respective committee members for the 2009 Organization of American Historians/

Abraham Lincoln Bicentennial Commission Doctoral Fellowship and the 2012 Hay-Nicolay Dissertation Prize.

A host of other people was essential to this project, some even before I formally started the work. Jim Ramsey encouraged my fascination with the Civil War and provided an outlet for my studies through my secondary school career. As an undergraduate, I spent four great years working at the Gettysburg College Civil War Institute as Gabor Boritt's research assistant. In addition to Dr. Boritt, Diane Brennan, Pam Dalrymple, and Tina Grim provided an enjoyable office atmosphere. Fellow students Tim Parry, Ian Harkness, and Katie Porch have remained loyal friends. Fellow alumnus Pete Vermilyea has become a close friend and trusted colleague who provided a thorough reading of the manuscript. In 2000, Harold Holzer and Frank Williams invited me to present a paper at the Lincoln Forum. It was that experience that eventually led me to apply to graduate school. In Danville, Virginia, Jason Gibson was more help than he knows. At Texas A&M, fellow graduate student William Francis Collopy was, and remains, equal parts mentor and friend; our frequent discussions about life and history over a "slice" are some of my fondest memories. At the Abraham Lincoln Presidential Library, James Cornelius was both kind and helpful and pointed me toward a number of new sources. Over the past two years, the good folks at the Lincoln Leadership Institute of Gettysburg—Steve Wiley, Angela Sontheimer, Shari Boyd, Jill Ingalsbe, Joe Mieczkowski, and General James Anderson—have become my colleagues and, more important, friends. Walt Besecker has served as a gracious mentor and advocate as I forayed into a new vocation.

Gettysburg College's Peter Carmichael was instrumental both in pushing me to finish the revisions and in assisting with the search for a publisher. At Southern Illinois University Press, editor Sylvia Frank Rodrigue has been wonderfully encouraging and professional. I will always appreciate her efforts to expedite things to get this book published in 2013. Additionally, the two outside readers offered comments best described as encouraging constructive criticism. The manuscript is much stronger due to their suggestions.

My family has been the greatest source of support and encouragement. I owe more than I can ever say to my grandmother Rebecca, who is convinced I am the best historian in the world, my mother, Kathy, and my father, Bernie, who all have supported and encouraged my Civil

War obsession from the age of twelve. Over the past six years, my wife, Melinda Wilson, has made life truly wonderful. Being with someone so special gives some perspective when I cannot track down that elusive source. My stepchildren, Trent and Allison, have also been encouraging, although I can tell they sometimes wish I talked about Lincoln a little less. The last round of revisions was completed with our family's newest member, baby Dawes, sitting in my lap. I expect his first words to be, "Four score . . ."

Associated Press Transcription of the Gettysburg Address

This is the version of the speech that most Americans saw in the 1860s as it was widely printed in newspapers around the country and, thus, is the version that is cited and used in chapters 1 and 2.

Four score and seven years ago our fathers brought forth upon this continent a new Nation, conceived in Liberty, and dedicated to the proposition that all men are created equal. [Applause.] Now we are engaged in a great civil war, testing whether that Nation or any Nation so conceived and so dedicated can long endure. We are met on a great battle-field of that war. We are met to dedicate a portion of it as the final resting-place of those who here gave their lives that that nation might live. It is altogether fitting and proper that we should do this. But in a larger sense we cannot dedicate, we cannot consecrate, we cannot hallow this ground. The brave men living and dead who struggled here have consecrated it far above our power to add or detract. [Applause.] The world will little note nor long remember what we say here, but it can never forget what they did here. [Applause.] It is for us, the living, rather to be dedicated here to the refinished work that they have thus far so nobly carried on. [Applause.] It is rather for us to be here dedicated to the great task remaining before us, that from these honored dead we take increased devotion to that cause for which they here gave the last full measure of devotion; that we here highly resolve that the dead shall not have died in vain [Applause]; that the nation shall, under God, have a new birth of freedom; and that Governments of the people, by the people, and for the people, shall not perish from the earth. [Long-continued applause.]

Lincoln, "Address Delivered at the Dedication of the Cemetery at Gettysburg," November 19, 1863, Newspaper Version, *CW*, 7:19–21.

Bliss Version of the Gettysburg Address

By the early 1900s, the "Bliss" copy of the Gettysburg Address, the fifth and final copy that Lincoln wrote out by hand on March 18, 1864, had become most prevalent. Robert Todd Lincoln announced his preference for this version, and it is the one that was inscribed on the walls of the Lincoln Memorial in 1922. Beginning with chapter 3, unless otherwise noted, all references to the speech use this version. Chapter 3 discusses the different versions of the speech and the move for an "authorized" text.

Four score and seven years ago our fathers brought forth on this continent, a new nation, conceived in Liberty, and dedicated to the proposition that all men are created equal.

Now we are engaged in a great civil war, testing whether that nation, or any nation so conceived and so dedicated, can long endure. We are met on a great battle-field of that war. We have come to dedicate a portion of that field, as a final resting place for those who here gave their lives that that nation might live. It is altogether fitting and proper that we should do this.

But, in a larger sense, we can not dedicate—we can not consecrate—we can not hallow—this ground. The brave men, living and dead, who struggled here, have consecrated it, far above our poor power to add or detract. The world will little note, nor long remember what we say here, but it can never forget what they did here. It is for us the living, rather, to be dedicated here to the unfinished work which they who fought here have thus far so nobly advanced. It is rather for us to be here dedicated to the great task remaining before us—that from these honored dead we take increased devotion to that cause for which they gave the last full measure of devotion—that we here highly resolve that these dead shall not have died in vain—that this nation, under God, shall have a new birth of freedom—and that government of the people, by the people, for the people, shall not perish from the earth.

Lincoln, "Address Delivered at the Dedication of the Cemetery at Gettysburg," November 19, 1863, Final Text, *CW*, 7:22–23.

The Long Shadow of Lincoln's Gettysburg Address

Introduction

> It will live, that speech. Fifty years from now American
> school-boys will be learning it as part of their education.
> —Mary Raymond Shipman Andrews, "The Perfect Tribute" (1906)

As the passengers neared Gettysburg on November 17, 1963, they must
have reflected, at least briefly, on events a hundred years in the past.
Just one day short of a full century earlier, Secretary of State William
Henry Seward accompanied President Abraham Lincoln to the dedication of the Soldiers' National Cemetery in Gettysburg. Seward was joined
by the ambassadors from France and Italy, with the Canadian minister
representing Great Britain. Now, Secretary of State Dean Rusk, French
ambassador Hervé Alphand, Italian ambassador Sergio Fenoaltea, and
British minister John Chadwick followed in their predecessors' footsteps
by returning to Gettysburg to celebrate the great speech. Though their
presence was a nod to the past, their mode of arrival most certainly was
not: The diplomats touched down in a helicopter.[1]

That three foreign dignitaries and the American secretary of state
would take the time to commemorate the Gettysburg Address in the
midst of the Cold War reveals how much meaning Lincoln's words had
taken on over the preceding century, both at home and abroad. In 1913,
British Earl George Curzon referred to the Gettysburg Address as "part
of the intellectual patrimony of the English-speaking race," and during
the world wars, a number of statues were erected across Britain featuring
lines from the speech.[2] Italy's Fenoaltea commented that day, "Lincoln's
address holds its rightful place among the immortal messages which the
idealism of the new World has conveyed to the old," echoing Giuseppe
Garibaldi's categorization of Abraham Lincoln in 1863 as the "pilot of
liberty," a comment that also aptly describes his famous speech.[3] Perhaps
most impressive, the constitution France adopted on October 4, 1958,

notes, "*Son principe est: gouvernement du peuple, par le peuple et pour le peuple* [Its principle is: government of the people, by the people, and for the people]."[4]

For his part, Rusk asserted, "Our commitments to freedom are the sources of our foreign policy. They explain . . . our concerns about our failures here at home to live up fully to our own great commitments. . . . [W]e will not be at ease until every one of our own citizens enjoys in full the rights pledged by the Declaration of Independence and our Constitution." As to how those commitments were known abroad, Rusk continued, "The central commitments of the American experiment are probably known to more people in other lands through the words of the Gettysburg Address than through those of the Declaration of Independence." Reflecting on why that particular speech held such a position, Rusk stated, "What makes it great and enduring is the simple eloquence with which it restates the ideas to which this nation is dedicated: 'liberty . . . the proposition that all men are created equal . . . government of the people, by the people, for the people.'"[5]

Finally, after a century, the majority of the nation had accepted Lincoln's complete message in the Gettysburg Address.

Though some historians have argued that the nation periodically forgot about the Gettysburg Address, the words never passed from view. But Lincoln's meaning did. In his 1992 Pulitzer Prize–winning *Lincoln at Gettysburg: The Words That Remade America*, Gary Wills contends the Gettysburg Address "not only put the Declaration in a new light as a matter of founding *law*, but put its central proposition, equality, in a newly favored position as a principle of the Constitution." Wills was certainly correct; Abraham Lincoln intended the Gettysburg Address as his most *eloquent* statement that a *democracy* could only persist with *equality* at its core. But Wills implies that this shift, "[o]ne of most daring acts of open-air sleight-of-hand ever witnessed by the unsuspecting," was almost immediately effective and "remade" America in the 1860s. Historian Gabor Boritt's *Gettysburg Gospel* slightly revises Wills and, as Boritt notes, "considers how Lincoln's speech rose to be American Gospel, the Good News, for it was not that at birth." According to Boritt, that rise began in 1876.[6] This book posits a different trajectory.

Since the nation as a whole was unready to commit to equality in 1863, neither was it ready to accept Lincoln's full message. In the ensuing century, groups wishing to advance a particular position utilized specific parts of the speech that echoed their stance while ignoring the rest, hijacking Lincoln's meaning for their own ends. Historian David Blight has discussed this "theft" of Lincoln: "Lincoln has long been infinitely malleable," in part due to his "essential ambiguity," as David Donald describes it.[7] Despite that, as the nation slowly moved toward fulfilling the promise of a democracy with equality, those invoking Lincoln's speech came ever closer to recovering his true purpose. That process culminated in 1963 at the height of both the Cold War and Civil Rights Movement when Americans rediscovered the central message of the Gettysburg Address as they increasingly accepted in their everyday life the inextricable link between a commitment to equality and the continuance of democratic government.

Thus, the Gettysburg Address did not "remake" America in the 1860s, as Wills posits, nor did it "rise" beginning in 1876, as Boritt suggests, culminating at the turn of the century when Americans would "begin to turn the text into a revered document, and find the meaning of their country there."[8] Rather, from the beginning, the words had been in the public eye but not until the 1960s would popular uses of the speech recapture Lincoln's original message and, thus, become a revered document essential to American national identity.

Scholars, including Wills and A. E. Elmore, have expertly and convincingly explored the ideas and words that shaped Lincoln's philosophy behind the Gettysburg Address, while William Barton, Louis Warren, Boritt, and others have examined the events that occurred in Gettysburg before, during, and after the dedication of the Soldiers' National Cemetery. This book covers those two topics but focuses on later invocations of the speech, predominantly in the twentieth century. Rather than covering every time period, the focus is on key moments that illustrate the evolving place of the Gettysburg Address in both American and international discourse. In his landmark work on French history, Pierre Nora comments that memories "buttress our identities, but if what they defended were not threatened, there would be no need for them."[9] Consequently, the Gettysburg Address has been most frequently invoked when the United States faced some type of turmoil, whether during domestic crises like the Populist, Progressive, or Civil Rights Movements or international affairs like the world wars or Cold War. In each case, historical actors introduced the Gettysburg Address to establish a connection between their position and Lincoln's iconic speech. In the 1960s, with the United States facing domestic issues dealing with race and international issues over democracy, the Address was referenced in the *New York Times* on 208 occasions. Over the next decade, when those issues receded, the Address was referenced just 96 times.

Before looking at those critical moments, this work begins with a review of the events that took place in Gettysburg from the end of the battle through the dedication ceremonies on November 19, 1863, arguing that one cannot understand the significance of Lincoln's words and the extent to which his message was lost for nearly a century without knowing what led him to Gettysburg and the specific words he and the other orators spoke that day. That Lincoln was likely asked to speak at the cemetery as early as August 28, 1863, and that his most famous line was pulled from an abolitionist orator are two revelations that should challenge how we think of both the organizers' and Lincoln's goals for his speech. The immediate responses to the day's events in New York, Gettysburg, Confederate Richmond, and London show how intensely parochial concerns and political affiliations shaped initial coverage of all the speeches delivered that day and even led to the censoring of Lincoln's words in some locales. The regional divisions established in this era persisted throughout the period under study.

After discussing the immediate responses to the speech, this book moves to 1901, the last time for over seventy years that a Southern African American would serve in Congress, and considers responses in the first twenty-two years of the twentieth century, closing with the dedication of the Lincoln Memorial in 1922. In this era, the dominant message was one of reunification (though not necessarily reconciliation), and the parts of the Gettysburg Address that could be used to advance that objective were invoked while the others were largely ignored. This was the first time since the end of the Civil War that a systematic use for the Gettysburg Address toward a particular end can be perceived. During the world wars, the speech was used to promote American democracy and rally the citizenry to defend that institution. As a result of the global nature of the period, it was during this time that the speech truly gained international status. In 1921, people from both sides of the Irish independence issue invoked the speech as supporting their side; in the 1940s, China's two competing leaders, Chiang Kai-shek and Mao Tse-tung, also saw the document as buttressing their particular beliefs against the other. Together, these two stories reveal the incredible reach of the speech and illustrate that those co-opting Lincoln's intended message did not solely reside in America.[10]

An international lens is essential to understanding the status of the Address during the Lincoln birth sesquicentennial and Civil War centennial commemorations from 1959 to 1963. The era suffered from strife at home due largely to the Civil Rights Movement and abroad with the Cold War, and interpretations of the Gettysburg Address depended on the speaker, audience, and subject. However, it was during this period that those invoking the speech began to do so in a way that preserved the coherent whole of Lincoln's argument rather than focusing on one component to the exclusion of others.

In addition to these dominant narratives, each era featured one or more counternarratives—in some cases, African Americans or their supporters who encouraged the nation to remember Lincoln's first line, in other cases unreconstructed Southerners who disavowed the speech's lines about democracy even in eras when most Americans supported Lincoln's call for "government of the people, by the people, for the people." The dominant narrative was ultimately controlled by those who were most successful in appropriating—or stealing, as Blight would say—Lincoln for their cause, while the counternarratives came from those whose invocations of Lincoln had not gained mainstream acceptance. Finally, the current volume's epilogue looks at the diversity of ways the speech has been interpreted and used since 1963, an era in which the speech has been invoked everywhere from the Camp David Summit of 1978 to the Hollywood comedy *Bill & Ted's Excellent Adventure*.

Every salesman needs a pitch, and over time, increasing numbers of Americans came to see the Gettysburg Address as the most effective way to sell the ideals of this country, both internally and externally. While early salesmen used *either* the passages about democracy *or* those about equality, later proponents realized the whole package was stronger than the component parts and reconnected Lincoln's original conception of the necessity of equality within a democracy. In so doing, the nation took one step closer to becoming the "city upon a hill" envisioned by its settlers over three centuries earlier.

1

The Final Resting Place: The Creation and Dedication of the Soldiers' National Cemetery

> It is the desire that, after the Oration, You as Chief Executive of the Nation formally set apart these grounds to their Sacred use by a few appropriate remarks.
> —David Wills to Abraham Lincoln, November 2, 1863

Three days of intense conflict, July 1–3, 1863, at Gettysburg, Pennsylvania, left the borough with a butcher's toll of fifty-one thousand casualties, including an estimated seven thousand dead humans and five thousand horses. Put another way, six million pounds of flesh lay on once peaceful farm fields. The horses were burned; most of the humans were buried by Union soldiers where they fell. The Confederates remained in their graves until the soldiers were moved to southern burial grounds in the early 1870s. Approximately fifteen hundred of the Union deceased were recovered and returned home, but the high cost of embalming and shipping bodies meant 70 percent of the Union dead remained in Gettysburg.[1]

At the end of July 1863, local lawyer David Wills described, "Our dead are lying on the fields unburied (that is no grave being dug), with small portions of earth dug up alongside of the body and thrown over it. In many instance arms and legs, and sometimes heads, protrude, and my attention has been directed to several places where the hogs were actually rooting out the bodies and devouring them."[2] When Pennsylvania Governor Andrew Curtin visited Gettysburg just days after the battle, he asked Wills to act as his local agent and to ensure the proper care for the state's fallen heroes. Thus began the process that brought Abraham Lincoln to Gettysburg four months later (see fig. 1.1).

Figure 1.1. *Abraham Lincoln*, Sunday, November 8, 1863. Photograph by Alexander Gardner. Prints and Photographs Division, Library of Congress.

This chapter details the development of the Soldiers' National Cemetery, but more important, it explores the fundamental question of why Lincoln went to Gettysburg, what message he tried to convey, and what factors ensured that his vision would be largely rebuffed in 1863. In the middle of a war whose direction consumed every possible moment of his time, Lincoln took nearly two days to travel to Gettysburg so that he could speak for fewer than three minutes. The Emancipation Proclamation, signed on January 1, 1863, had dealt slavery a blow but only a half blow, for it made no mention of equality and was written in such a pragmatic and legalistic tone that historian Richard Hofstadter once commented it had "all the moral grandeur of bill of lading."[3] Lincoln clearly wanted to go further, telling Congress in December 1862, "We know how to save the Union. The world knows we do know how to save it. We—even *we here*—hold the power, and bear the responsibility. In *giving* freedom to the *slave*, we *assure* freedom to the *free*—honorable alike in what we give, and what we preserve."[4]

Nearly a year later, many had not accepted Lincoln's vision, and, consequently, he intended the Gettysburg Address as his most eloquent statement that a democracy could only persist with equality at its core. Lincoln was not the only speaker at Gettysburg, however, and to understand the immediate reactions to his speech (outlined in chapter 2), one must know not only his intent but also what the other orators said.

The job facing Wills was unimaginable in scope but would prove himself up to the task. An 1851 graduate of Pennsylvania College, Wills went on to study law under the abolitionist Congressman Thaddeus Stevens and gained admission to the bar in 1854. That same year, Wills became the first superintendent of the Adams County Public Schools, showing his prominence in the community. As befitted a Stevens protégé, Wills was a pro-abolition Republican. It was not surprising when the politically like-minded Governor Curtin appointed Wills his local agent just a week after the battle.[5]

Until at least July 20, no plan existed to create a cemetery for the soldiers in Gettysburg. In those first few weeks, Wills attempted to locate and identify the remains of Pennsylvanians and return them to their families. Theodore Dimon, New York's agent in charge of taking care of the state's deceased soldiers at Gettysburg, claimed a national cemetery was his brainchild:

> It seeming to me impracticable to have *all* these removed to their former homes, and especially in the case of the more distant States. I concluded, after much consideration of the matter to present it to several gentlemen, from the various States interested, who were at Gettysburg. At my request, therefore, a meeting was held at the office of David Wills, Esquire, agent of the State of Pennsylvania. At this meeting I presented a proposition that a portion of the ground occupied by our line of battle on Cemetery Hill should be purchased for a permanent burial place for the soldiers.[6]

Wills maintained that the idea was his. It is unlikely that anyone will ever know for certain who originated the idea for the cemetery, but on

July 24, 1863, Wills submitted a plan to Governor Curtin identifying Cemetery Hill, the key to the Union position during the battle, as the ideal location for the cemetery. The lawyer urged Curtin to act quickly as he "was afraid the owners of the land might be operated on by speculators." Curtin agreed and authorized Wills to begin purchasing the land.

Wills's fear of speculators proved a reality. On July 25, David McConaughy, a Republican lawyer and the president of the local Evergreen Cemetery, told Curtin he had purchased the land in question and was attaching it to the town cemetery, where he would bury the soldiers at a cost of $5 per body. Additionally, McConaughy announced a plan to raise a monument in the cemetery and boldly asked the governor to make the first contribution.[7]

On August 3, Wills notified Curtin that he and the other state agents agreed that the cemetery needed to be national in outlook and "independent of local influences and control," such as those McConaughy was trying to exert. Realizing that Curtin would not allow the burial of Pennsylvania's dead in the town cemetery, McConaughy offered the land to the state at cost. On August 13, Wills notified Curtin that he and the other state agents had agreed that the expense of the cemetery would be shared by all the states according to their representation in Congress.[8] In 1872, the cemetery would be ceded to the Department of War, but the original plan was for this to be a cemetery inaugurated and run by the individual states that had soldiers at the battle. By mid-August, Wills had purchased five parcels of land comprising seventeen acres atop Cemetery Hill and adjacent to the Evergreen Cemetery and called on William Saunders, a landscape gardener and rural architect from the Department of Agriculture, to design the cemetery. By arranging the graves in a semi-circle, Saunders took advantage of the oddly shaped land while ensuring that no state received a more privileged position than any other.[9]

While Saunders designed the cemetery, Wills gave serious thought to the dedication ceremonies. In late August, Governor Curtin implored Wills to see to "the proper consecration of the grounds."[10] There was little question as to who should give the dedicatory oration; sixty-nine-year-old Edward Everett was the obvious choice. In 1863, Everett held no political office but was invited to Gettysburg because he was the foremost orator of the day. After graduating from Harvard at the age of seventeen in 1811, Everett served five terms in the House of Representatives, won four terms as the governor of Massachusetts, was the secretary of state in 1850, and served in the U.S. Senate for eighteen months. A staunch Whig and Unionist, Everett was the vice-presidential candidate of the Constitutional-Union Party in 1860 and, thus, had run against Lincoln. Despite these offices, Everett was more known for his speaking ability, as evidenced by the four volumes of his speeches then in print. His oration on George Washington, which he delivered 134 times in the 1850s, earned nearly $70,000 towards the purchase and preservation of the first president's home, Mount Vernon. All told, Everett earned over $100,000 in royalties for his speeches. Everett combined oratorical excellence with political insight, making him an ideal choice to deliver the dedicatory address.[11]

On September 23, Boston Mayor F. W. Lincoln privately inquired whether Everett would prepare and deliver an oration at the dedication of the cemetery. Everett indicated his acceptance, and that same day, Wills sent a formal invitation. Everett replied that he would be happy to take part in the ceremonies but could not possibly prepare an appropriate address before November 19. Wills agreed to the change.[12]

On November 2, 1863, Wills sent President Lincoln the following:

> Sir,
> The Several States having Soldiers in the Army of the Potomac, who were killed at the Battle of Gettysburg, or have since died at the various hospitals which were established in the vicinity, have procured grounds on a prominent part of the Battle Field for a Cemetery, and are having the dead removed to them and properly buried.
>
> These Grounds will be Consecrated and set apart to this Sacred purpose, by appropriate Ceremonies, on Thursday, the 19th instant.
>
> Hon Edward Everett will deliver the Oration.
>
> I am authorized by the Governors of the different States to invite you to be present, and participate in these Ceremonies, which will doubtless be very imposing and solemnly impressive.
>
> It is the desire that, after the Oration, you, as Chief Executive of the Nation, formally set apart these grounds to their Sacred use by a few appropriate remarks.[13]

Traditionally, historians cite this as Lincoln's first invitation to Gettysburg and, due to the late date, conclude that the organizers did not really want Lincoln at the event—either because he was a poor stump speaker or because he would steal the show—or at least did not envision more than a ceremonial role for him. The idea of a late invitation worked hand-in-hand with the myth of Lincoln writing his address on the back of an envelope on the train to Gettysburg to show that his remarks were essentially off the cuff. In reality, nothing could be further from the truth.[14]

On October 13, nearly three weeks before the formal invitation, the *Philadelphia Inquirer* reported that Wills told its Baltimore correspondent that Lincoln was "expected to perform the consecrational service" at the cemetery's dedication. Two days later, Gettysburg's *Star and Banner* ran a column titled "Consecration of the Soldiers' National Cemetery" that noted, "Edward Everett is to deliver the dedicational oration. President Lincoln will also be present and participate in the ceremonies." On October 19, Gettysburg's *Compiler* printed the identical column that had appeared four days earlier in the *Star and Banner*. An early article on the upcoming ceremonies published in the October 6 *Adams Sentinel* reported that Everett would deliver the oration but made no mention of Lincoln or any role he might play. It seems the press became aware of Lincoln's intended role in the ceremonies between October 6 and October 12.[15]

Another piece of circumstantial evidence supports the case for an earlier invitation. On August 28, Curtin visited Lincoln in Washington, D.C. Newspapers the following day stated that the men discussed draft quotas for Pennsylvania, but a letter Curtin wrote Lincoln on September 4 hints at another topic. The four-paragraph letter is entirely concerned with the fall election and the bad effect the draft was having on Republican chances. But, Curtin stated, all was not lost: "We can carry the election beyond all question, by an active and vigorous canvass, and the cordial support of all the Departments of the Government."[16] Curtin could have been referring to any number of things, but two months later when Lincoln travelled to Gettysburg, he brought along the heads from three of the seven "Departments of the Government": William Henry Seward from State, John P. Usher from Interior, and Montgomery Blair from the Post Office. If the same method was employed to ask Lincoln to participate in the ceremonies that was used with Everett in September, it is likely that Curtin broached the subject at this late-summer meeting. Between August 28 and October 13, the date when newspapers announced Lincoln's participation, this was the only meeting between Lincoln and anyone involved with the Soldiers' National Cemetery.[17] Given Curtin's role in the establishment of the cemetery and its dedication, it is difficult to imagine he would miss this opportunity to ask Lincoln to grace his state with a visit.

It seems probable that by September, Lincoln had already agreed to be in Gettysburg and that Wills's November 2 letter was not an initial invitation to the ceremonies but a *formal* invitation. The organizers likely followed the same method as they had with Everett—a private invitation and an understanding of acceptance preceding the official request so as to avoid embarrassment in the case of a rejection. Lincoln never responded to the letter, possibly because he had already indicated his willingness to participate.

Rarely did Lincoln leave Washington, D.C., making clear that he viewed the speech at Gettysburg as an important opportunity to make a midcourse correction and define the meaning of the war. In the immediate reactions to the ceremonies, many reporters commented that as Lincoln had played only a minor role at Gettysburg, his words should be passed over lightly. However, if Lincoln was asked to participate in the dedication of the Soldiers' National Cemetery nearly a month before Everett was invited, there is a strong case to be made that the ceremony organizers conceived of Lincoln's role as a major one, perhaps even *the* major one.

The days leading up to the dedication at Gettysburg were busy with preparations. On October 15, Wills solicited bids for the removal of the bodies from the battlefield, and Frederick W. Biesecker won with a rate of $1.59 per body. In a letter to Curtin that was also printed in the local papers, Wills said, "The Contractor commenced the work on the 26th ult, and has been removing about sixty bodies daily." Originally, Wills planned to move the bodies to the cemetery after the dedication ceremonies, but since Everett moved the date back by nearly four weeks, the work had already begun before the consecration in mid-November.[18]

As the burials began, the town prepared for visitors. Wills invited the key figures to stay at his house and soon was anticipating more than thirty guests. On November 9, the *Compiler* announced a meeting to arrange accommodations for those expected to attend the cemetery dedication. Three days later, the *Star and Banner* reported, "The Committee have issued an appeal to our citizens generally to throw open their houses on the 18th and 19th and invite all who intend on furnishing eating or sleeping accommodations for compensation to send in their names. . . . [W]e take the liberty of suggesting that some uniform price should, if possible, be agreed upon—not to exceed, say, 50 cents per meal, and the same for lodging."

Harvey Sweney, a Gettysburg resident living on the town's main street, noted that in the days before the dedication ceremonies, "Nothing scarcely could be heard but the loud snort of the iron horse and the rumble of the long and heavy trains. . . . [E]very building public or private was filled and for miles around town the houses were filled with the congregated throng." With a population of twenty-four hundred, the little town overflowed with visitors. "All the rooms in the hotels were engaged several weeks ahead but our old town roused up to action. . . . Churches, public schools, town halls, all the private dwellings, barns, etc. were thrown open to receive them," Sweney wrote.[19] The townspeople provided lodging and victuals for their guests, but transportation was another matter. A reporter from the *Indianapolis Daily Journal* scoffed, "If getting away from Gettysburg is half as hard as getting to it, we shall probably have to go to Hagerstown to get across the street. Our excursion from Harrisburg was certainly the worst conceived, arranged and executed expedition of the war, not excepting the Peninsula campaign."[20]

In Washington, Lincoln worked through the morning of November 18 before boarding the train for Gettysburg at noon. Accompanying the President were cabinet members William Seward, Montgomery Blair, and John Usher. French ambassador Henri Mercier, Italian minister Joseph Bertinatti, Canadian minister William McDougall, presidential secretaries John Nicolay and John Hay, Charlotte Everett Wise (Everett's daughter), several lower-ranking public officials, military personnel, and reporters loyal to Lincoln were also on the train. That three cabinet members came to the ceremonies merely as spectators further underscores the importance of the event and that of the political situation in Pennsylvania.

A large crowd formed at the train station in Gettysburg, eager to glimpse Lincoln's arrival. Wills, Everett, and a receiving committee met and escorted Lincoln the block to Wills's house, where a formal dinner awaited. Everett, who had been in town for several days, likely anticipated an uncomfortable meal. As the Constitutional-Union Party vice-presidential candidate in 1860, Everett had run on a ticket opposing

Lincoln and had once held a low opinion of the man. In response to Lincoln's speeches during his inaugural tour, Everett commented in his journal, "These speeches thus have been of the most ordinary kind, destitute of everything, not merely of felicity and grace, but of common pertinence. He is evidently a person of very inferior cast of character, wholly unequal to the crisis." Everett had met Lincoln earlier but only briefly and was getting his first sustained exposure to him. That Charlotte Everett Wise had come to Gettysburg on the President's private train and Lincoln's genial nature at such occasions likely forestalled the potential awkwardness.[21] The President had been inside the Wills home for just a few moments when citizens called for a speech. After several minutes, Lincoln appeared in the doorway, briefly acknowledged their presence, and ducked back inside the house. The crowd was not discouraged, and during dinner, even more well-wishers congregated on the square.[22]

Meanwhile, some of Lincoln's traveling partners were having a more spirited evening. Hay commented, "McVeagh young Stanton & I foraged around for a while—walked out to the College got a chafing dish of oysters then some supper. . . . [W]e found [editor John] Forney and went around to his place Mr. Fahnestocks and drank a little whiskey." As befitted a future secretary of state (1898–1905), Hay had clearly learned to mix drinking and politicking at an early age.[23]

J. Howard Wert, a Gettysburg resident and a future historian of the era, remembered, "The square upon which the [Wills] house fronted was one dense mass of people eagerly awaiting the appearance of Mr. Lincoln. And when he did appear, never did mortal have a more enthusiastic greeting."[24] The recollections of those present are at odds as to the location of the speech; some recalled that Lincoln spoke from a second-floor window or balcony; others asserted that Lincoln stood in the doorway. Perhaps the confusion originates from the fact that Lincoln had twice already poked his head out to acknowledge serenades and possibly appeared from multiple locations over the course of the evening. Regardless of where he stood for this appearance, Lincoln waited for the crowd to quiet and then spoke but a few words[25]:

> I appear before you, fellow-citizens, merely to thank you for this compliment. The inference is a very fair one that you would hear me for a little while at least, were I to commence to make a speech. I do not appear before you for the purpose of doing so, and for several

very substantial reasons. The most substantial of these is that I have no speech to make. [Laughter.] In my position it is somewhat important that I should not say any foolish things.

A VOICE—If you can help it.

MR. LINCOLN—It very often happens that the only way to help it is to say nothing at all. [Laughter.] Believing this is my present condition this evening, I must beg of you to excuse me from addressing you further.[26]

In holding his tongue, Lincoln was likely remembering several embarrassing moments in the past two years when he had made impromptu remarks. Just the day before, during an eight-minute delay at Hanover Junction, Pennsylvania, he had responded to a crowd that gathered around his train, "Well, you have seen men, and according to general experience, you have seen less than you expected to see." Laughter ensued, but soon subsided when Lincoln asked rhetorically, "You had the Rebels here last summer, hadn't you?" The crowd responded in the affirmative, to which Lincoln playfully asked, "Well, did you fight them any?" Stunned silence permeated as those present likely remembered the nineteen Union cavalrymen who had died defending Hanover and now lay buried in the local cemetery. The mood of those present never quite recovered before Lincoln's train began moving again to traverse the remaining few miles to Gettysburg.[27]

Lincoln would make no such mistake that night in Gettysburg. The *Adams Sentinel* reported favorably on his comments, noting that Lincoln "made but a few remarks, but they were characteristic of the pure and honest President."[28] Hay was more straightforward in his evaluation: "The President appeared at the door and said half a dozen words meaning nothing." A number of Southern papers reported this speech as "The Gettysburg Address," convincing their readers that Lincoln really was an uncouth jokester incapable of seriousness even at a funeral. The poor opinion some would hold of the Gettysburg Address in subsequent years began here, as the result of sloppy reporting.[29]

After listening to Lincoln, the crowd went next door to the residence of Robert Harper, where Seward was staying, calling for the statesman to speak a few words. Seward leaped at the chance. On November 14, Wills had written Seward, "In the event of [Lincoln's] not being able to be present that duty would, I think, naturally devolve on you."[30] Most likely, it seems, this was the speech Seward delivered. Over the ensuing days, many newspapers at home and abroad scrutinized his words even more closely than Lincoln's:

> *Fellow Citizens*—I am now sixty years old and upwards; I have been in public life practically forty years of that time, and yet this is the first time that ever any people or community so near to the border of Maryland was found wiling to listen to my voice and the reason was that I said forty years ago that slavery was opening before this people a graveyard that was to be filled with brothers falling in mutual political combat. I knew that the cause that was hurrying the Union into this dreadful strife was slavery, and when I did elevate my voice it was to warn the people to remove that cause when they could by constitutional means, and so avert the catastrophe of civil war that now unhappily has fallen upon the nation, deluging it in blood. That crisis came, and we see the result. I am thankful that you are willing to hear me at last. I thank God that I believe this strife is going to end in the removal of that evil which ought to have been removed by peaceful means and deliberate councils. (Good.) I thank my God for the hope that this is the last fratricidal war which will fall upon the country—a country vouchsafed by Heaven—the richest, the broadest, most beautiful, most magnificent and capacious ever yet bestowed upon a people, that has ever been given to any part of the human race. (Applause.) And I thank God for the hope that when that cause is removed, simply by the operation of abolishing it, as the origin of the great treason that is without justification and without parallel, we shall thenceforth be united, be only one country, having only one hope, one ambition and one destiny. (Applause.) Then we shall know that we are not enemies, but that we are friends and brothers, that this Union is a reality, and we shall mourn together for the evil wrought by this rebellion. We are now near the graves of the misguided, whom we have consigned to their last resting place with pity for their errors and with the same heartful of grief with which we mourn over the brother by whose hand raised in defence of his government, that misguided brother perished. When we part to-morrow night let us remember that we owe it to our country and to mankind that this

war shall have for its conclusion the establishing of the principle of democratic government—the simple principle that, whatever party, whatever portion of the Union, prevails by constitutional suffrage in an election, that party is to be respected and maintained in power until it shall give place, on another trial and another verdict, to a different portion of the people. (Good.) If you do not do that, you are drifting at once and irresistibly to the very verge of the destruction of your government. But with that principle this government of ours—the freest, the best, the wisest and the happiest in the world—must be, and, so far as we are concerned, practically will be, immortal. (Applause.)[31]

According to Henry Jacobs, a student at the local college, the statesman's implication that south-central Pennsylvania was full of Southern sympathizers offended the townspeople. The county had, after all, given a majority of their votes to Lincoln in the 1860 presidential election. In the following days, Southern newspapers would take issue with Seward's comments that slavery was the true cause of the war. Jacobs also observed, "There is, we think, a trace of [Seward's] having been apprised of what Mr. Lincoln was to say the next day."[32] If, however, Hay's evaluation of the speech is accurate, few shared either of Jacobs's thoughts: "[Seward] spoke so indistinctly that I did not hear a word of what he was saying." After leaving Seward, the crowd sought out other officials willing to entertain.[33]

The special correspondent of the *New York World* observed, probably accurately given the descriptions of the evening's festivities, "There seemed to be among the great crowds many who came to Gettysburg simply to have a good time, and to them it did not matter much whether the occasion was a funeral or a marriage."[34] Two such men were the President's personal secretaries: Hay said that he "went back to Forney's room having picked up Nicolay and drank more whiskey."[35]

Forney, now fortified with alcohol, decided it had come time for him to address the roving crowd, and so Nicolay set off to find a band to serenade the newspaperman and whip up a crowd. Forney, editor of the *Philadelphia Press* and *Washington Morning Chronicle*, had been a Democrat in the 1850s but slowly turned Republican and was clearly in Lincoln's camp by December 1860. During the war, Forney was "the nearest thing to an administration organ," according to historian Mark E.

Neely Jr., and many referred to Forney as "Lincoln's dog." When Forney eventually had an audience, the speech he gave was rambling and rather incoherent. He alternated between berating the crowd for not cheering Lincoln louder during the President's earlier speech, defending his own opposition to Lincoln in 1860 as a political move designed to damage the Democratic Party, and suggesting that Stephen Douglas (whom he had publicly supported for the presidency in 1860) had died at the right time.[36] Hay's diary makes clear that he viewed Forney as a nuisance, and historian J. Cutler Andrews offers perhaps the most concise statement of the man's character: "He enjoyed public speaking, especially his own, and frequently went on the stump. The Democrats detested him cordially and called him a renegade when they called him no worse."[37]

While hundreds of people made their rounds, Lincoln remained in his room accompanied by William Johnson, his African American servant. According to Wills, "The President sent his servant to request me to come to his room. I went and found him with paper prepared to write, and he said that he had just seated himself to put upon paper a few thoughts for to-morrows exercises, and had sent for me to ascertain what part he was to take in them, and what was expected of him. After a full talk on the subject I left him." Around 11:00 P.M., Lincoln made his way next door to Seward's room to talk about what he had written. Wills stated, "The next day I sat by him on the platform when he delivered his address, which has become immortal, and he read it from the same paper on which I had seen him writing it the night before."[38]

Controversy surrounds the question of when Lincoln wrote the Gettysburg Address. Did he compose it in Washington before November 18, on the train on November 18, or at the Wills house on the night of November 18, or did he deliver it extemporaneously? The amount of time that Lincoln spent preparing his remarks gives a sense of the importance he ascribed to the occasion. Mostly likely, Lincoln wrote a partial draft in Washington, and, in fact, one visitor noted that Lincoln recited a snippet of the speech to him on November 12, while painter and journalist Noah Brooks, who was working in the Executive Mansion in the fall of 1863, later recollected that Lincoln told him around the same time that the speech was written but not finished. This reinforces the notion that Lincoln began the speech in Washington, put the finishing touches on it at the Wills house, and added a few words extemporaneously. Jacobs's statement supports this time frame, Nicolay also remembered it that way. Observations of Ward Hill Lamon, a personal friend and body-guard, about Lincoln's writing style offer further circumstantial evidence: "When Mr. Lincoln had a speech to write, which happened very often, he would put down each thought, as it struck him, on a small strip of paper, and, having accumulated a number of these, generally carried them in his hat or his pockets until he had the whole speech composed in this odd way, when he would sit down at his table, connect the fragments, and then write out the whole speech on consecutive sheets."[39]

The nineteenth of November boasted a blue sky and a temperature of 52 degrees.[40] At 7:00 A.M., artillery pieces on Cemetery Hill fired a salvo and inaugurated a day of festivities. Already, many visitors were out on the battlefield touring and looking for mementos.[41] The *Adams Sentinel* noted, "The ground in these vicinities is yet strewn with remains and relics of the fearful struggle—ragged and muddy knapsacks, canteens, cups, haversacks, threadbare stockings trodden in the mud, old shoes, pistols, holsters, bayonet sheaths, and here and there fragments of gray and blue jackets. . . . [H]ides and skeletons of horses still remain upon the ground. Grave marks of unrecognized heroes were in every quarter of the field, and rows of graves ranged along the line of the stone or wooden fences."[42] Lincoln and Seward spent the wee morning hours touring the battlefield.[43]

The procession to the cemetery lined up at 9:00 A.M. As President Lincoln made his appearance on the square, he surely noticed the national flag flying at half-mast. Eight-year-old William C. Storrick remembered the scene well. The square was "rife" with people who were "awed by the appearance of the great tall man. . . . We and others shook hands with him and then Mr. Lincoln walked to the curb and mounted a horse."[44] The horse, one observer remembered, was tiny, creating a situation that "was next to the humorous, and no one seemed more conscious of it" than Lincoln.[45] Daniel Skelly, a local boy who ran next to Lincoln as the procession made its way to the cemetery, believed, "Mr. Lincoln was the most peculiar-looking figure on horseback I had ever seen. . . . but he was perfectly at ease."[46] Sweney related that the procession was "a living sea of human beings" with Lincoln at its center: "He sat gracefully bowing with a modest smile and uncovered head to the throng of women, men and children that greeted him from the doors and windows."[47] Directly behind Lincoln was a contingent of college and seminary students, including many who eventually recorded their recollections of that day.

The program called for music, a prayer, more music, Everett's oration, even more music, and then the dedicatory remarks of President Lincoln. Reverend Thomas H. Stockton, chaplain of the House of Representatives, opened the ceremonies with a moving prayer. The *Adams Sentinel* reported, "The President evidently felt deeply, and with the venerable statesman and patriot, Hon. Edward Everett, who was by his side, seemed not ashamed to let their sympathetic tears be seen."[48] As was his custom, Hay offered a rather cynical evaluation: "Mr Stockton made a prayer which thought it was an oration." The minister had taken every opportunity to castigate the Rebels who had invaded Pennsylvania, "Prepared to cast a chain of Slavery around the Form of Freedom."[49]

After Stockton's lengthy prayer, Everett rose. Lincoln had likely already read Everett's address. On November 14, Everett had sent his speech to the *Boston Daily Advertiser* to be printed both for his own use and to facilitate distribution to various newspapers in advance of the ceremonies. Given the length of the oration, such a measure was necessary to ensure that the speech would appear in print the day after the ceremony. In two later articles, Brooks claimed that Lincoln had received a copy of Everett's speech as early as November 14 and that it is visible on a table next to Lincoln in a photograph Mathew Brady took that day. While this timetable is improbable, as Edward Everett himself did not even have the typeset speech until 5:00 P.M. that night, it does seem likely that Lincoln received a copy of the speech before he left Washington, D.C., on November 18.[50]

Everett opened what would be a two-hour oration with a call for patience: "Standing beneath this serene sky, overlooking these broad fields now reposing from the labors of the waning year, the mighty Alleghenies dimly towering before us, the graves of our brethren beneath our feet, it is with hesitation that I raise my poor voice to break the eloquent silence of God and Nature. But the duty to which you have called me must be performed;—grant me, I pray you, your indulgence and your sympathy." Beginning with an explanation of funerals in ancient Athens, Everett then discussed the causes of the war, the first two years of the struggle, the three days at Gettysburg, and finally offered his thoughts regarding the meaning of the great events.[51] The oration was exactly what the state officials had envisioned when they asked Everett to speak. After an hour and fifty-seven minutes, Everett finished his oration. Lincoln stood, grasped Everett's hand, and exclaimed, "I am grateful to you."[52]

Those present generally commented favorably on Everett's speech, though some later deemed it too long for the occasion. Henry Jacobs said, "[T]he [length], however, would have been pardoned, and the speech have been commended as being what its author intended, viz. the crowning effort of his life, if President Lincoln had not been there." After a brief musical selection, Lamon, chief marshal for the event, rose and announced, "The President of the United States!"[53]

Lincoln stood, clutching a piece of paper in his hand. Charles Baum, a nine-year-old sitting on the steps of the speakers' platform and suffering from an attention span diminished by Everett's performance, feared "now we are in for it again."[54] An older and more perceptive Sweney sensed "the dreadful responsibility that this nation and this wicked rebellion has cast upon him, has had its marked effect. . . . He feels the terrible responsibility that rests upon him." The dedication ceremonies gave Lincoln a chance to share that burden with the nation, and he took full advantage of it.[55]

Joseph Gilbert, the Associated Press reporter at the dedication ceremonies, offered perhaps the best description of Lincoln's delivery of the speech: "He stood for a moment with hands clasped and head bowed in an attitude of mourning—a personification of the sorrow and sympathy of the nation. Adjusting his old fashioned spectacles, a pair with arms reaching to his temples, he produced from a pocket of his Prince Albert coat several sheets of paper from which he read slowly and feelingly. His marvelous voice, careering in fullness of utterance and clearness of tone, was perfectly audible on the outskirts of the crowd. He made no gestures nor attempts at display, and none were needed."[56]

Four score and seven years ago our fathers brought forth upon this continent a new Nation, conceived in Liberty, and dedicated to the proposition that all men are created equal. [Applause.] Now we are engaged in a great civil war, testing whether that Nation, or any Nation so conceived and so dedicated, can long endure. We are met on a great battle-field of that war. We are met to dedicate a portion of it as the final resting-place of those who here gave their lives that that nation might live. It is altogether fitting and proper that we should do this. But in a larger sense we cannot dedicate, we cannot consecrate, we cannot hallow this ground. The brave men living and dead who struggled here have consecrated it, far above our power to add or detract. [Applause.] The world will little note nor long remember what we say here, but it can never forget what they did here. [Applause.] It is for us, the living, rather to be dedicated here to the refinished work that they have thus far so nobly carried on. [Applause.] It is rather for us to be here dedicated to the great task remaining before us, that from these honored dead we take increased devotion to that cause for which they here gave the last full measure of devotion; that we here highly resolve that the dead shall not have died in vain [applause]; that the nation shall, under God, have a new birth of freedom; and that Governments of the people, by the people, and for the people shall not perish from the earth. [Long-continued applause.][57]

Since 1863, the speech has been invoked so often and recited on such a variety of occasions that it is often forgotten that Lincoln was delivering a funeral oration and that there were established elements of such a ceremony. In the mid-nineteenth century, a good and noble death was extremely important to the families of the deceased; Lincoln, therefore, sought to assure listeners and readers that their fallen husbands, sons, brothers, and fathers "shall not have died in vain." Historian Drew Faust notes that a good death meant "the deceased had been conscious of his fate, had demonstrated willingness to accept it, had shown signs of belief in God and in his own salvation, and had left messages and instructive exhortations for those who should have been at his side." Lincoln tried to satisfy each of those criteria, thereby honoring the men who were buried just yards away while assuring their families that the sacrifice was purposeful.[58]

Offering reassurance on the one hand, Lincoln sought a rededication on the other. After two years of conflict, the outcome was still quite uncertain, but it is clear that Lincoln had shifted positions from a simple restoration of the 1861 status quo to the creation of a stronger nation. As Gary Gallagher so convincingly shows in *The Union War*, by the 1860s, democratic republics had failed almost universally, and the continuance of the United States truly was "the last, best hope of earth," as Lincoln once said. Simply preserving the gloriously democratic Union would be in itself a sublime result even were slavery to remain intact, for a division would set back republican government the world over.[59]

By 1863, however, Lincoln concluded that the only way the Union could stabilize and persist was by placing equality at its core. As Gary Wills argues in *Lincoln at Gettysburg,* "He would cleanse the Constitution. . . . He altered the document from within, by appeal from its letter to the spirit, subtly changing the recalcitrant stuff of that legal compromise, bringing it to its own indictment. By implicitly doing this, he performed one of the most daring acts of open-air sleight-of-hand ever witnessed by the unsuspecting."[60] Peace without emancipation, Lincoln and many other Northerners came to realize, would offer no longer an armistice than had the failed Compromise of 1850.[61] But neither was emancipation alone enough, for without equality the nation would soon fall prey to further civil strife. That Lincoln never once mentioned slavery in the speech but focused instead on equality and "a new birth of freedom" evinces that he had moved beyond thinking about simple emancipation or abolition.

From his earliest days as a politician, Lincoln grappled with these questions. Several times in the 1830s and 1840s, Lincoln publicly announced his desire for universal freedom, and as he matured, he took that argument further and argued for some measure of equality.[62] Increasingly, Lincoln drew on the Declaration of Independence, the document Hay called the President's "political chart and inspiration."[63] In 1861, Lincoln himself proclaimed, "I have never had a feeling politically that did not spring from the sentiments embodied in the Declaration of Independence."[64] Indeed, as Wills argues, at Gettysburg, Lincoln "not only put the Declaration in a new light as a matter of founding *law,* but put its central proposition, equality, in a newly favored position as a principle of the Constitution."[65] As the sectional crisis deepened in the 1850s, white Southerners came to rely increasingly on the Constitution and its clauses that protected slavery and strengthened the slaveholding states, while the Northern states looked to the Declaration and its disavowal of the ethics of human bondage.[66] In 1852, Lincoln observed, "An increasing number of men, who, for the sake of perpetuating slavery, are beginning to assail and to ridicule the white-man's charter of freedom—the declaration that 'all men are created free and equal.'"[67] This line is critical; for Lincoln, freedom and equality were connected, one impossible without the other.

In an 1854 speech at Peoria, Illinois, Lincoln attacked Douglas for opening the territories to slavery, declaring, "My ancient faith teaches me that 'all men are created equal,' and that there can be no moral right in connection with one man's making a slave of another. . . . Let us re-adopt the Declaration of Independence, and with it, the practices, and policy, which harmonize with it. Let north and south—let all Americans—let all lovers of liberty everywhere—join in the great and good work. If we do this, we shall not only have saved the Union; but we shall have so saved it, as to make, and to keep it, forever worthy of the saving. We shall have so saved it, that the succeeding millions of free happy people, the world over, shall rise up, and call us blessed, to the latest generations."[68] A private 1855 letter to his best friend, Joshua Speed, reveals that Lincoln was not merely publicly invoking the Declaration to make political hay but that he was also considering the document in his personal life: "As a nation, we began by declaring that '*all men are created equal.*' We now practically read it 'all men are created equal, *except negroes.*' When the Know-Nothings get control, it will read 'all men are created equal, except negroes, *and foreigners, and catholics.*' When it comes to this I should prefer emigrating to some country where they make no pretence of loving liberty—to Russia, for instance, where despotism can be taken pure, and without the base alloy of hypocracy."[69]

Historian Douglas Wilson contends that phrases from the Constitution including, "Liberty," "consent of the governed," or the "pursuit of happiness," all argue against slavery and were at that time more palpable for most Americans, who, even if they opposed human bondage, did not believe "all men are created equal." But, at Gettysburg, Lincoln passed by these halfway attacks and took up that which was potentially most damaging, both to himself and to his opponents.[70] His reasoning is best illustrated in a letter Lincoln sent to Illinois politician James N. Brown in 1858 just three days after the last of Lincoln's famous debates with Douglas: "I believe the declara[tion] that 'all men are created equal' is the great fundamental principle upon which our free institutions rest; that negro slavery is violative of that principle; but that, by our frame of government, that principle has not been made one of legal obligation."[71] That summer, he had urged, "So I say in relation to the principle that all men are created equal, let it be as nearly reached as we can."[72]

Writing on the bicentennial of the Declaration of Independence, philosopher and public intellectual Eva Brann made clear the reason for Lincoln's devotion to that document: "To Lincoln the Declaration was not simply announcing independence, but also a principle, that all men are created equal, thus giving it the transcendent character that a mere declaration of independence would not have contained."[73] Indeed, in his speech at Independence Hall in Philadelphia on George Washington's birthday in 1861, Lincoln declared that the Declaration gave "liberty, not alone to the people of this country, but hope to the world for all future time. It was that which gave promise that in due time the weights should be lifted from the shoulders of all men, and that *all* should have an equal chance. . . . If this country cannot be saved without giving up that principle—I was about to say I would rather be assassinated on this spot than to surrender it."[74]

That penultimate line is crucial. Lincoln, a man of his times, did not believe the races were equal but that they should be treated equally. Only a nation that assured equality of *opportunity* would survive, Lincoln had come to believe. Shortly after the *Dred Scott* decision declared that African Americans were not citizens of the United States, Lincoln articulated his vision in a speech to his Springfield neighbors: "In some respects [an African American woman] certainly is not my equal; but in her natural right to eat the bread she earns with her own hands without asking leave of any one else, she is my equal, and the equal of all others. . . . I think the authors of [the Declaration of Independence] intended to include *all* men, but they did not intend to declare all men equal *in all respects*. They did not mean to say all were equal in color, size, intellect, moral developments, or social capacity. They defined with tolerable distinctness, in what respects they did consider all men created equal—equal in 'certain inalienable rights, among which are life, liberty, and the pursuit of happiness.' This they said, and this meant. They did not mean to assert the obvious untruth, that all were then actually enjoying that equality, nor yet, that they were about to confer it immediately upon them. In fact they had no power to confer such a boon. They meant simply to declare the right, so that the enforcement of it might follow as fast as circumstances should permit."[75] Scholar Richard Carwardine succinctly summarizes Lincoln's political philosophy as "a belief in meritocracy: in the right of all individuals, through their industry, enterprise, and self-discipline, to rise in an increasingly market-oriented society."[76] Both Lincoln's own views and those of his constituents prevented him from calling for immediately legal opportunity, instead settling on the far more publicly acceptable notion of equality of opportunity.

Lincoln struggled in the 1850s and into his presidency with the gap between the ideal and the reality and for a while thought that colonization—encouraging African Americans to migrate to Africa or South America—might offer a solution. How sincere Lincoln was in his support for the plan is difficult to discern. On the one hand, he secured a Congressional appropriation of $600,000 for the effort but then barely touched that fund and privately made clear that all he really wanted was a "commencement" to emigration that would appease white people and ease the path toward emancipation and abolition. Gabor Boritt concludes that Lincoln's colonization plans were "a lullaby for the antiblack majority of the political spectrum," while Carwardine comments that for Lincoln, "colonization was the sugar around the pill of emancipation." However, new evidence pieced together by historians Phillip Magness and Sebastian Page indicates that Lincoln engaged in semi-secret negotiations with Great Britain to resettle African Americans to British Honduras *after* he signed the Emancipation Proclamation and that the plan only failed due to bureaucratic infighting and budget cuts. The episode raises more questions than it answers. Perhaps, Boritt, writing long before Magness and Page made their discovery, offers an answer: Lincoln believed "if it were not possible [for African Americas] to be free, equal, and prosperous in United States, it should be made possible elsewhere."[77]

On August 26, 1863, Lincoln sent a letter to longtime friend James C. Conkling to be read at a Springfield, Illinois, meeting of Union supporters who were, Lincoln acknowledged, "dissatisfied with me about the negro." In justifying the Emancipation Proclamation, Lincoln continued, "Negroes, like other people, act upon motives. Why should they do any thing for us, if we will do nothing for them?" Following Lincoln's logic, only a promise of equality would bring a full commitment to the Union by the nation's five million African Americans. Lincoln concluded, "There will be some black men who can remember that, with silent tongue, and clenched teeth, and steady eye, and well-poised bayonet, they have helped mankind on to this great consummation; while, I fear, there will be some white ones, unable to forget that, with malignant heart, and deceitful speech, they strove to hinder it."[78] Lincoln had already seen evidence of how difficult it would be to get the nation to accept black soldiers; that summer, loyal Republican ally Curtin had himself fallen into this category. On June 15, 1863, as Confederate troops bore down on Pennsylvania, David Wills telegraphed Governor Curtin, "There can be a company of sixty colored volunteers obtained here—Will they be accepted[?]" Curtin responded, "We have no authority to accept colored men in this new service. Authority must first be obtained from the War Dept." When an African American company from Philadelphia headed for Harrisburg to help defend the state from Robert E. Lee's army, Curtin ordered, "Have the negroes stopped at once," and then again, "Stop Negroe volunteers now at West Chester from leaving," but both times his messages arrived too late. Upon reaching Harrisburg, however, the volunteers were told their service was not needed.[79] Eventually, 180,000 African Americans would serve in the Union army, and they, too, helped shape Lincoln's thinking about equality. Just six weeks after his speech at Gettysburg, Lincoln proposed African American suffrage "on the basis of intelligence and military service," an idea he would also broach with the governor of Louisiana in March 1864.[80]

As historian Gary Wills demonstrates, on that November day in 1863, the President sought to identify the Declaration not the Constitution as the central statement of American ideals. Of the eleven clauses in the Constitution pertaining to slavery, ten protected the institution and all the inequalities that came with it.[81] However, the Declaration had no legal standing in 1863, and, as such, when Lincoln issued the Emancipation Proclamation a year earlier, he had to base it on the legalistic argument that it was a military necessity rather than the humane argument, supported by the Declaration, that it was morally just. But Lincoln could not tolerate that half measure, and that is why he seized the opportunity to come to Gettysburg in late 1863 to reorient the nation's past and future. Those who cite Lincoln's waffling on emancipation and abolition during this period should remember that one of Lincoln's greatest skills as a lawyer was in giving up six points in order to win the seventh and deciding issue.

Lincoln clearly knew what he wanted to say. He desired neither fancy words nor originality, instead aiming for simplicity and familiarity. As A. E. Elmore shows in his work on the Gettysburg Address, Lincoln invoked some of the most common words and phrases from the King James Bible—which Carwardine calls Lincoln's "all-purpose anti-slavery manual"—and the Book of Common Prayer, including *score*, *dedicate*, *consecrate*, and *hallow*. David Wills's November 2 letter also includes the words *consecrate* and *brave*. Parson Weems's biography of George Washington, one of Lincoln's favorites, used the line "not in vain." Lincoln's use of words in common usage ensured that those listening and reading both understood what he said and would remember his words.[82]

Of all the phrases in the speech, the one most quoted in the ensuing years would be that final assertion "that Governments of the people, by the people, and for the people shall not perish from the earth." Like many of Lincoln's earlier sentiments, this one was also adapted from other writers and one that he had already used in a slightly different form.[83] Over the years, historians put forth a number of possible sources for this line. Writing in 1919, Henry Jacobs, who had been present at the speech, suggested a source: "Nor should the words of [Chief Justice John] Marshall's great colleague and friend, Justice Story, be overlooked. . . . 'It was made by the people, made for the people, and is responsible to the people.'"[84] More recently, Eugenio Bagini suggests that Lincoln "echoed Giuseppe Mazzini's 1833 statement that Young Italy sought revolution 'in the names of the people, for people, and by people,'" and notes that Lincoln received a volume of Mazzini's writings in 1862.[85] A great many favor Daniel Webster, who commented in 1830 that the federal government was "made for the people, made by the people, and answerable to the people."[86]

The man who most likely served as Lincoln's inspiration for this line was Theodore Parker, an ardent abolitionist and nationally known speaker from Massachusetts. Beginning in 1850, Parker frequently referred to democracy as "a government of all the people, by all the people, for all the people." William H. Herndon, Lincoln's law partner, both corresponded with Parker and had a volume of the man's works in their office. Lincoln himself told friend Jesse Fell that he thought much of Parker. Historians of the Gettysburg Address overlook the fact that Parker visited Springfield (at Herndon's invitation) and gave an address, titled "The Progressive Development of Mankind," on October 24, 1856. Though this speech was not reprinted in any of the local papers, a similar Parker speech, "Some Thoughts on the Progress of America" declared, "A government is to be of all the people, by all people, and for all the people."[87] Lincoln was in Springfield the night of Parker's speech, and it is likely that he would have attended the event. At any rate, it seems clear Parker had come to Lincoln's attention. In the famous 1858 speech in which he declared, "A house divided against itself cannot stand," Lincoln invoked the biblical phrase "every city or house divided against itself shall not stand." However, Lincoln used language closer to that Parker employed in an 1854 sermon: "There can be no national welfare without national unity of action. This cannot take place unless there is national unity of idea in fundamentals. Without this a nation is a 'house divided against itself;' of course it cannot stand." If Lincoln borrowed his final phrase from an abolitionist who demanded a government "of *all* the people" (emphasis added), the line takes a different tone and further demonstrates Lincoln's conception of democracy and equality as intertwined. By invoking the abolitionist Parker but removing that one word—*all*—Lincoln appealed to each of the members of the North's fragile war-time coalition of abolitionists, former Whigs, and War Democrats.[88]

Ultimately, the Gettysburg Address set the wheels in motion for a new America. Beyond reorienting the relative place of the Constitution and Declaration in the American political tradition, Lincoln took a step further and modified even the Constitution. It is fitting that a man whose life would span that of both Thomas Jefferson and Woodrow Wilson would construct a plan for the future that focused on what a government *should* do, rather than just those things, as had the Declaration, that it should *not*.[89]

As Lincoln spoke, Associated Press reporter and shorthand expert Gilbert started to write down the Address. Over fifty years later, Gilbert recalled, "He had not been known to prepare his speeches in advance and as he was expected to speak extempore, I was relied upon to take shorthand notes of his remarks." But the reporter was unable to fulfill his assignment: "Fascinated by his intense earnestness and depth of feeling, I unconsciously stopped taking notes and looked up at him." The frequent breaks for applause in Gilbert's account indicate that the audience was similarly impressed. The reporter for the *Chicago Tribune* noted even greater applause than Gilbert had observed.[90]

The Address was a sharp contrast to the two-hour oration that had preceded it, and it was not at all what the audience was expecting. No one knew exactly what Lincoln would say, or for how long he would speak, but his theme and brevity were both a surprise. This was, after all, the man who had delivered an address of more than fifteen thousand words during the Lincoln-Douglas debates.

Despite the applause observed by Gilbert and the *Chicago Tribune* reporter, many historians argue that the audience did not applaud when Lincoln finished his speech, citing this supposed silence to argue that the Gettysburg Address of 1863 was a failure and that the positive evaluations of it did not come until later. However, the recollections recorded by the citizens of Gettysburg overwhelmingly indicate that there was applause. Pennsylvania College student T. C. Billheimer simply noted the Address was met with applause, but student Jacobs and young Baum both said the applause was "hearty." H. C. Holloway noted that the applause was delayed, but for a good reason: "The speaker had, as we thought, but barely commenced when he stopped. That clear, ringing voice ceased before we were ready for it. There was a pause between the closing of the address and the applause because the people expected more; but when it was apparent that the address was really concluded, the applause was most hearty."[91] Baum agreed: "To my great surprise, after a few sentences, he completed his remarks." Even those who argued that there was no applause gave the seriousness of the occasion as the reason and not any dissatisfaction with the oration. Baum perhaps best summarized the crowd's reaction when he said that the Address was met with "profound silence, followed by hearty applause."[92]

After the ceremony, Gilbert looked at Lincoln's original manuscript and completed his transcription of the Address. In the ensuing months, Lincoln received many requests to produce copies of the Address that could be published or sold to raise funds for the war effort, and he complied on several occasions. Of the five versions now in existence, most argue that the last one Lincoln penned, now known as the Bliss copy, gets closest to what Lincoln wanted to say. At any rate, the differences are more cosmetic than consequential. Gilbert's report is quoted above because it was the most widely circulated at the time.[93]

After a dirge and closing prayer, the crowd dispersed. Lincoln retired to the Wills house for a late lunch. Shortly thereafter, the President made an appearance on the square to shake hands with the many well-wishers. With the train back to Washington not scheduled to leave for a few more hours, Lincoln had one special request. He wanted to meet John Burns, the citizen who had taken up arms and joined the Union forces during the July 1 fighting. A committee quickly brought Burns to the Wills residence. After talking with the old man for a short while, Lincoln, Seward, and Burns walked two blocks to the Presbyterian Church to listen to an address by Governor-elect Charles Anderson of Ohio. The journey to the church was, according to Billheimer, a most humorous one: "I laughed and laughed aloud. Lincoln took enormous strides and Mr. Burns could not take strides like that. He could not keep step with the President." While attending the church service with President Lincoln was the most cherished moment of Burns's life, it was apparently not stimulating enough to keep the old man awake, for within minutes he fell sound asleep next to President Lincoln. Before Anderson finished, Lincoln and his party arose and left, arriving back in Washington, D.C., at one o'clock the following morning. As Lincoln journeyed back to Washington, the reporters at Gettysburg scrambled to find an open telegraph.[94]

Lincoln's role in the great drama was over. In less than three hundred words, he put moral force behind the Emancipation Proclamation and made explicit his belief that democracy could not persist without equality, thus achieving his goal in coming to Gettysburg. For support, Lincoln had invoked the Declaration of Independence, reminding his listeners and eventual readers that the nation had strayed from its founding promise and that it must "highly resolve that the dead shall not have died in vain; that the nation shall, under God, have a new birth of freedom," that included equality of opportunity for all. The reporters present now had more control over his words than Lincoln did, and what they reported, both of his speech and the others delivered that day, shaped how the public remembered the dedication of the Soldiers' National Cemetery and what they made of Lincoln's speech. Unfortunately, as the following chapters show, Lincoln's meaning was lost for nearly a century.

2

The Luckless Sallies of That Poor President Lincoln: Responses to the Gettysburg Address, 1863

President Pericles, or rather Abe, made the dedicatory speech;
but had to limit his observations within small compass, lest he
should tell some funny story over the graves of the Immortals.
—Richmond Enquirer, November 27, 1863

Newspaper coverage of the dedication ceremonies and Abraham Lincoln's address commenced the very next day, November 20. More than any other person, Associated Press reporter Joseph Gilbert shaped those early stories. Most papers around the country picked up his account of the ceremonies and accompanying transcription of Lincoln's speech. The initial coverage typically covered the nuts and bolts of the procession to the cemetery, the scenery, and crowd reactions to the speeches, underscoring that the dedication ceremony was an event, not just a series of speeches.

From there, the coverage diverges. This chapter examines the ways that local editors in New York, Gettysburg, Richmond, and London— four cities that dominated the news in their region—shaped their coverage in quite distinct ways by honing in on the aspects most likely to interest their readers and reinforce their local or regional political and social affiliations. Looking through a local lens, Richmond papers rejected Lincoln's use of the Declaration to link democracy with equality and therefore refused to print the speech, while editors in New York and London typically reprinted Lincoln's words but reserved the bulk of their editorial comment for Edward Everett. There was no dominant narrative of this era but rather a series of intensely local and political responses focusing largely on something other than Lincoln's words. Those initial responses show the origins of attitudes towards the Gettysburg Address that persisted for a century, in some cases, and precluded

the acceptance of Lincoln's call for a greater commitment to both democracy and equality.

When the press corps left the dedication ceremonies, they scrambled
to get reports back to their home papers the quickest way possible. Just
three decades earlier, journalism had entered an era of increased access to
information from afar and of decreased transmission times. In an attempt
to speed the retrieval of news, a service using carrier pigeons connected
London and Paris in 1835. That same year, Samuel Morse invented a code
to transmit messages across telegraph wires. Also in 1835, James Gordon
Bennett began publication of the *New York Herald*, the first modern newspaper, and inaugurated the trend of gathering news from far and wide. In
1844, the telegraph successfully transmitted a message from Baltimore,
Maryland, to Washington, D.C., making it easier for distant reporters
to provide stories for their home papers. Within two years, the telegraph
connected Richmond, Virginia, and Washington, D.C.

Although a tremendous tool, the telegraph was prohibitively expen-
sive. To send a two-thousand-word column from Washington to New
York cost around $100. A similar message sent from New Orleans to
New York incurred a bill of $450.[1] This was an era when a typical laborer
made perhaps $1 per day. To combat these high costs, several New York
newspapers formed the New York Associated Press in 1849, a group that
reorganized in 1856 as the General News Association of the City of New
York. Subscribers could use any of the association's reports in their papers as long as they paid part of the telegraph fees, thereby dividing the
expense and making the service affordable. By 1860, fifty thousand miles
of telegraph wires crisscrossed the United States. The telegraph had opponents, however. President James Buchanan worried it would increase the
instances of inaccurate reporting: Telegrams "are short and spicy, and can
easily be inserted in the country newspapers. In the city journals they can
be contradicted the next day," an impossibility for the country weeklies.[2]

By 1860, twenty-five hundred journalists worked in the United States,
a third for Southern papers. The country boasted 4,051 newspapers, about
10 percent of which were dailies. These papers were not ashamed to borrow stories from one another. George Smalley's account of the Battle of
Antietam originally appeared in the *New York Tribune*, but a reported
fourteen hundred newspapers reprinted the story.[3] According to one
authority, in order to put together the paper for each day's edition, the

editor "would first select two important newspapers from each of the larger cities represented among his newspaper exchanges and clip a dozen or so small articles. . . . [T]hen he would clip articles for solid matter, leaving just enough space for the lead editorial. When the printer told him enough material had been found for the day's edition, he would knock off the editorial rapidly." Most editors saw no need to rewrite an article that had appeared in another paper.[4]

Approximately 5 percent of Americans subscribed to a paper, and an even larger percentage read the papers of friends or family members.[5] Readers usually selected papers based on political affiliations, and 80 percent of the journals identified with a particular party, usually announcing their loyalties in the masthead. Due to low subscription prices, proprietors only made money by winning government contracts to print legislative journals and state laws, necessitating the political affiliations.[6]

The reporters congregated in Gettysburg on November 18–19 came from papers large and small, urban and rural, Democratic and Republican, nearby and faraway (though, obviously, none were from the Confederacy). In the 1960s, Ronald Reid examined reporting of the Gettysburg Address in 260 Northern newspapers and found that 98 percent of the dailies covered the event, typically with multiple articles, while just 56 percent of the weeklies offered coverage. Predictably, Republican papers printed five times as much content on the ceremony as Democratic papers. Papers devoting a small amount of space to the dedication excerpted Lincoln, while papers with greater coverage gave more consideration to Everett. Consequently, although more people read Lincoln's words than Everett's, the latter was the subject of more editorial comment.[7]

Despite the multitude of cities represented in Gettysburg on November 19, New York stood above the rest. The dedication ceremonies at Gettysburg received more coverage in New York City than anywhere else in the world, even in Gettysburg itself. But beyond a simple reprinting of what the President had said, the city's editors largely ignored Lincoln's words and instead focused on Everett. In this city, the political affiliation of the papers wholly determined which speeches they commented on and the tenor of those remarks. Because the New York papers circulated throughout the world—the transcript of Lincoln's address printed in Gettysburg's *Adams Sentinel* on November 24, 1863, actually came from the *New York Herald* of November 20—New York editors largely shaped the national and even international responses to the Gettysburg Address.

In many ways, New York City in 1860 had more connections to the South than the North, particularly in commercial terms. That year, the city carried out $200 million in trade with the five leading cotton states. Democratic Mayor Fernando Wood stated on several occasions that he considered New York's rise to prominence a product of slave labor, asserting that without the commercial ties to Southern plantation owners the city would still rank behind Boston and Philadelphia. Wood so valued those connections that in January of 1861 he proposed the city secede, proclaim its independence, and carry on trade and normal relationships with both the North and the South. By 1863, Wood represented New York in Congress, where he continued to argue and vote against continuing the war.[8]

The mayor had company in his views on slavery. Bennett of the *New York Herald* warned his readers that if elected, Lincoln would free the slaves, who would then flock north and take their jobs. In 1860, the state of New York went Republican by over fifty thousand votes, but the city returned a thirty thousand majority against Lincoln. In an editorial just three days after Lincoln's inaugural address, Bennett referred to abolitionism as "nigger worship" and asserted that slavery provided a comfortable existence for those in bondage. Bennett had spent time in the South as a young reporter for the *Charleston Courier* and had evidently picked up some of the region's racial views.[9]

Initially, most New York newspapers suggested allowing peaceful secession. In some cases, the editors felt their Southern brethren would back down; in others, they genuinely felt the Union would remain strong even if reduced by a handful of states. Many with commercial interests did not think business affairs would change in the least due to secession. However, when the shooting began, most papers quickly backed the Union. This did not mean, however, that Lincoln had unconditional support. Henry Raymond, editor of the *New York Times*, was an ardent Republican, but even he berated Lincoln in early 1861 for having no plan to deal with secession or the war. The issuance of the Emancipation Proclamation polarized the New York press. William Cullen Bryant of the *Evening Post* and Horace Greeley of the *Tribune* both supported the measure, but the majority of New York's editors did not. Bennett, as is easily surmised from his earlier comments, opposed emancipation, as did the editors of the *World*, *Express*, *Frank Leslie's*, and the *Irish-American*.

The proclamation inaugurated a tumultuous year in New York City. The Battle of Gettysburg produced casualty lists the likes of which America had never seen. In June, two nearly simultaneous events had primed the city for explosion: the drawing of the first names for the federal draft on June 11 and the breaking of a strike of Irish stevedores by African Americans. Ten days after Gettysburg, draft riots broke out in the city resulting in 119 deaths, 2,000 injuries, and property damage of $1.5 million. The targets were overwhelmingly Republicans and African Americans, and the rioters mainly Irish and Catholics. The riot was clearly a rejection of the war and a fear that emancipation would lead to greater economic competition of the city's poorest classes with the newly freed slaves. Those poor were already suffering from wartime inflation. Retail prices in the city increased by 43 percent, and food expenses tripled, while wages grew only 12 percent. Some men made fortunes from war contracts, but the conflict also increased the wealth gap and further overburdened already crowded tenements.[10]

Into this environment arrived the first reports of the ceremonies at Gettysburg. Outside Gettysburg, New York City had perhaps the most natural interest in the dedication ceremonies. Of the 2,576 men buried at Gettysburg whose origins are known, 886 came from New York, 340 more than any other state. Additionally, Secretary of State William Henry Seward hailed from New York and his role in the ceremonies garnered attention. In 1863, nearly all of New York's dailies belonged to the Associated Press, by then a fairly well-oiled machine. The editors of most daily papers set aside a column or two for the usually short messages that came across the telegraph wires. On November 18, the *Herald* and *Times* both printed a notice from Pennsylvania Governor Curtin especially inviting the veterans of the War of 1812 and the war with Mexico to attend the ceremonies and noting that the flag would fly at half-mast at government installations. The *World* carried the same story the following day. On the day of the ceremonies, the *Herald*, *Tribune*, and *World* all printed an announcement that several representatives of France and Italy would accompany Secretary of State Seward to Gettysburg. On November 20, most of the city's daily papers provided a straightforward review of the dedication events and words from those days based on Gilbert's report. Then—sometimes later in that same edition but more often in the ensuing days or even weeks—an editorial offered extended thoughts on one or more of the orations.

Gilbert's account, telegraphed to the city on the night of November 19 in time for the editions the following day, covered the activities of November 18 with a four-paragraph-long review of Lincoln's arrival and that of the other distinguished guests in Gettysburg and included transcriptions of both Lincoln's and Seward's words that night. The coverage of November 19 began with a three-paragraph review of the procession to the cemetery before offering the text of Reverend Thomas H. Stockton's prayer. An account of Lincoln's speech followed, with applause markers and the comment, "Three cheers were here given for the President and the Governors of the States." Finally, Gilbert provided the speech that New York Governor Horatio Seymour delivered on the afternoon of November 19.

The *Evening Post, Herald, Times, Tribune,* and *World* all carried Gilbert's account, though they used it in different ways. Some foregrounded the events of the nineteenth and pushed those of the eighteenth to the end of the column. The *Herald* held off running its coverage until the third page, but the other papers put the stories on page 1, above the fold, highlighting the focus they placed on the dedication. In all four cases, the editors printed Everett's complete speech, undoubtedly from the version he sent out in the preceding days.

In addition to the reporting by the Associated Press, most of the papers had a special correspondent at the ceremonies who provided more-detailed accounts in the ensuing days. The only daily paper without additional coverage or editorials was Bryant's *Evening Post.* A very brief column in the 4:00 P.M. edition of November 19 mentioned which dignitaries were present and that Everett had spoken. The following day, the *Evening Post* simply reprinted the two principal speeches. The dearth of coverage perhaps signaled that the editor, who did not support Lincoln in his reelection bid the following year, had already grown dissatisfied with the President.

The *New York Herald* offered the most extensive, and earliest, of these supplemental reports. Though overshadowed in elite political circles by rival editors Raymond and Greeley, Bennett had no peer when it came to capturing the ear of the masses. In addition to pioneering the art of long-distance newsgathering in the decades preceding the war, Bennett also popularized sensational news of grizzly crimes and scandals, indulging the guilty pleasures of the masses. Walt Whitman wrote that Bennett was "[a] reptile marking his path with slime wherever he goes, and breathing

mildew at everything fresh or fragrant; a midnight ghoul, preying on rot-
tenness and repulsive filth; a creature, hated by his nearest intimates, and
bearing the consciousness thereof upon his distorted features, and upon
his despicable soul; one whom good men avoid as a blot to his nature—
who all despise, and whom no one blesses." The cost of Bennett's paper, a
penny, helped ensure a circulation estimated as high as 105,000. In turn, he
spent $500,000 to $750,000 on newsgathering during the war. A chunk of
that bill came from the correspondent who telegraphed Bennett literally
thousands of words on the ceremonies in Gettysburg.[11]

On November 20, the *Herald* printed the fullest account of the dedication ceremonies of any paper in the world. This was also the first paper
with information on the ceremonies to arrive in both Richmond and
London, making its view of the ceremonies the most influential. The
Herald's coverage opened on page 3 with a four-column-wide map of the
borough of Gettysburg and the hills south of the town containing the
cemetery. An accompanying column, "The National Necropolis," used
the following subheads:

THE NATIONAL NECROPOLIS

Our Heroic Dead at Gettysburg.

Consecration of a National Cemetery for the Union Soldiers who Fell There.

Arrival of the President and Cabinet.

Speeches by Mr. Lincoln, Mr. Seward and Gov. Seymour.

SOLEMN AND IMPRESSIVE CEREMONY

Imposing Civil and Military Procession.

THE CROWDS OF THE BATTLE FIELD.

ORATION BY EDWARD EVERETT.

History of the Three Days' Fighting at Gettysburg.

Upon Whom the Responsibility of the War Rests.

The Question of the Restoration of Concord Between
the North and the South, &c., &c., &c.,

The column offered a brief review of the battle before describing the
cemetery grounds. Much of the Associated Press account appeared on the
following page, including the review of Lincoln's journey to Washington,

the President's remarks on the night of November 18, and the transcription of Seward's address. John Forney's speech of November 18 was also briefly summarized: "[Forney] declared that the reason he had not supported Mr. Lincoln for the Presidency in 1860 was that he wanted to break up the slaveowning democracy, that he was really in favor of his election, but did not want to let it appear, so that he might the better accomplish his purpose." This paragraph in particular would catch the eye of Richmond's editors. An explanation of the parade and the order of procession to the cemetery followed. Finally, Everett's speech took up the rest of the fourth page and most of the fifth.

The tenth page contained a much more detailed recounting of the day's ceremonies. Bennett again invoked the Associated Press account, both for its version of Lincoln's Gettysburg Address and the speech by Governor Seymour. A brief overview of the events following the dedication ceremonies up to the time Lincoln left to return to Washington, D.C., brought the coverage to a close.

Figure 2.1. *Newsboy in Camp*, Culpeper, Virginia, November 1863. Photograph by Alexander Gardner. Prints and Photographs Division, Library of Congress.

Both that day and the next, the *Herald* offered a commentary that focused on Everett's speech, not that of President Lincoln. Comparing Everett's effort to a recent speech by Henry Ward Beecher, a prominent abolitionist orator whom Bennett commonly dismissed, the editor commented, "It is not necessary to compare this oratorical wet blanket with such giants as Webster. He seems dwarfish even when compared to Ward Beecher." The *Herald* criticized Everett for his lack of emotion: "He had written his essay in his library and he said that which he had written. . . . An inaccurate account of the battle gave occasion for kindly little puffs of Hooker and Meade, when, as every one knows, Gettysburg was a soldiers' battle—won not by Meade's generalship, but by the privates and the corps commanders." Though the editor did not reference the President, his description of Everett's oratorical style contrasts completely with that of Lincoln: "Seldom has a man talked so long and said so little. . . . He gave us plenty of words, but no heart. His flowers of rhetoric were as beautiful and as scentless and as lifeless as wax flowers." That Bennett focused so much of his energy eviscerating Everett is not surprising. Bennett had supported the Constitutional-Union Party in the 1860 election with John Bell as the presidential candidate and Everett as the vice president. When the war began, Everett viewed publicly supporting the President as the only proper thing to do and, consequently, came out in favor of Lincoln, a man Bennett despised as the antithesis of everything for which the Democrats stood. Thus, Bennett was all too happy to use Everett's speech as an opportunity to denounce the man he had once supported. Amongst his Democratic readers, such a sentiment would have been common and offered Bennett another opportunity to give his audience what they wanted.[12]

The daily *World* was even more ardently Democratic than the *Herald* and a typically harsher critic of Lincoln. An editorial on November 20 states that Everett had fallen short of expectations and wondered if "the hand of age begins to lie heavy on his faculties, or whether the natural coldness of his temper never permitted him to stir the fountains of human feeling to their profound depths." The thrust of the complaint was that Everett's speech was a mere recitation of history that did not stand up to other great American orations, such as Daniel Webster's at the laying of the Bunker Hill Monument cornerstone in 1825. Like the *Herald*, the *World* editor on November 20 invoked a flower analogy: "His rhetorical flowers are artificial and elaborately finished, surprisingly like, no doubt, but fed by no life-giving sap and filling the air with no self-produced fragrance."

The following day, the *World* ran a descriptive account of the events of November 18 and 19 from their special correspondent "Sidney." The reporter found much of the behavior of the crowd on the night of the eighteenth "in bad taste and out of place" and provided an extensive overview of Forney's speech. Forney, as a Democrat-turned-Republican, received a great deal of scorn from many of the Democratically affiliated papers that reported on the dedication ceremonies. But of more importance than "Sidney's" account was the *World*'s editorial that day: "Mr. Everett on 'State Sovereignty' and 'Reserved Rights.'" Noting that "there are many points in his speech at Gettysburg which call for criticism," the editor announced that his primary concern was Everett's "attempt to make it appear that state sovereignty is peculiarly a southern doctrine, and furnishes the pretext for this atrocious rebellion." To clarify his position, the editor continued, "That the rebels have proceeded on a perversion of the doctrine of state sovereignty, and have deduced from it consequences that do not legitimately follow, is no valid argument against the doctrine itself." The ensuing paragraphs measured Everett's words and the Constitution, with the purpose to "furnish positive proof that the states are sovereign."

The *World* took up the theme of adherence to the Constitution again on November 27, this time in response to Lincoln's subordination of that document to the Declaration of Independence. The column began by reciting Lincoln's first sentence of the Gettysburg Address and then accused him of "gross ignorance, or willful mis-statement, of the primary fact in our history by a President of the United States." Why? Because "the Constitution not merely does not say one word about equal rights, but expressly admits the idea of the inequality of human rights." The editor also took issue with Lincoln's comment that "our fathers had brought forth a new nation" and stated instead that the Declaration made the colonies "free, sovereign, independent states." The *World* argued that slavery was not abolished by the Constitution because doing so would have precluded any attempts at union, and in that sense nothing had changed since 1787.

As the only New York daily to criticize the ideas of the Gettysburg Address, the *World* holds a unique position. In 1992, Gary Wills called Lincoln's assertion that the Declaration rather than the Constitution was the nation's founding document "one of the most daring acts of open-air sleight-of-hand ever witnessed by the unsuspecting." But Lincoln did not fool or convince papers like the *World*. Rather, the editor felt that his readers would find abhorrent Lincoln's interpretations on democracy, equality, and slavery.[13]

These Democratic papers were influential but far from unrivaled. Greeley's *New York Tribune* was just as fervently Republican as the *Herald* and *World* were Democratic. The paper published a daily edition for distribution around New York, a semi-weekly version for those a bit farther out, and a weekly that circulated from California to Maine. All told, the paper boasted three hundred thousand subscribers and probably a million readers.[14] On November 20, the *Tribune* carried the telegraphic report from the Associated Press and the next day ran a series of letters from field reporter John Davenport describing the town and cemetery and the public officials who had arrived. In contrast to the harsh criticism leveled at Everett by the *Herald*, Davenport judged his speech "one of the gentleman's best efforts." Then, as it had the day earlier, the *Tribune* printed the complete text of Lincoln's address with applause markers, an unusual step that makes one wonder whether Greeley tried to emphasize Lincoln's words by printing them twice. Greeley had long been a proponent of emancipation, and his plea with Lincoln the previous summer to do something toward this end remains one of the more famous editorials in history. In this light, it is inexplicable that Greeley passed up the chance to analyze or even praise the speech after years of talking about the need for equality.

Raymond's *New York Times* was less sensational than Bennett's *Herald* and although still Republican was more politically moderate than Greeley's *Tribune*. The *Times'* initial coverage also came from the Associated Press account. Like the *Herald*, the *Times* offered an early evaluation of Everett's address, noting that his "narrative of the marches manoeuvres, skirmishes and strategy . . . will tend to confuse and repel those who are less familiar with the events than himself, and crowd out those 'glittering generalities' which he or any other great orator might be expected mainly to deal in on such an occasion." The editor softened his criticism with the conclusion, "After he gets through with this, however, Mr. Everett does justice to his subject and himself."

On November 21, the *Times* printed Seward's oration, a part of the Associated Press account that it had left out the previous day, along with a column penned by "our Special Correspondent." The correspondent noted the large number of visitors in town and expressed the opinion that many came for reasons other than the speeches, for even while Everett spoke the crowds roaming the battlefield equaled those listening to the dedication ceremonies. And in a line that reveals, perhaps, why the newspapers spent so much of their columns reviewing the battle and battlefield, the author observed of the crowd, "They seem to have considered, with President Lincoln, that it was not what was *said* here, but what was *done* here, that deserved their attention." Whether the writer intentionally paraphrased Lincoln or if the observation was an original thought is unclear. Although many of his colleagues wrote about the parts of Lincoln's speech dealing with democracy, this journalist focused on those dealing with freedom: "But little over four months have passed away since the champions of Slavery and Freedom met here in deadly strife."

Weekly journals of the mid-nineteenth century tended to provide fewer news items but longer articles, giving each piece more substantial thought. They also typically included a great deal of literature and travel narratives. This shift in emphasis, as well as their less frequent publication, meant that the weeklies left out a great many news items covered by the dailies.

New York's weeklies typically covered the cemetery dedication and accompanying speeches through special dispatches or editorials rather than the blow-by-blow reporting offered by the dailies. The *Ledger*, a journal declaring itself "Devoted to Choice Literature, Romance, the News, and Commerce," leaned Republican and contained an extended editorial on the ceremonies covering Everett's oration. The journal left little doubt as to what it thought of the speech: "The discourse of Mr. Everett was marked by that fine sense of propriety, of fitness, which is an unfailing characteristic of his public efforts." The first half of the column gushed over Everett's oratorical skills; the second half touched more specifically on the context of his two-hour-long speech. The *Ledger*, unlike the *World*, believed Everett's explanation of the political and legal factors of the war: "In the political exposition which forms an integral portion of the discourse Mr. Everett shows his usual temperance of statement, his keen sagacity of view, and his peculiar aptness in enforcing his argument by historical parallels." Such a careful position, the *Ledger* noted, was in line with Everett's attempts to bring peace both through his spot on the Constitutional-Union ticket in 1860 and in his quest for British mediation of the conflict early in the war. But the speech at Gettysburg revealed Everett's transformation, or so the *Ledger* surmised: "Haunted by a sad foreboding of the consequences of war between the North and the South, he has, as he gracefully expresses it, perhaps tried too long in the path of hopeless compromise. . . . But now he has no terms to make with rebels. Eloquently does he insist on the first duty of the patriot to stand by the Union. Bravely does he urge the people of America to prosecute the war to a successful issue, to establish peace upon a permanent basis by victory over the armed hosts of revolt. . . . Never did Mr. Everett utter a more generous, a more electric, a more thrilling word." The *Ledger* commended Everett's change of stance on the war, something for which the Richmond and London papers, as well as the Democratic New York papers, condemned him. Taken with the *World*, the reporting in the *Ledger* supports the contention that editors viewed the ceremonies at Gettysburg, including the speeches, through their preexisting worldview and found little to change their minds.[15]

The two most famous weeklies during the war, *Harper's Weekly* and *Frank Leslie's Illustrated Newspaper*, were both profusely illustrated, New York–based journals that leaned Republican. On December 5, *Leslie's* offered two pages of illustrations from Gettysburg, including scenes of Union graves, the town itself, Rebel graves, a large spread of the "Dedication Ceremony" taking up half the page, depictions of Meade's headquarters, the Round Tops and another picture of Union graves. Two pages later, a column titled simply "The Gettysburg Celebration" covered the ceremonies with a fairly straightforward narrative and little commentary other than a favorable remark on the entire commemoration. *Leslie's* also included the text of Lincoln's address as reported in the *Philadelphia Inquirer* of November 20. That version differs from the Associated Press transcription in several places and is generally viewed as less accurate. There is one significant difference in this transcription, which is the reporting of Lincoln's final line as government "for all the people." The final line is typically construed as emphasizing democracy, but the addition of *all* echoes Theodore Parker, changes the tone, and makes it the third statement about black equality and freedom rather than the first about democracy. Philadelphia's *Christian Recorder* of November 28 also used this phraseology. In later years, people focused on that final line to talk exclusively about democracy, but in 1863, at least one reporter thought Lincoln referenced equality.

THAT POOR PRESIDENT LINCOLN

Like *Frank Leslie's*, *Harper's Weekly* also printed its first account of the dedication ceremonies on December 5. These illustrated journals, having to plan the bulk of their content far in advance in order to secure the drawings and prepare them for the press, could not offer immediate responses to the Gettysburg ceremonies the way the dailies and nonillustrated weeklies could. On December 5, *Harper's* ran a five-paragraph account of the cemetery dedication that included responses to the two major speeches. Of Everett, *Harper's* observed, "The oration by Mr. Everett was smooth and cold. Delivered, doubtless, with his accustomed graces, it yet wanted one stirring thought, one vivid picture, one thrilling appeal." The President came in for a better review: "The few words of the President were from the heart to the heart. They can not be read, even, without kindling emotion. 'The world will little note nor long remember what we say here, but it can never forget what they did here.' It was as simple and felicitous and earnest a word as was ever spoken." Nearly a month later, on January 9, 1864, *Harper's* again quoted that line in its column on "The New Year" but offered no new thoughts. In that initial report of December 5, *Harper's* skipped over Seward's speech, but two weeks later, it rectified that omission. *Harper's* took issue with Seward's classification of the Confederates as "misguided brethren" and with the general idea that negotiations remained a possibility: "They are men to conquer or be conquered." For the most part, Seward escaped criticism from his home-state papers, an omission that the Gettysburg journals rectified.

One of the more specialized weeklies to cover Gettysburg was the New York–based *National Anti-Slavery Standard*. On November 28, the journal printed an excerpt of Everett's speech, the Associated Press version of Lincoln's address, Seward's remarks, and a brief explanation of the events following the dedication ceremonies excerpted from the *New York Times* of November 21. An editorial letter penned on November 22 by the journal's Washington correspondent, identified only as "Avon," considered what Seward's speech revealed about the administration's stance on abolition. Seward had recently made several comments that greatly concerned the antislavery elements in the North. However, his statements about the war mercifully ending slavery left the journalist to conclude, "It is very difficult to find out just what his real opinions are upon the slavery question," because Seward carefully considered his thoughts before speaking, and his words "came from the lips of a shrewd political diplomatist, and not from an earnest man's heart." In the fall of 1863, abolitionists believed Lincoln's efforts to keep the Border States in the union would lead him to make concessions effectively nullifying emancipation. But declaring that "Mr. Lincoln and Mr. Seward are on the most intimate terms of friendship, and *they understand each other*," Avon concluded, "The Gettysburg speech from Mr. Seward is encouraging not only in reference to himself, but also in reference to the president." A week later, Avon offered another letter reiterating his earlier missive. Noting the successes of the western armies, he concluded that militarily the cause of freedom rested on sounder ground than it had earlier in the fall: "When Mr. Seward finds it necessary to come out, as he did at Gettysburg, and avow his opposition to slavery, Mr. Lincoln, who, ever since the war broke out, has at all times been in advance of his Secretary of State, may be relied upon." Given Seward's long history as an antislavery Republican and the context of his speech, it was natural for most of the antislavery papers to focus on his words. William Lloyd Garrison's *Liberator*, a Boston-based journal, highlighted Seward's remarks by placing them at the beginning of the column. A brief introduction of just three sentences preceded Seward's words. Gilbert's version of Lincoln's oration followed, along with an overview of the day's other events.[16] The names of these two papers suggest, perhaps, why they focused on Seward's words rather than Lincoln's. In a time when the great majority of the nation's African Americans were still enslaved, the *Liberator* and the *Anti-Slavery Standard* were more concerned with ending the institution of slavery permanently and throughout the entire nation, something Seward addressed directly, than securing equality—a phrase filled with multiple and contested meanings.

Some of the other weeklies had less coverage. The *New York Dispatch* printed a poem about the Battle of Gettysburg on November 29 but nothing else, though two weeks later it would call Lincoln's annual message to Congress "compact, simple, truthful, and sometimes even eloquent."[17] Similarly, the *Irish American* printed nothing about the Address; perhaps, the paper's Democratic sympathies and frequent tirades against Lincoln were weighed against the knowledge that he was speaking over the graves of many Irishmen who had fought and died at Gettysburg.

As with many other issues during the war, the tenor of a New York newspaper's coverage of the dedication ceremonies at Gettysburg and of Lincoln's Gettysburg Address was dependent upon the paper's political leanings. The Democratic papers, such as Bennett's *Herald* and the *World*, focused most of their venom on Everett. The Democratic editors despised Everett for his stance in support of the Republican administration once the war began. In a city that toyed with the idea of secession, Everett's denunciation of state sovereignty also provided fodder for the Democratic editors and ensured that they would focus their venom on him. The Republican-leaning papers, on the other hand, generally commented favorably on Everett's effort, though they focused more on his oratorical skills than his content and were more likely to offer praise for Lincoln's speech. In short, the war led to little evolution in the views of New York editors, but, rather, they adhered to their prewar political divisions and offered a range of responses to Everett's speech. The one thing they all seemed to have agreed upon, however, was that it was Everett more than Lincoln who demanded comment.

Due to publishing frequency, New York papers had already reached Gettysburg carrying reports of the dedication ceremonies before the local papers put out their own accounts. This delay of four days certainly stole some of the thunder from the Gettysburg papers, but it also allowed them to include more material and to excerpt and respond to outside articles. While all of the cities discussed in this chapter were more interested in the events at Gettysburg than the speeches, the local papers were the most extreme in this regard, passing over any real consideration of the speeches and devoting all their space various festivities in *their* town.

The *Compiler* was the first local paper to report the events of November 19. The paper declared itself "A Democratic and Family Journal," and editor Henry Stahle strongly disliked the current administration and the chief executive. On August 13, 1860, Stahle referred to Lincoln as a "Fifth rate lawyer" with "no experience in legislation, no claims to Statesmanship." In the months and days leading up to the election, Stahle reprinted articles from Democratic papers proclaiming Lincoln's supposed alliance with the abolitionists and predicting impending doom should the Republican triumph. When Lincoln proposed both the permanent establishment of paper currency and compensated emancipation in his second annual message to Congress, Stahle commented, "We cannot persuade ourselves that Mr. Lincoln really believes that either of them can be carried out. If he does, then he is weaker than we supposed him to be." The issuance of the preliminary Emancipation Proclamation two months earlier left a sour taste in Stahle's mouth, and he would later comment, "Lincoln is for war and the nigger." Shortly after the fighting at Gettysburg, Union authorities arrested Stahle for allegedly aiding the enemy, a spurious charge in every way. Stahle found himself incarcerated for weeks at Fort McHenry in Baltimore, an ironic place to lose his liberty given that "The Star Spangled Banner" was penned in that very location a half century earlier. After his release, Stahle attacked Lincoln's administration for allowing the mistreatment of Pennsylvanians, both by the invading army and by their own government.[18]

On November 23, Stahle proclaimed November 19 "a great day in the history of Gettysburg—second only in interest to the eventful first, second and third days of July last." After a brief review of the hustle and bustle accompanying the ceremonies and the parade to the cemetery, Stahle said that Everett's address "was an exceedingly elaborate and ornate production." The *Compiler* reprinted Everett's opening paragraphs and closing paragraphs in full and summarized the middle part of his speech. When it came to Lincoln's role, Stahle commented simply, "The Chief Marshall then introduced the President of the United States, who, after the applause had subsided, spoke as follows." Unlike many of his fellow Democratic editors, Stahle printed Lincoln's address. However, rather than adopting the Associated Press version of the speech, the *Compiler* used that from the Republican *Philadelphia Inquirer* of November 20. Despite his earlier incarceration at the hands of Lincoln's government, Stahle did not denigrate the President's speech at Gettysburg, a restraint suggesting this editor understood that for many of his readers, their town's connection to the great events and the President's speech would trump their normal partisanship for at least a day.[19]

One day later, the *Adams Sentinel* offered its evaluation of the ceremonies and Lincoln's speech. Republican editor Robert Harper lived next to David Wills and had hosted Seward on November 18. Like the *Compiler*, the *Sentinel* of November 24, 1863, carried the complete text of Lincoln's speech. Despite Harper's training as a newspaperman, he did not furnish an original version of Lincoln's speech, instead utilizing the Associated Press transcription. In contrast to Stahle, who gave no evaluation of Lincoln or his speeches, Harper noted, "The President was serenaded twice during the evening, and his appearance excited bursts of enthusiasm—showing the strong hold he has upon the affections of the people. He made but few remarks, but they were characteristic of the pure and honest President."

The *Star and Banner*, Gettysburg's third local paper, offered a report of the ceremonies on November 26. The paper declared itself to be "Devoted to the Interests of the People: 'Fearless and Free'" and leaned heavily Republican. The first page covered Everett's oration. After printing the words Lincoln spoke on the night of November 18 (without the interruption from the audience), the *Star and Banner* said, "The President was most enthusiastically greeted, and when he retired, he did so amid prolonged applause." The paper offered a long review of the events of the night of November 18 and the procession to the cemetery on November 19 before providing the Associated Press version of Lincoln's speech. At the end, the *Star and Banner* related, "Long applause. Three cheers given for the President of the United States and Governors of the States. . . . We heard of several gentlemen being robbed of considerable sums of money, by pickpockets on the occasion of the Dedication of the National Cemetery. . . . Two or three of these long-fingered gentry were arrested by the Detective and lodged in jail."

Coverage of the ceremonies did not quickly pass from the local papers. On December 1 and 3, the *Adams Sentinel* and *Compiler*, respectively, carried the illustration of the cemetery's layout that had first appeared in the *New York World* on November 20. The *Sentinel* of December 1 also carried two further items relating to the events of the nineteenth, revealing the range of activities that had taken place. The first, a column from Philadelphia's *Lutheran & Missionary*, noted the honorable performance of the town and its people both during the battle and the dedication ceremonies. The second was another article on the pickpockets.

On December 14, the *Compiler* reprinted an extensive column titled "Mr. Seward at Gettysburg," clipped from Philadelphia's *Age*, a Democratic paper that usually had little time for Lincoln or his administration. In a marked departure from its usual critiques of Lincoln, two days following the dedication ceremonies the *Age* declared, "[T]he speech of the President is the best he has ever made." Seward came in for harsher treatment: "Mr. Seward, after the fighting was over, went to Gettysburg to do what is more in his line than fighting—make a speech and have a 'lively time.'" The editor condemned Seward for steadfastly denying during the antebellum years that a war would touch Pennsylvania but then declaring in his Gettysburg speech that "he anticipated forty years ago that the battle of freedom would be fought upon this ground, and that slavery would die." The writer concluded that Seward either lied at

Gettysburg or had for the better part of his life and that in either case he was culpable for the deaths of so many. Now, Seward was tarnishing their memories: "When they are cold in the ground and cannot resent the slander—comes the demon who had falsely entrapped them, and, standing on their bodies, denies their patriotism, denies them their life's opinion, and degrades a triumphant sacrifice at the holiest of altars into a barbarous quarrel for a cause that the majority of these dead patriots hated and despised." Though Stahle did not write this editorial, he offered his approval by reprinting it without comment.

A week later, on December 21, Stahle reprinted another editorial attacking a speaker at Gettysburg. Decrying John "the dog" Forney's assertion that Stephen Douglas had died at the right time, the *Allentown Democrat* steamed, "If Mr. Douglas had not died at the time he did, we should never have had this war." The paper asserted that Forney had no loyalties and simply flattered anyone with patronage to dispense. With this, the *Compiler*'s coverage of the dedication ceremonies came to a close.

Less overtly partisan than the newspaper accounts is a letter written by Gettysburg resident Harvey Sweney to his brother on November 29. Sweney felt that Lincoln's "modest appearance and dignified manners, to say nothing of the noble speeches he made here, has endeared him to the hearts of the people and added thousands of friends to him on that day."[20] Another piece of evidence also leads one to believe that the citizens of Gettysburg came away impressed with the Address and with Lincoln in general: the election returns from 1860 and 1864. In 1860, the presidential race contained four contenders: the Reading Ticket, Abraham Lincoln, Stephen Douglas, and John Bell. The Reading Ticket was an anti-Lincoln, pro-Democratic ticket. The electors could vote for any Democrat so as to give them the best chance of defeating Lincoln.[21] In Gettysburg, the Reading Ticket received 43.6 percent of the vote and Lincoln 54.4 percent. Four years later, Lincoln increased that margin, outpolling Democrat George Brinton McClellan 60 percent to 39.8 percent, an overall increase of about 10 percent. Considering how poorly Republicans fared in Adams County the year before, these results take on added significance. In the 1863 gubernatorial election, Republican Andrew Curtin lost Adams County by 228 votes, three times more than in 1860. Curtin's weak polling reflected, the *Compiler* argued, the burdens placed on the county during the Gettysburg Campaign. By 1864, the war was on an improved footing, which no doubt partially explains

Lincoln's better showing, but it is hard to believe voters in Gettysburg would have supported Lincoln if his speech had disappointed them.[22]

In most other locales, the news of the dedication ceremonies quickly passed after an initial report or two and maybe an editorial. In Gettysburg, on the other hand, the event was both of national *and* local importance, and, consequently, the story had legs in south-central Pennsylvania that it lacked elsewhere. Most of the immediate response to the dedication ceremonies focused on the role the town played in hosting such a grand event rather than the words spoken by the various dignitaries. Gettysburg's editors offered fewer of their own comments on the speeches than had their New York brethren, instead choosing to reprint editorials from other papers, but as in New York, these tended to fall strictly along party lines. As for Lincoln's Gettysburg Address, while the editors generally announced their respect for the man and his attendance at the ceremonies, they offered no more evaluative comments on the President's words than had the New Yorkers.

By the fall of 1863, Richmond, Virginia, housed the Confederate government, was protected by the South's most famous and successful army, and was economically the most important city in the seceded states. During the war, the city's population swelled from thirty-seven thousand in 1860 to over one hundred thousand at the peak of the war. The newspapers of the city dominated those of the Confederacy, particularly when it came to reporting Northern events. The Richmond press used that dominance to censor reports of the dedication ceremonies at Gettysburg and Lincoln's speech. While early reports of the event confused Lincoln's role at Gettysburg, later pieces omitted the words that Lincoln spoke. By quoting the Declaration, Lincoln had invoked Thomas Jefferson against his fellow Virginians, and they could not disavow his message without casting aspersions on one of their own. Richmond's editors were careful to not print what Lincoln said that day, lampooning him personally and generally before moving on to Everett's many statements with which they could take issue. Examining the spread of reporting about the dedication ceremonies throughout the South shows that the rest of the Confederate press relied almost totally on the coverage in the Richmond papers, allowing those five editors to shape the reporting on the event throughout the entire region and keep everyone in the dark about what Lincoln had said.

In 1860, the major Southern newspapers belonged to the Associated Press, but the inauguration of war and the June 1, 1861, suspension of telegraphic service between Richmond and Washington, D.C., ended that affiliation. Shortly thereafter, the Southern Associated Press came into existence, but high costs and poor reports led to its demise. In the fall of 1862, the Richmond papers formed the Richmond Press Association. This organization provided cheaper reporting than the Southern Associated Press, but the quality remained poor. Finally, in the early spring of 1863, several major Southern dailies formed the Press Association of the Confederate States of America (also known as the Confederate Press Association). By May of that year, forty-four of the Confederacy's papers belonged, including all the daily Richmond newspapers. Because of the importance of Richmond, the association hired John Graeme Jr. to facilitate news gathering in the Confederacy's capital, and it was likely he who wrote the following November 24 article that appeared in the *Richmond Dispatch*, *Richmond Examiner*, *Richmond Sentinel*, and *Richmond Whig*.[23]

> Several columns of the *Herald* are occupied with a description of the "National Necropolis," or cemetery at Gettysburg. Lincoln, Seward, several foreign ministers, and other dignitaries were present. Lincoln was serenaded the night preceding the day on which the ceremony took place. He declined to make a speech on the ground that "in his position it was somewhat important that he should not say foolish things." A voice—"If you can help it." Lincoln—"It very often happens that the only way to help it is to say nothing at all." (Laughter.)
>
> Seward was also serenaded and responded in an anti-slavery speech. He thanked God for the hope that when slavery is abolished the country will be again united.
>
> The notorious Forney was also serenaded. In his speech he declared that he was in favor of Lincoln's election in 1860, but did not want it to appear so, that he might the better accomplish the breaking up of the Democracy.
>
> Everett's oration is published at length in the *Herald*, occupying six columns of small type. He predicted the reconstruction of the Union.[24]

But where did Graeme get his story? A regular exchange of newspapers between the lines allowed Richmond editors to procure Northern papers within a few days of their publication. According to the *Richmond*

Dispatch of November 24, the accounts of the dedication of the Soldiers' National Cemetery in the Richmond papers that day came from "Northern papers . . . through the courtesy of the officers of the Exchange Bureau."[25] Richmond editors received Northern newspapers within three days of their publication, astonishingly fast considering that the papers had to pass through enemy lines. This exchange also worked in the opposite direction, and the *New York Times* and *Chicago Times* frequently reprinted items from the *Richmond Examiner.*

Nearly all the information from Graeme's account came directly from the *New York Herald*'s subheads, making it difficult to escape the impression that Graeme skimmed that paper's report and did not read the tenth page, which discussed Lincoln's part in the ceremonies. Perhaps, the sentence that Everett's oration consumed "six columns of small type" in the *New York Herald* explains how the writer missed the small column on Lincoln. The editor of the *Richmond Dispatch* commented that he found the news from the North, including Graeme's account, "Not of much interest."[26]

The *Richmond Examiner* of November 25, 1863, contained some of the most extensive reporting of the events accompanying the dedication ceremonies. Noting an abundance of coverage in the "Yankee papers," editor John Moncure Daniel promised "to give only the portion of their accounts likely to interest our readers." Daniel was born on October 24, 1825, in Stafford County, Virginia. After stints reading the law in Fredericksburg and serving as a librarian in Richmond, he found his true calling as a journalist, first for the *Southern Planter*, then the *Richmond Examiner.* Due to his staunchly Democratic editorials, Daniel fought several duels before and during the war. In 1853, President Franklin Pierce appointed Daniel the minister to the court of Victor Emmanuel in Turin, Italy. At this time, a New Yorker sued Daniel for libel on the basis of an editorial Daniel wrote before leaving Richmond. Daniel lost the case and paid several thousand dollars in damages. The outcome of the trial soured Daniel to the North and its citizens, a prejudice that frequently appeared in his writings. The Virginian returned home at the beginning of the Civil War and cast his lot with his native state. He served on General Ambrose Powell Hill's staff until wounded in June 1862, at which time he returned to edit the paper he owned, the *Richmond Examiner.* Daniel preferred to let others compose the paper's editorials but then edited them so heavily their authors did not recognize them. Nothing made it into the *Examiner* that Daniel did not approve. A known racist, Daniel would have found Lincoln's assertion that "all men are created equal" repugnant.[27]

Daniel's biases appeared in the paper's November 25 editorial on the Gettysburg Address. The first part recounted the parade on the morning of November 19. The *Examiner* noted that Stockton's prayer, Everett's oration, and Lincoln's address had already been published, but, in fact, no Richmond newspaper previously printed the speeches. In contrast to the lack of coverage of these three central speeches is the full reprinting of the dirge and benediction that concluded the ceremonies. The following section was titled "LINCOLN'S RECEPTION AT GETTYSBURG—HE MAKES A SPEECH." Yet, rather than the Gettysburg Address, the column discussed Lincoln's remarks of November 18. While complimenting the crowd for their respect and orderliness, Daniel chided Lincoln for behaving in a "humorous manner" despite the "solemnity and reverence" that such an occasion required.

Three days later, the *Examiner* condemned the ceremonies as "the substitution of glittering foil and worthless paste for real brilliants and pure gold." Daniel opined, "The Yankees have an invincible conviction that they are the successors of the Romans in empire, and of the Athenians in genius." Edward Everett "'took down his THUCYDIDES,' and fancied himself a PERICLES."[28] The *Examiner* continued, "The play was strictly classic. . . . A vein of comedy was permitted to mingle with the deep pathos of the piece. This singular novelty, and the deviation from classic propriety, was heightened by assigning this part to the chief personage. Kings are usually made to speak in the magniloquent language supposed to be suited to their elevated position. On the present occasion Lincoln acted the clown." However, the following line asserted that Lincoln "declined to speak for fear he should perpetrate a folly," revealing that the speech in question was that of November 18. The following sentences confirm that point by mentioning the disappointment of the crowd that Lincoln would not speak. The editorial also pointed out the comments of the heckler who joked that Lincoln "could only avoid talking nonsense by holding his tongue." What promised to be an evaluation of the Gettysburg Address quickly revealed itself instead as a reference to Lincoln's November 18 remarks. On December 8, the Democratic *Chicago Times* reprinted the *Examiner*'s editorial of November 28 on the front page, giving it an audience in the North.

On November 25, the *Richmond Dispatch* published an account of "THE GETTYSBURG CEMETERY CELEBRATION—THE SPEECHES." It appears that the *Dispatch* obtained a copy of the *New York Herald* the day after its initial report on the dedication. Derisively calling the ceremonies "entirely Yankeeish," the paper gave a rundown of the speeches on November 18, including the text of Lincoln's comments and a summary of Seward's speech before reprinting parts of Everett's oration.

Founded just a decade before the war, the *Dispatch* broke with the other Richmond papers in claiming no political affiliation and vowing that news would stand superior to politics on its pages. The journal cost only a penny and quickly attracted the younger crowd in the city and surrounding areas. By 1860, it had a circulation of eighteen thousand, the largest of any paper in the state, and was probably the third-largest daily in the South, just behind two of the New Orleans papers.[29] The *Richmond Dispatch* focused most of its editorial on "Edward Everett, of 'Boasting,' [Boston] that secondary and most disgusting edition and representative of the Pilgrim Fathers." Everett had contended that he did not believe "there has been a day since the election of President Lincoln when, if an ordinance of secession could have been fairly submitted to the mass of the people, in any single Southern State a majority of ballots would have been given in its favor." This predictably drew fire from the editor of the *Dispatch*, who exclaimed, "the stiff corpses of one thousand two hundred and eight eighty men lying in a semi-circle around him, killed dead," served the "purpose of giving the lie to all such statements." The editor disingenuously asserted Virginia's unity on the question of secession as the state did not secede until after the armed conflict had started at Fort Sumter, and the *Dispatch* did not fully support secession until 1861. Two years into the war, however, the past was glossed over in the name of unity and Confederate nationalism. The account ended after Everett's oration with no discussion of Lincoln's speech on November 19.

Many Virginians despised Everett before his comments at Gettysburg. Much like the man who followed him that day at Gettysburg, Everett opposed slavery but feared the dissolution of the Union should steps be taken against the institution. In the 1860 presidential election, Tennessee, Kentucky, and Virginia pledged their electoral votes to Bell and Everett's Constitutional-Union Party ticket, only to see Everett throw his support behind Lincoln and the government's war policies after Fort Sumter.

The man that many Virginians had voted for as their choice to hold the second-highest office in the nation had turned his back on them. In short, Southern comments about Everett's oration probably had as much to do with his past as his words at Gettysburg.[30]

On November 27, the editor of the *Richmond Dispatch* devoted a whole column to Everett, beginning, "Everett's oration at Gettysburg is what might have been expected of that unreal, metaphorical, moonlight orator. It matters little to him what the facts." In this case, the facts Everett supposedly twisted revolved around the levels of support for secession. Much like the *Richmond Examiner*, the *Dispatch* made no mention of Lincoln's role in the dedication ceremonies and his speech. The *Liberator*, the famed abolitionist paper published in Everett's hometown, picked up this editorial and reprinted it verbatim on January 1, 1864, as "A Rebel View of Edward Everett's Gettysburg Oration."

Founded in 1804, the *Richmond Enquirer* was the oldest of Richmond's papers. In 1863, Democrats Nathaniel Tyler and William J. Dunnavant owned and edited the paper.[31] On November 27, the *Enquirer* reported that Lincoln had played a part in the dedication ceremonies and offered Richmond's first direct reaction to Lincoln's speech of November 19. The paper identified Lincoln as the "stage manager and Edward Everett as the 'Orator of the day.' . . . Mr. Everett produced the expected allusions to Marathon and Waterloo, in the best style of the sophomores of Harvard." Everett's affiliation with Harvard made the reference both personal and pointed. The editorial further commented, "After the Orator of the day, President Pericles, or rather Abe, made the dedicatory speech; but had to limit his observations within small compass, lest he should tell some funny story over the graves of the Immortals." In stating that Lincoln spoke after Everett, the *Enquirer* demonstrated an understanding of Lincoln's role in the ceremonies on November 19. However, the *Enquirer* never explicitly discussed the words Lincoln spoke at Gettysburg, instead denigrating Lincoln for the brevity of his comments. In referencing Pericles, as had Daniel of the *Examiner*, the *Enquirer* editor signified his own erudition while suggesting that Lincoln was not being original but rather copying a two-thousand-year-old speech.

Two of Richmond's dailies, the *Whig* and the *Sentinel*, carried the Confederate Press Association's account of the cemetery dedication on November 24 but offered no further reports. While the other three dailies all printed at least one other substantial article on the dedication

THAT POOR PRESIDENT LINCOLN   57

ceremonies, none of the papers reprinted the words that Lincoln spoke at the dedication ceremonies. In marked contrast, in both 1861 and 1865, the *Richmond Dispatch* reprinted Lincoln's inaugural addresses. In 1861, the paper carried substantial commentary on the U.S. presidential inauguration, while the reporting in 1865 consisted of a simple description. In both the inaugurals and the Gettysburg Address, Lincoln advocated a strong national government and indicated his personal opposition to slavery, but only in the Gettysburg Address did Lincoln assert the equality of all men. It cannot be mere coincidence that Richmond's papers censored the speech containing this assertion, even though the text was available to them. As is often the case, what the newspapers omit is as significant as what they print.[32]

From Richmond, news of the events at Gettysburg spread to the rest of the state and the Confederacy. On November 27, 1863, the Lynchburg *Virginian* offered extensive reporting on "THE CEMETERY—SPEECH AND WIT OF LINCOLN." After a full column on the parade to the cemetery, the *Virginian* related, "The dedication ceremonies were then performed, the oration being delivered by Edward Everett, after which the crowd dispersed." A description of the cemetery ensued. This account is full of details, making it remarkable that it contains nothing on the part President Lincoln played. The reference in the headline to a speech by Lincoln was to an entirely different event that had taken place on November 18 in Hanover Junction, Pennsylvania, before Lincoln even arrived in Gettysburg.

The *Virginian*'s editor corrected his earlier omission on December 4 in a story "Old Abe's Last." Taking the account from the *New York World*, the editor quoted the opening sentence of Lincoln's Gettysburg Address, the only paper in the Old Dominion to quote any part of the speech. Despite reporting part of Lincoln's oration, the Lynchburg editor thought no more of Lincoln than his Richmond colleagues: "Really, the ignorance and coarseness of this man would repel and disgust any other people than the Yankees. . . . What a commentary is this on the character of our enemies."[33]

The *Staunton Vindicator* of December 4 provided additional comments on Everett and his "unkind criticism" of the South based wholly on the reporting of the *Richmond Dispatch*. Noting that "many of our contemporaries are much disturbed at the consecration of the field at Gettysburg as a huge Yankee Necropolis and give vent to unkind criticism of the part taken by Edward Everett," the *Vindicator* editor admitted that he had not read Everett's oration or a report of it. Yet, he indicated distaste for the man whom they had once admired. The paper sarcastically told Everett to come dedicate the final resting places of Union soldiers who had fallen in Virginia. There were a good many, the editor noted, and more would join them if the North persisted in its action. The entire story in the *Staunton Vindicator* centered on Everett's role in the dedication ceremonies; not once did Lincoln's name appear. Staunton's other paper, the *Spectator*, offered no coverage on the dedication ceremonies.

As the news of the dedication of the cemetery at Gettysburg made its way across the Confederacy, the Southern press followed Richmond's lead. The piece authored by Graeme appeared in many Confederate newspapers over the following ten days. Between November 24 and November 29, the *Atlanta Daily Constitutionalist, Atlanta Daily Intelligencer, Atlanta Southern Confederacy, Augusta Daily Chronicle & Sentinel, Charleston Mercury, Daily South Carolinian, Macon Telegraph, Memphis Appeal, Mobile Daily Advertiser & Register, Savannah Daily Morning News*, and *Wilmington Daily Journal* published either Graeme's account or, more often, an abbreviated version.

A few days after the appearance of these telegraphic accounts, the other Southern newspapers began receiving copies of the Richmond papers and quickly copied their Virginia brethren. In its edition of November 30, the *Memphis Appeal* reprinted the *Richmond Enquirer*'s account of three days earlier. On December 2, the *Atlanta Daily Intelligencer* carried that same account. The *Macon Telegraph* reprinted the account from the November 25, 1863, *Richmond Dispatch*. The *Mobile Daily Advertiser & Register* reprinted another account from the *Richmond Dispatch* focusing entirely on Everett's oration and did not mention either Lincoln or his speeches. None of these papers wrote their own editorials about the events surrounding Lincoln's Gettysburg Address and the dedication of the Soldiers' National Cemetery. Instead, they simply reprinted articles written by the Richmond newspapers, revealing the influence the Richmond editors had, particularly over events originating in the North. Richmond, therefore, represents Southern reporting on the Gettysburg Address. This position of national prominence was already well-established. Following the battle of Chancellorsville in May 1863, the *Savannah Republican* and *Wilmington Daily Journal* both complained that the Richmond papers had not printed the casualty lists from out-of-state regiments or discussed their roles in the battle, evidencing their conception of the Richmond papers as a national press, much like today's *New York Times* or *Washington Post*.[34]

The New Orleans press alone among Southern papers did not follow Richmond's lead. By fall 1863, Union forces had occupied the city for a year and a half. Southern editors ran most of the city's papers, with one exception. When Union General Benjamin F. Butler took command of New Orleans, the editor of the *New Orleans Crescent*, J. O. Nixon, belonged to the Confederate army. Butler confiscated the paper and had it sold to Unionists, who rechristened the paper the *New Orleans Times*.[35]

Because of New Orleans's shipping activity and its occupation by the Union, the city's editors frequently received New York papers sooner than those from other places in the Confederacy. The city's *Daily True Delta* carried Lincoln's Gettysburg Address on December 1 and three days later reprinted the *New York World*'s editorial of November 21 criticizing Everett and "his arguments against State sovereignty and reserved rights."[36] On December 3, the daily *New Orleans Bee* noted that it had received the *New York Herald* of November 21, probably courtesy of a Union ship. The editor, like many of his counterparts in Virginia, ignored the role Lincoln had played in the dedication ceremonies and focused on Everett. Calling Everett a "wet blanket," the paper echoed the *Herald*'s assertion that Everett did not match up to Webster and had not performed well during his dedicatory oration. The *Bee* did not comment on Lincoln's speech.[37] The *New Orleans Times*, the only Union paper in the city, reprinted the *New York Tribune*'s November 20 coverage on December 1, including transcriptions of both of Lincoln's speeches in Gettysburg. In an editorial the following day, the paper commented, "The President's speech at the Gettysburg inauguration excites universal remark and commendation."[38] Memphis, Tennessee, had also fallen into Union hands during the fall of 1863, a fact reflected by the extensive, positive coverage given to the ceremonies by the *Memphis Daily Bulletin*. Like the *New Orleans Daily True Delta*, the *Memphis Daily Bulletin* reprinted Lincoln's address.[39]

Although all the Richmond papers mentioned the events in Pennsylvania, it seems as though few people paid any attention to those accounts. Confederate President Jefferson Davis offered no comments on the Address. Nor did John B. Jones, the famous Confederate war diarist, who wrote about nearly everything newsworthy. Josiah Gorgas, head of Confederate ordnance, also remained silent, as did famous diarists Mary Chesnut and Judith McGuire.[40] Virginia newspapers mentioned Lincoln in nearly every issue, eventually desensitizing their readers to stories about the Union president. Such stories include a December 8, 1863, article from the *Richmond Dispatch* titled "Lincoln Sick." The article related, "Yankee papers say that 'Lincoln has got the varioloid,'" and wondered, "What the varioloid has done that Lincoln should 'get it,' we cannot imagine, but it is just like Lincoln to seize some harmless object, and just like the Yankee papers to make a grand fuss over it." With daily articles like this, it is little wonder that most readers found Southern reporting of the dedication ceremonies to be so commonplace as to merit passing over without comment.

As a result of the censorship by the Richmond editors, few Southerners in 1863 had any idea what Lincoln said at the dedication of the cemetery in Gettysburg. While the Richmond papers reprinted Lincoln's inaugurals in both 1861 and 1865, they never provided their readers with the text of Lincoln's words at Gettysburg. Some Northern papers, such as the *New York World*, also chastised Lincoln's speech, but they, at least, printed his words so their readers could form their own judgments. Lincoln's affirmation "that all men are created equal" and his call for "a new birth of freedom" invoke Virginian Thomas Jefferson to link the Gettysburg Address to the Emancipation Proclamation, and as a result, the Richmond editors lampooned Lincoln's appearance and words without ever telling their readers what he said.

The editorials proffered south of the Mason-Dixon line focused wholly on Everett's speech with its assertions about the legitimacy of secession. The Old Dominion had a special relationship with the Massachusetts man, having supported his bid for the vice presidency in 1860, and his seeming betrayal earned him the lion's share of the editorial criticism. Unlike New York and Gettysburg, where a functioning second-party press provided at least some editorial variety, the editors in Richmond sang the same tune. The domination of the Richmond press ensured that their version of the ceremonies disseminated throughout the Confederacy, and, thus, Confederates associated Everett, not Lincoln or Seward, most closely with Gettysburg.

On December 2, 1863, a ship named the *Edinburgh* arrived in Queenstown, Ireland, carrying copies of the New York papers dated November

20 and 21 and at least one letter for the *Times* of London written by its special correspondent in New York. In 1858, the United States and Great Britain had laid an underwater cable across the ocean floor to allow telegraphic communication between the two nations and continents. Unfortunately, after just a month in operation and a total of four hundred messages sent and received, the cable stopped working. The year after the Civil War ended, another cable once again linked the nations and enabled communication within hours rather than days. But, in 1863, news traveled no faster than the ships. Within hours of the *Edinburgh's* arrival, agents read those New York papers and sent a summary to London via telegraph.[41]

After those living in North America, the people most concerned with the outcome of the Civil War lived in England. The focus here is specifically on England as both Scotland and Ireland had different stances on the war than that commonly found in England.[42] The United States and England shared a bond that remained strong despite frequent animosities. The two countries did more trade with each other than anyone else. In 1860, the English cotton industry employed five million people, and England's importation of cotton provided economic support for slavery, a great irony as it had abolished that institution throughout the empire a generation earlier and took great pride in opposing slavery to the point that Englishmen purchased more copies of *Uncle Tom's Cabin* than their American cousins.[43] On the other hand, as historian Jay Sexton has shown, Confederate diplomats "argued that secession was an act of self-determination, a principle that had much traction in liberal quarters of Europe." But such sympathy would gain little momentum, for the Confederacy's "economic blackmail of the cotton embargo antagonized British statesmen," who both had greater financial ties to the North and were concerned that support for secession in the United States would come home to roost in both Ireland and India.[44]

In terms of gaining English support, the North was its own biggest enemy. In his first inaugural address, Lincoln reaffirmed his earlier declaration during the Lincoln-Douglas debates, "I have no purpose, directly or indirectly, to interfere with the institution of slavery in the States where it exists. I believe I have no lawful right to do so, and I have no inclination to do so."[45] This may have reassured pro-Union slaveholders of Lincoln's intentions, but it certainly did not help his cause overseas. On October 5, 1861, London's *Saturday Review* commented, "England is slandered if it is said that she does not with her whole heart hate slavery and desire its extinction, or that she would not be cordially with the North if it were against slavery that the North was fighting. The North, however, vehemently disclaims any such imputation."

English suspicions of Northern complicity in maintaining and perpetuating slavery had a long history. Despite officially ending its participation in the Atlantic slave trade in 1808, the United States made minimal efforts to prevent illegal trading. After 1842, the country provided no monies for the purpose of enforcement and levied no significant punishments against offenders, turning a blind eye to the slave trade and infuriating the English. The Royal Navy took the lead in preventing the trade, patrolling the coast of Africa and stopping suspicious ships. After a time, the Royal Navy started boarding American ships they suspected carried slaves. The Northern Democratic press—led by the *New York Herald*—protested most vehemently, not necessarily because they supported slavery but both because Northerners owned and operated most of the maritime fleet and because they objected to British usurpations of American sovereignty. As a result, the English came to see the North as allowing the continuation of the slave trade, a conclusion supported by the fact that between 1857 and 1861 over seventy slave-trading expeditions left from New York City. Further, just two days before Lincoln's inauguration, Congress adopted the Morrill Tariff, a protective measure that doubled the taxes collected on imported goods. At the time, the United States imported 40 percent of its manufactured goods from England, and Englishmen saw the tariff as a direct attack on their country. The tariff effectively privileged the North's manufacturing over the South's export economy, belying the notion that the government was working to bring the seceded states back into the fold. Finally, Lincoln's selection of Seward as his secretary of state did little to ameliorate English feelings toward the North. In the 1850s, Seward steadfastly opposed negotiating over the border of the Oregon Territory and simultaneously agitated for the annexation of Canada—no small threat considering what the United States had done in Mexico less than a decade earlier. During the secession crisis, Seward proposed declaring war on England in order to reunify the United States, a suggestion that soon leaked.

When the war broke out, most English citizens were disgusted with both sides, and many, to quote historian R. J. M. Blackett, "declared a pox on both houses" and supported neither side.[46] In a *National Review* editorial published in July 1861, editor William Rathbone Greg opined: "We cannot be very zealous for the North; for we do not like her ambition; we are irritated by her insolence; we are aggrieved by her tariffs; but we still have much feelings of kinship and esteem. We cannot be zealous at all for the South; for though she is friendly and free-trading, she is fanatically SLAVE, and Slavery is the object of our rooted detestation."[47] As the war dragged on, events led the English to one side and then the other. In December 1861, the *USS San Jacinto* stopped the English mail steamer *Trent* and removed two Confederate diplomats, outraging Englishmen, who viewed the action as an attack on their sovereignty. The two nations almost came to blows for the third time in less than a century before Lincoln resolved the situation by releasing the two diplomats. Though resolved peacefully, the *Trent* affair hardened anti-Northern sentiments.[48]

Despite domestic expectations, the Emancipation Proclamation did not swing English support to the North. The *London Morning Post*, *London Morning Herald*, and *London Daily Telegraph* all attributed the Emancipation Proclamation to blatantly political motives that stripped it of any moral authority. Lincoln's claims that the war was not about slavery and that he would discuss an end to the conflict that left the institution intact opened him up to such criticisms. While the Proclamation deprived the South of some of the sympathy it previously enjoyed, no immediate increase in support for the North ensued. Lincoln's almost exclusive appointment of abolitionist-minded men to the diplomatic posts in Britain likewise had little effect.[49]

As Seward, Everett, and Lincoln spoke in Gettysburg, Englishmen looked for one side to stake out a worthy position. Much like New York in the United States, London was the center of news in England. Foreign news would first appear in the daily and semi-weekly papers aimed at the middle class. Typically, on the first day of coverage, these papers would run the basic outlines, frequently excerpted from other papers. For important stories, an editorial followed within a few days. The weekly, monthly, quarterly, and annual journals popular in the country covered weightier issues. This, combined with their calmer tone, gave these journals more political influence. As in America, papers passed among multiple readers, oftentimes at dens or libraries where people congregated to read and discuss the news.

Of the daily papers, the *Times* of London reached the widest audience, with a circulation as high as sixty-five thousand. That paper had been rather skeptical of Lincoln to this point, a result of his failure to move against slavery purely on a moral basis. After the Emancipation Proclamation, the *Times* commented that Lincoln had an "utterly inefficient, though possibly well-meaning Administration," one "that mismanages everything which it touches; that inspires few people with respect, and no one with confidence." Furthermore, the *Times* called the Emancipation Proclamation "hopelessly in his way." The *Times'* editors rarely held back when perceiving a chance to denigrate Lincoln and what they viewed as his half-hearted strikes against slavery.[50]

On December 3, the *Times* printed a descriptive account of the ceremonies at Gettysburg that noted the presence of Lincoln, Seward, and Everett and offered a full reprint of Lincoln's speech but without the breaks for applause that most of the New York papers of November 20 included. In concluding, the columnist summarized Everett's fifty-page speech in a single sentence: "Mr. Everett made a long speech recapitulating the events of the campaign which terminated with the battle of Gettysburg." The great battle, the subject of Everett's speech, appealed more to American readers than to Englishmen three thousand miles away, resulting in this short recap of Everett's very lengthy address.[51]

The following day, the *Times* carried two more stories about the dedication ceremonies. The first fell under the heading "The Field of Gettysburg." After a two-sentence introduction, the *Times* printed the Associated Press version of Lincoln's speech with the applause markers. A two-sentence transition led into an excerpt from Everett's speech describing the location and geography of the cemetery and concluded with a full transcript of Seward's speech of November 18. Of the three speeches reprinted, Lincoln's was the last delivered yet the first in the story. The positioning of the speech and the inclusion of the applause markers in this version suggest the importance assigned to it by the journalist and editor.

Three pages later followed a three-column article, "The Civil War in America," by its New York correspondent, about a third of which covered the activities at Gettysburg. The correspondent revealed his distinct lack of respect for both principal speakers, saying that the ceremony was "rendered somewhat flat by the nature of Mr. Everett's lecture, and ludicrous by some of the luckless sallies of that poor President Lincoln." That comment was a reference to Lincoln's comments on November 18, for the writer later noted that Lincoln's November 19 words were "got up in a somewhat different style from his extempore effusion of the eve." The writer commented that Seward "spoke rather more to the purpose" and ascribed the cause of the war to slavery. Lincoln had attacked slavery, too, and, in fact, had gone further and argued for a measure of equality, but he had done so by invoking the Declaration of Independence, and perhaps this English writer chose not to remind his countrymen of their loss of the American colonies eighty-seven years earlier. As Blackett notes, references to the Declaration would have brought up "a deep sense of betrayal that many still felt at the loss of the American colonies." Thus, in quoting Jefferson's Declaration of Independence, Lincoln silenced both Richmond and London.[52] The conservative *Times* was more willing to consider Seward's and Everett's comments about abolition than Lincoln's about equality.

Then came the punch line: "The Hon. Edward Everett is a lady's orator." His speech "reads tame beyond belief, and is such a performance as would scarcely win the prize for composition over the common run of undergraduates." The journalist complained that the speech recounted the battle in boring detail and offered an unsophisticated pontification on the causes of the war: "Anything more dull and commonplace, anything less calculated to call forth deep or lively or lasting emotions, it would not be easy by the most fastidious taste, the most unwearied industry, and the most consummate scholarship without a soul to it to produce." In the land of Wellington, the exploits of Meade hardly justified a two-hour oration.

On December 3, both the *London Daily Telegraph* and *London Morning Post* offered a short column, courtesy of Reuters: "Mr. Lincoln, Mr. Seward, and the Corps Diplomatique were present at the dedication of the Gettysburg cemetery. Edward Everett made an oration."[53] While that was the only mention in the *Telegraph* of the dedication ceremonies, the *Morning Post* carried another story the next day, this one consisting of a paragraph-long overview of the ceremonies along with a full transcription of Lincoln's address without any marks for applause. The paper also printed a brief excerpt of Seward's remarks on the night of November 18 but nothing from Everett's oration. On December 19, the *Leeds Intelligencer* printed a story on the Gettysburg Address largely from the December 4 *Morning Post* account with a few minor changes. When it came to reporting international events, the smaller, outlying newspapers frequently excerpted the columns from the London papers rather than write their own.

On December 12, the *Morning Post* made up for its earlier, skimpy coverage of Everett. As the mouthpiece of Prime Minister 3d Viscount Palmerston, this column in the *Morning Post* is the closest thing to an official response to the dedication ceremonies and the speeches. The New York correspondent began, "The tergiversation of the Northern politicians in this crisis has been much discussed." Before the outbreak of the war, Everett had vigorously opposed compelling the Southern states to remain in the Union against their will, demanding, "In the name of Heaven, let them go in peace." But then, without any reason, according to the columnist, Everett "coolly changed sides . . . [and] has been foremost among those who have encouraged the Administration to persist in its policy, and have stimulated the brutal passions of its soldiery." And now, Everett again showed his immorality: "He must have been more than ever satisfied, as he thought of the fruitless carnage of the two preceding years, that it was 'preposterous' to expect 'to hold 15 States in the Union by force.' But he nevertheless vehemently urged the further prosecution of this war." The columnist lamented that Everett accused the Confederacy of "covering the sea with pirates," responding that the world would not think less of the Confederacy simply because Everett "designates its cruisers as 'pirates.'"[54] In taking particular exception to this point, the author brought the issue home. The Confederacy had contracted with English shipbuilders to build and outfit warships. As a neutral government, England could not allow warships to be built for the Confederacy, but English ambivalence toward the North made them less than diligent in preventing these deals. Although the British government had started confiscating these ships in late 1863, their change in position was not yet widely known.[55]

The *Morning Post* columnist scoffed that Everett "knew his audience. The North echoes his words with acclamation." Herein lay the problem: "If Mr. Everett were but one of many prominent men who had pursued the same disgraceful course, his conduct would have called for no further comment than a disparaging remark or two upon his individual character. But when it is remembered that at least ninety-nine out of every hundred Northern politicians who opposed the election of Mr. Lincoln subsequently manifested as little sense of duty or of decency as Mr. Everett, the subjects suggest reflections of a general and serious nature. . . . Something must be rotten in a nation which presents so sad a spectacle to the world."[56]

The modest coverage of the dedication of the Soldiers' National Cemetery in the daily papers dwarfed that offered by the weeklies and monthlies. Most of these publications consistently dedicated space to the war in America, but among London's weekly papers, only three, the *Englishman*, *Reynolds's Newspaper*, and *Illustrated London News* covered the Gettysburg Address. On December 5, 1863, the *Englishman* carried the same brief Reuters account that had appeared in the *Daily Telegram* and *Morning Post* of December 3. On December 8, the *Illustrated London News* printed the same piece. On December 6, *Reynold's* printed the Gettysburg Address, though it removed the middle portion.

Other papers did not offer even this limited coverage. The *Bee-Hive*, a pro-Confederate paper, frequently printed stories about pro-emancipation meetings in London, Bury, Manchester, and Liverpool but ignored Lincoln's speech. So did the *Spectator*, which had commented on November 28, "It is not easy to be too thankful for the Providence which substituted Lincoln for Seward in the Presidential chair." The *Saturday Review of Politics, Literature, Science, and Art* echoed those sentiments on December 12: "Mr. Lincoln has personally abstained from the offensive language which has been recklessly used by many of his Ministers and political associates." Here, the *Review* intended to remind its readers of Seward's 1861 proposition that the United States invade Canada as a way of reuniting the North and South. But neither these weeklies nor the *Albion*, *Athenaeum*, *Miner & Workman's Advocate*, or *Punch* mentioned the Address. The omission is puzzling given that many of these papers expressed pro-Northern sentiments or at least antislavery ones and theoretically agreed with Lincoln's statements at Gettysburg.[57] It seems likely that these papers, most of whose editors had believed the Emancipation Proclamation to be not a moral act but an expedient one, were just as skeptical of Lincoln's sudden call for equality and, thus, did not know what to make of the speech.

The monthlies offered no more extensive coverage. *British Workwoman Out and at Home*, *Eclectic Review*, *Fraser's Magazine*, *MacMillan's Magazine*, and *New Monthly Magazine* contained largely the same mixture as the weeklies and also ignored completely the events at Gettysburg. The *British Quarterly Review* and *Annual Register* also remained silent. The journals that published less frequently were more selective in which stories they covered, a practice necessitated no doubt by page limits and the need to trim coverage rather than bulk it up. When compared with the other news coming from America concerning the military situation in Tennessee and the annual messages of both Lincoln and Davis in December, the Gettysburg Address simply did not rate as a particularly newsworthy item in the eyes of London's editors.

Overall, the coverage in the London papers was a hybrid of that offered in New York and Richmond. Like most of the New York papers, London editors printed the text of the Gettysburg Address with some brief comments about the ceremony in Gettysburg. Like their counterparts in the American cities, London editors breezed over Lincoln's words with a quick line or two, if at all, and focused most of their attention on Everett. Like Richmond, London had more of a tie to Everett than to Lincoln, for Everett had been a foreign minister assigned to Britain in the 1840s and also proposed asking England to mediate the sectional conflict in 1860 and 1861. Everett's hawkish stance at Gettysburg shocked Englishmen. Further, his portrayal of the Confederacy as a rogue collection of states without legal standing implicitly scolded England for giving covert support to the South. On the other hand, Lincoln had gone even beyond the mere abolition that Englishmen supported and called for a measure of equality, but in basing that argument on the Declaration of Independence, he ensured that his message would not garner wide comment amongst a nation still sensitive about the loss of their one-time colonies. As in Richmond, Everett's comments about the immediate issues ensured the editors would analyze his assertions, while Lincoln's more general tone and invocation of the Declaration meant that most editors were unwilling to grapple with the implications of his words.

All four cities, New York, Gettysburg, Richmond, and London, covered the dedication of the Soldiers' National Cemetery and the accompanying speeches in a similar way. Except for Gettysburg, the initial accounts came from telegraphic dispatches and tended toward a neutral reporting of the actual occurrences and speeches with little editorial comment. In about half of the daily papers reviewed, the editors offered further commentary within the next few days or weeks. The weeklies in all places were less likely to cover the ceremonies, a result of having too much news and too little space. Gettysburg is the obvious exception, as its journals printed significantly more articles and articles of much greater length than the papers of these other cities. New York, Richmond, and London soon turned their attention to other events in America, such as the raging debate over prisoner exchanges and the condition of prisoners, the faltering economy, military actions in Tennessee, a speaking tour by abolitionist Beecher, and, finally, the annual messages of both President Davis and President Lincoln. In Gettysburg, however, the event had local as well as national significance and remained a topic of conversation longer.

Two striking observations emerge from these four cities. The first is the extent to which Gilbert of the Associated Press shaped how the nation and the world, in 1863 and even today, think about the Gettysburg Address. What if Gilbert had offered an inaccurate reporting of Lincoln's words? Or what if he had completely ignored them, as did Richmond's editors? If Northern reports in 1863 ignored Lincoln's words, what would Americans think of them today? Second, given the common origin of all these news items and editorials, the different responses to the speeches are notable. In all four locations, Gettysburg included, the editors reacted to the events at Gettysburg in ways that advanced, in descending order of importance, their own political agendas, then those of their cities, regions, and nations. In Gettysburg, the editors sought to remind the wider readership of the place of the town in the nation's history. The town had borne the experience of battle and birthed a commemoration of epic proportions and was careful to maintain hold on that claim.

In the 1860s, New York had only recently taken the role of leading city from Boston and in many ways remained uneasy in that position. At any rate, a tremendous rivalry existed between the two cities. Republicans and abolitionists dominated Massachusetts, and Boston in particular, while the pro-slavery Tammany Hall Democrats ruled New York City. Everett was a natural target for the New York editors, regardless of his words. That he had switched from a Democrat-friendly political position in 1860 to a Republican-oriented view by 1863 was further ammunition for New York City editors. The substance of Everett's oration, a long explanation of the battle and its significance, was old hat to New Yorkers. With seventeen daily papers publishing during the war, people in the city had seen numerous accounts of the great battle. In smaller towns with fewer papers, Everett's oration seemed new and fresh but not so in New York. Further, while New Yorkers comprised over a quarter of the common soldiers in the Army of the Potomac, Everett focused his speech more on the generals. At the Battle of Gettysburg, the high-ranking officers who performed well did not come from New York, so Everett largely left the state out of his narration. In their responses to Everett's speech, New York's editors sought to reassert the correctness of the city's position on secession and their preeminence in political and military affairs by dismissing his implied assertions to the contrary. While the war had smoothed out many of the party and regional rivalries that existed within the South, it had little effect on those divides in the North, as evidenced by the comments of these New York editors in response to the speeches at Gettysburg.

In Richmond, the editors highlighted Everett's comments about the divisions within the Confederacy to rally support for the war and increase Confederate nationalism by bringing their constituents together in a common hatred of the Yankees. On the other hand, they suppressed Lincoln's words about equality and freedom, unable to find a way to disavow them without denigrating their own Thomas Jefferson.[58] It would be another generation before most Southerners were even aware of what Lincoln had said in Gettysburg.

Londoners, and Englishmen in general, had much less at stake in the American Civil War than New York, Gettysburg, or Richmond, but there remained plenty in the Gettysburg ceremonies to catch their attention. Londoners could not ascertain the level of Lincoln's sincerity in his increasingly frequent antislavery statements so the city's editors largely left his address alone. He had quoted the Declaration of Independence, a document aimed at their king less than a century earlier. But Everett's charges of English impropriety in flaunting the rules of war and of the sea offended these editors, particularly as they viewed Everett, a man they knew from his time as ambassador, as a turncoat. He had attacked their country's honor, and so they attacked his as a way of skirting the allegations and advancing national interests.

Thus, in New York, Gettysburg, Richmond, and London, editors evaluated the dedication ceremonies at Gettysburg—specifically, the speeches by Seward, Everett, and Lincoln—on the basis of their own political affiliations and how the words affected the people in those cities. This trend would continue in the ensuing years. Not even London, a city three thousand miles away and without a formal ally in the conflict, remained impartial enough to evaluate the speeches based on their messages rather than their deliverers. As a result, though many editors offered quick comments either lauding or condemning the Gettysburg Address, usually for its literary qualities, few offered any consideration of the controversial, even revolutionary, ideas that Lincoln proposed. The general nature of Lincoln's comments gave them relevance across both time and space but meant that in 1863, readers found little that *demanded* a response in the same way as Everett's oration. Baum best summed up the world response to the Gettysburg Address with the observation that it was initially met with "profound silence."[59]

3

—

A Prophet with a Vision: 1901–22

> The gaze of the younger persons of the audience fastened on
> those silver heads and furrowed features, listening to the remi-
> niscences of participants in the older scenes, enabled them with-
> out the aid of much imagination to consider themselves a part
> of, and witnesses to, the soul-stirring scene of fifty years ago.
> —*Gettysburg Star and Sentinel*, November 26, 1913

On July 4, 1913, President Woodrow Wilson addressed a crowd of veterans and spectators at Gettysburg. Marking the fifty years that had passed
since the battle, the native Virginian commented, "How wholesome and
healing the peace has been! We have found one another again as brothers
and comrades in arms, enemies no longer, generous friends rather, our
battles long past, the quarrel forgotten—except that we shall not forget
the splendid valor, the manly devotion of the men then arrayed against
one another, now grasping hands and smiling into each other's eyes."[1]
But not everyone saw the past half century and current situation through
such rose-colored glasses. Some Union veterans were upset by Wilson's
comments, feeling he had whitewashed the traitorous history of secession
and rendered soldiers on both sides equally heroic. More pointed, the
following day the *Baltimore Afro-American Ledger* wondered "whether
Mr. Lincoln had the slightest idea in his mind that the time would ever
come when the people of this country would come to the conclusion that
by the 'People' he meant only white people."[2]

    The period from 1901 to 1922 is best described as an era of sectional re-
unification and marked the first time the Gettysburg Address was really
put to work, so to speak, in a systematic way toward a specific cause. A
process that began with the ouster of North Carolina's George H. White
from Congress, the last Southern African American to serve in that body
until 1973, came to fruition with the dedication of the Lincoln Memorial.

As the Civil War generation began passing away in large numbers and the need for national unity intensified in the internationally focused twentieth century, leaders on both sides worked toward reunification if not complete reconciliation. Historian Barbara Gannon concludes, "It was not the [veterans] who conceded; instead it was their children and grandchildren who accepted the fundamental tenets of the Lost Cause to advance their own cause—reunion and reconciliation." At times, reunification and reconciliation were vastly different aims; at others, they nearly aligned. Sectional reunification required turning a blind eye to the rollback of rights for Southern black people.[3] Representative White's ouster was emblematic of a larger disenfranchisement of black voters: In Louisiana, for example, the number of registered African American voters declined by nearly 99 percent from 130,000 in 1896 to 1,342 in 1904. Of greater consequence were the thousands of African Americans who were lynched during the period, including 105 in 1901 alone.[4]

During this era, the Gettysburg Address became a tool used by both those trying to promote sectional reunification at any cost and the minority on the other side who sought to remind the wider nation of Lincoln's vision and the extent to which it had not been fulfilled. The majority used the speech to bind the nation together, while the minority used it to point out its flaws. The particular and divergent parts of the speech both sides invoked set a pattern that would persist throughout the ensuing half century.

In *The Gettysburg Gospel*, Gabor Boritt notes that in the generation after the war, "Lincoln's words were mostly forgotten," and that it was not until "late in the century [that] Americans would rediscover Lincoln's remarks in their own right, call them by the name we still know, begin to turn the text into a revered document, and find the meaning of their country there."[5] But the evidence, much of which Boritt cites, suggests that Lincoln's words were far from forgotten in the years after the war.

As early as 1864, *Harper's Weekly* commented, "What President Lincoln said upon the field of Gettysburg in that speech, whose rare felicity not Pericles nor any orator every equaled, is said by every faithful American heart as it contemplates the battle-fields of the last fortnight in Virginia and Georgia." Significantly, the short news item was reprinted by the *Hartford Courant*, a Democratic journal that had declined to comment on the speech six months earlier and had opined in reference to Lincoln's 1863 annual message to Congress, "Mr. Lincoln is not distinguished for elegance or perspicuity of style."[6] Along the same lines, in April 1864, the *Boston Daily Advertiser* observed that the Gettysburg Address was "frequently pronounced the most felicitous of the President's occasional speeches."[7]

Lincoln's assassination brought a huge number of public tributes and eulogies, many of which either referred to the President's speech at Gettysburg or quoted specific lines. The public speakers who produced those tributes most often commented on Lincoln's eloquence more than his ideas, a predictable tactic given that the authors were themselves writers striving for beautiful words and that having just won the Civil War, many were loath to reopen the debate over the causes. A great number of the eulogies invoked Lincoln's final paragraph only, a selection that allowed them to add Lincoln to the roll of those who "shall not have died in vain" and simultaneously appeased ex-Confederates by suggesting the war was solely about the preservation of democracy: "that government of the people, by the people, for the people, shall not perish from the earth."[8] There were, of course, dissenters on both extremes. Senator Charles Sumner of Massachusetts titled his Lincoln eulogy "Promises of the Declaration of Independence, and Abraham Lincoln." Sumner, the ardent abolitionist who did his best to tug Lincoln toward the radicals, predictably cast the war as one about *"the Liberty and Equality of all men."* Sumner said that at Gettysburg, "The President, with unconscious power, dealt another blow, second only to the Proclamation of Emancipation," and "his few words will live long as Time." Sumner offered a prophetic vision of the speech's future significance: "That speech, uttered at the field of Gettysburg, and now sanctified by the martyrdom of its author, is a monumental act. . . . The battle itself was less important than the speech."[9] Predictably, not all agreed, and although both Southern and overseas papers reported Lincoln's passing, most did not use his Gettysburg Address in their tributes.[10]

On July 4, 1865, organizers laid the cornerstone for a monument in the center of the graves in the Soldiers' National Cemetery at Gettysburg. The monument honored the soldiers, not Lincoln, and featured statues representing liberty, war, history, peace, and plenty.[11] General Oliver Otis Howard, the general posted on Cemetery Hill during the battle, delivered the main oration at the dedication. While Howard performed unevenly in combat, his commitment to abolition and rights for African Americans never wavered. Thus, it is not surprising that Howard recited

Lincoln's entire Gettysburg Address that day. Indeed, the Address would find a prominent place in the national cemeteries after the war.

At the unveiling of the completed monument four years later, Oliver Morton, then a U.S. senator and formerly the wartime governor of Indiana, also invoked Lincoln and the Gettysburg Address. In his speech, Morton reminded the audience of Lincoln's commitment both to equality and democracy. He quoted Lincoln's call for the nation to have a "new birth of freedom" and reasserted that government "of the people, by the people, and for the people, shall not perish from the earth." Much like the newspaper coverage of the original cemetery dedication six years earlier, the press skewered the main speaker.[12] A *New York Times* editorial on July 2, 1869, commented, "We pronounce [Morton's] speech of yesterday a great disappointment—a disappointment greater even than we experienced in listening to the speech of EDWARD EVERETT at the same place." In 1863, the *New York Times* said little about Lincoln's oration at Gettysburg, but in 1869, the editor noted, "Neither MORTON's speech nor EVERETT's, at Gettysburg, is worth much; but when we recall the brief and immortal speech delivered at the same place by President Lincoln, we are satisfied with the one supreme gem of eloquence which Gettysburg has called forth." The paper also reprinted Lincoln's address on the front page.[13]

Sumner, Howard, Morton, and the editor of the *New York Times* stand in marked contrast to the editors from 1863 who refused to consider Lincoln's comments about the central place of equality in a democracy. They also represent a break with most commentators over the ensuing half century, who managed to avoid that subject. But in the immediate aftermath of the war, when the new constitutional amendments promised real change, and Reconstruction had not yet failed, Lincoln's goal of democracy with equality came closer to fruition than at nearly any point in the next century.

Funeral orations did not monopolize references to the Gettysburg Address in the decades after the war. In 1879, cartoonist Thomas Nast produced a work in *Harper's Weekly* "Death at the Polls and Free from 'Federal Interference'" (see fig. 3.1). The cartoon features a skeleton holding a rifle and captions filling the space between the skeleton and the perimeter of the sketch. One play on words is, "1775–1776 Liberty or Death. 1879–1880 Death to Liberty," another asks, "Is 'A Government of the people, for the people, and by the people,' to be shot to DEATH?"

Nast had opposed slavery and racial segregation and decried the leniency shown former Confederates. This cartoon was just one of several Nast created to point out continuing problems in the wake of the restoration of the former Confederate states to the Union and the full reinstatement of their political privileges, including the end of federal oversight into state matters. Nast's cartoon was thematically similar to an 1874 iteration "Worse Than Slavery," but the earlier version did not invoke Lincoln. Democracy was losing, Nast seemed to caution, and only federal intervention would allow the meaningful application of the Fourteenth and Fifteenth Amendments.[14] In 1882, the city of Buffalo, New York, put the last paragraph of the speech on its Civil War monument.[15] Three years later, on the other side of the Atlantic Ocean, *Reynolds's Newspaper* began carrying the motto "government of the people, by the people, for the people" on its masthead.[16]

In the 1890s, many people used the Gettysburg Address to criticize the government, partially due, no doubt, to the sudden proliferation of books on Lincoln and in part to the rise of the Populists. Dedicated to the common man, the Populists and like-minded reformers frequently quoted Lincoln's final line of the Address: "That government of the people, by the people, and for the people, shall not perish from the earth." In 1890, Mary Lease, famed for allegedly exhorting Kansas farmers to "raise more hell and less corn," categorized the United States as "a nation of inconsistencies. . . . It is no longer a government of the people, by the people, and for the people, but a government of Wall Street, by Wall Street, and for Wall Street."[17] In 1896, the *Denver News* carried an article, reprinted in the *Atlanta Constitution* on April 17, stating, "Lincoln ought to rise from the grave and make one more speech at Gettysburg in recognition of the fact that government by the bosses, for the bosses and of the bosses has pretty effectually supplanted government by the people."[18]

As these articles suggest, Boritt is right that it was not until the turn of the century that Lincoln's speech became known as "*the* Gettysburg Address."[19] However, that change was more reflective of the decreasing interest in and significance attributed to Edward Everett's speech at Gettysburg than a rising fascination with Lincoln's words. A *New York Times* keyword search for "Gettysburg Address" for the period 1890 to 1899 results in only 12 hits, but searching for "Lincoln" *and* "Gettysburg" returns 105, indicating that people were referring to and invoking the speech long before settling on its now-accepted name.

Figure 3.1. *Death at the Polls, and Free from "Federal Interference,"* Harper's *Weekly*, October 18, 1879. Illustration by Thomas Nast. Prints and Photographs Division, Library of Congress.

On the centennial of Lincoln's birth, famed Populist orator William Jennings Bryan declared, "His Gettysburg Address is not surpassed, if equaled, in simplicity, force, and appropriateness by any speech of the same length of any language. It is the world's model in eloquence, elegance, and condensation." That was high praise from the man who delivered arguably the nineteenth century's second-greatest American oration, the "Cross of Gold" speech at the 1896 Democratic convention.[20] Underlying this Populist rhetoric was the implication that the Gettysburg Address guaranteed everyday Americans equality with the elite.

Though Lincoln was little discussed during the sordid Gilded Age with its dirty politics and triumph of the elite, the reemergence of the common man, beginning with the Populist Movement, returned the sixteenth president to the limelight. The increased interest in Lincoln brought more attention to his greatest speech, in part because its timelessness allowed its application to events far distant from the cemetery dedication in November 1863. The timelessness of Lincoln's words also allowed their use as a tool of the reunification that would consume the first two decades of the twentieth century.

The wave of immigration sweeping the country in the late 1800s and early 1900s also had an impact on invocations of the Gettysburg Address. By 1900, immigrants and children of immigrants in the United States represented one third of the population. Many leaders saw education as a way to turn immigrants into both Americans *and* productive workers, two major concerns at the turn of the century. Whereas just over 50 percent of the nation's school-aged children attended school in 1870, that number rose to 60 percent in 1900, and 80 percent in 1920. The number of children flocking to schools required a new conception of the educational experience; no longer were curricula designed only for the children of elites. Teachers used two basic resources to educate students in the late nineteenth and early twentieth century: readers and textbooks.[21]

In the nineteenth century, most students learned about the past somewhat incidentally through readers, a result of both the lack of history courses taught in schools and teachers' early efforts at multidisciplinary education. The *Riverside Literature Series* is a typical pamphlet that includes the Gettysburg Address among its lessons. A monthly publication put out by Boston's Houghton Mifflin, the January 1888 edition features "The Gettysburg Speech and Other Papers by Abraham Lincoln and an Essay on Lincoln by James Russell Lowell." The following year, the Parker Publishing Company of Taylorville, Illinois, put out a brief pamphlet, *Lincoln's Gettysburg Speech. With Suggestive Exercises on Teaching Synonyms, Word-Analysis, Figures of Speech, Etc.* This pamphlet belong to *Parker's Lessons in Literature*, a series of approximately three hundred leaflets "Famous throughout the United States as the best regular or supplementary reading obtainable" and "prepared expressly for supplementary reading in schools." A similar set, *The Little Classic Series*, was published by the A. Flanagan Company of Chicago, which, in 1905, produced *Speeches by Lincoln* as a part of the eighth-grade readers.[22]

By the turn of the century, more districts offered history courses and, consequently, bought history textbooks, though that term applies in only the most general sense. The conventions that made a book a textbook included the numbering of paragraphs for easy reference, bolded vocabulary words, and the inclusion of a page or so of questions at the end of each chapter. The 1890s were a particularly eventful decade in the evolution of Southern textbooks. That era saw the founding of the Sons of Confederate Veterans in 1889 and the United Daughters of the Confederacy in 1894. Echoing the concerns voiced by one ex-soldier in the pages of *Confederate Veteran*, a popular monthly magazine, "These long-legged Yankee lies will continue to run until we write our own history and print our own books," these groups formed committees to make sure that the books adopted in the South agreed with the Confederate interpretation of the war.[23]

In 1896, Baltimore publisher R. H. Woodward Company brought out *School History of the United States*, a textbook authored by J. William Jones. Jones identified himself as "born, reared, and educated on Southern soil, following for four years with youthful devotion the battle-flag of the Southern Confederacy, for twelve years secretary of the Southern Historical Society. . . . For many years I have been solicited to write a School History of the United States which, while fair to all sections, would do full justice to the Southern States." Due to his aforementioned autobiography, Jones felt, "I may modestly claim that I have had some facilities for knowing, and some qualifications for preparing, a history of the United States which shall be acceptable to the South and fit to be taught in her schools." When published, Jones's book became the favored history text in the South, though not in the North. Jones makes no mention of the Gettysburg Address in his work, a pattern his successors would follow.[24]

Jones's book was preeminent in the South until the 1899 publication of Susan Pendleton Lee's *New School History of the United States*.[25] The Virginia Superintendent of Public Instruction deemed Lee's book the *only* U.S. history text approved for use in the state's public schools for 1904–5.[26] Echoing Jones, Lee revealed, "The author is encouraged to hope that this history will meet the approval of the wise and experienced educators of American children, and supply the want, so often expressed in the South, for an *unprejudiced* and *truthful* history of the United States." Following in Jones's footsteps, Lee made no mention of the Gettysburg Address. An examination of the readers and other books approved by the Virginia Superintendent of Public Instruction for that year indicates no others that included the Gettysburg Address, continuing, whether intentional or not, the exclusion of the speech from the Old Dominion.[27]

These textbooks infuriated Union veterans, who felt that the books did not, in their minds, accurately portray the Confederacy as the offending side.[28] In contrast to the recalcitrance to discuss Lincoln's speech and all of its implications in Virginia was Michigan's *Lincoln at Gettysburg*, a 1915 bulletin published by the State Superintendent of Public Education. Superintendent Fred Keller penned an introductory letter: "We are confident that the study of Lincoln's immortal speech will impress the boys and girls of Michigan what a privilege it is to be an American citizen." The bulletin features a facsimile of the Gettysburg Address, a brief overview of the cemetery and Lincoln's Address by O. T. Corson, another article by John Morrow, present at the cemetery in 1863, and some suggestions for lessons centered on the speech by Elinor Gage, an English teacher in Traverse.[29]

Albert Bushnell Hart's *School History of the United States* (1918) became the nation's most popular American history textbook in the 1920s and 1930s. Hart, a professor of government at Harvard University, conscientiously sought inclusiveness, with his frontispiece consisting not of the traditional image of George Washington but, instead, featuring a boat of immigrants passing the Statue of Liberty as they sailed into New York. Taking a page from the Southern-oriented textbooks of the era, Hart played up the sectional reunification after the Civil War, noting that Lincoln "was born in Kentucky, and he understood the southern people." Hart said, "His brief speeches are full of noble spirit, of thoughts as true for the South as for the North," before quoting several of Lincoln's more memorable lines, including "government of the people, by the people, for the people shall not perish from the earth."[30]

A book published that same year garnered more popularity in the South, however. John Holladay Latané taught history at Johns Hopkins University. His 1918 work, *A History of the United States*, sympathizes with the Southern interpretation of the war and Reconstruction, evidenced by his comment in the preface: "The slavery contest was economic in its origins and development." Latané presented a benign and likeable Lincoln but, like Lee before him, made no mention of Lincoln's most famous speech. Latané also commented, "The [Emancipation] proclamation was strictly a war measure," and quoted Lincoln's famous letter to Horace Greeley for support. Latané presented Lincoln's own words to make this point, but by omitting Lincoln's stipulation at the end of the Proclamation that emancipation constituted "an act of justice" and by failing to consider the Gettysburg Address, Latané ignored evidence of Lincoln's moral opposition to slavery. Because of this avoidance, Latané appealed to the South as well as the North, making his book one of the first to achieve a national circulation.[31]

When it came to covering the Gettysburg Address, textbooks of this era offered quite distinctive coverage depending on which regional audience they targeted. Essentially, Southern textbooks passed over Lincoln's most famous speech, and Northern-focused tomes made sure to include the words. But writers in both regions aimed to advance sectional reunification through their coverage of the speech. Though unwilling to praise Lincoln's Gettysburg Address, Southern writers refrained from condemning the speech, thereby slowly helping to dissipate the conflict between the regions. On the other hand, while Northern writers cited and praised the Gettysburg Address, they did so either because of its eloquence or because of its defense of a democratic form of government, two ideas acceptable to Southerners in the era. They studiously avoided any invocations of Lincoln's lines regarding equality or new births of freedom. Coming from two very different angles, the majority of textbook writers in this era shared a similar end goal.

One writer who tried to bridge the gap between the various strains of memory was Mary Raymond Shipman Andrews. In 1906, Andrews penned a reunification-themed short story, "The Perfect Tribute," that would become the widest circulated and arguably most influential piece on the Gettysburg Address of all time. A Mobile, Alabama, native, Andrews married a New York Republican in 1884 and spent her adult life in that state. One day, her son came home from school and relayed a story from his teacher that the great Gettysburg Address had been written on a scrap of brown paper on the train to Gettysburg. Andrews, her son later recalled, felt "some tribute to [Lincoln] ought to be written by a Southerner" and set out to do so. In July 1906, she submitted "The Perfect Tribute" to *Scribner's Magazine.*[32]

In Andrews's story, a depressed Lincoln travelling to Gettysburg wondered, "Of what use was it for such a one to try to fashion a speech fit to take a place by the side of Everett's silver sentences?" Despite this, Lincoln borrowed a pencil from Secretary of State William Henry Seward and composed an address on a "bit of brown paper." At the conclusion of Lincoln's speech on November 19, Andrews wrote, "Not a hand was lifted in applause. . . . In Lincoln's heart a throb of pain answered it. His speech had been, as he feared it would be, a failure."[33]

Back in Washington the following day, Lincoln was, according to Andrews, dragged to a hospital by a young boy determined to find a lawyer to make out a will for his dying brother, a mortally wounded Confederate captain from Georgia named Carter Hampton Blair. Blair did not know his guest's identity and in the course of their talk declared that the previous day, President Lincoln "[m]ade one of the greatest speeches of history." Blair predicted, "It will live, that speech. Fifty years from now American school-boys will be learning it as part of their education."[34]

Andrews had struck gold. The reunification narrative, combined with the tragic hero of the martyred president unaware of his own greatness, resonated with a nation trying to gloss over the remaining sectional tensions and simultaneously bemoaning the lack of leaders in their own time.[35] The story generated such demand that in September 1906, it came out as a brochure just in time for the beginning of a new school year, marking its transition from an article to a reader. In 1909, the centennial year of Lincoln's birth, *Scribner's* printed a school edition. This was just the beginning. In 1943, Lincoln scholar Gerald McMurtry related that the book boasted twenty-five distinct editions with more than fifty-seven printings and a total output of over half a million copies.[36] More than any other work, this book introduced American schoolchildren in both history and literature classes to the story of Lincoln's Gettysburg Address. It also seems likely that Andrews's phrase "perfect tribute" influenced Charles Baum, the nine-year-old sitting near Lincoln, who in 1935 categorized the reception of the speech as "profound silence."[37]

In 1935, Metro-Goldwyn-Mayer Studios produced a half-hour movie based on Andrews's work, starring Charles "Chic" Sale as Abraham Lincoln. Adapted for the silver screen by Ruth Cummings and directed by Edward Sloman, the film began with a man carving the words of the Gettysburg Address onto a stone but then followed the Andrews story.[38] In addition to its immediate impact, the film appeared on a number of suggested resource lists for schools during the Civil War centennial in the 1960s, stretching its reach past the half-century mark.[39]

Ultimately, Andrews's story proved just a little too good. The Confederate army never enrolled a Carter Hampton Blair. And although the story remains popular, Lincoln did not write the Gettysburg Address on a scrap of paper on the train to Gettysburg. Rumors that he borrowed a pencil from a young train engineer named Andrew Carnegie are also untrue, despite Carnegie's claims to the contrary. While it is easy to cite circulation numbers, it is hard to judge the real impact of Andrews's story on the hearts and minds of her young American readers in 1906 and after. What can be said, however, is that Andrews's story was part of a growing theme of reunification narratives that would become more predominant in the ensuing years, a number of which used the Gettysburg Address as a tool to promote that end.

Although this reunification theme is the dominant narrative in textbooks of the era, there is a strong counternarrative. In 1919, the United Confederate Veterans issued a pamphlet penned by Mildred Rutherford demanding that states "reject a text-book that glorifies Abraham Lincoln and vilifies Jefferson Davis."[40] Four years later, Rutherford wrote another exposé, *The South Must Have Her Rightful Place in History*. The book attacks Abraham Lincoln and those who had written about him in the preceding sixty years. Chapters with titles such as "Abraham Lincoln Not the Preserver of the Union" and "Violations of the Constitution by Lincoln" dominate. Rutherford's premise is, "False history accepted as truth destroys civilization. For over sixty years the civilization of the South has been almost destroyed by the falsehoods written about it. . . . The time has fully come when the South especially should know the truth about Abraham Lincoln."[41]

These truths include the "fact" that Lincoln "headed the list of subscribers to John Brown's raid in Kansas and Virginia, advocating murder and arson." Rutherford takes particular care to dispel the notion that the Gettysburg Address came from Lincoln's genius: "Lincoln's biographers pose him as a highly educated literary personage, and the Gettysburg speech which Seward wrote afterwards is put into every collection of great speeches and attributed to Lincoln, not Seward." At the end of her pamphlet, Rutherford explains exactly what she wants: "We of the South are not advocating the adoption of any one text book, but we are advocating that those text books unjust to the South shall be ruled out of our schools, out of our homes, out of our public and private libraries, and that new encyclopedias and books of reference now being sold be carefully examined before placed in our homes or public or private libraries."[42]

Southern white women at this time often had a greater ability to voice a counternarrative than their male counterparts. Historian Caroline Janney shows that it was the ladies' memorial associations, not their male counterparts, that were at the fore of commemorating the war. Thus, Rutherford's counternarrative suggests that those Southern white people who were aware of Lincoln's words disapproved of them, but they were simply outmanned by the national urge to move past sectional conflict. Perhaps, nowhere was that reunification narrative on greater display than at the semi-centennial anniversary of the battle in 1913.[43]

Intermittently for nearly five years, state and local officials, as well as the various veterans' organizations, planned a fiftieth-anniversary commemoration of the Battle of Gettysburg. Organizers invited veterans from states on both sides of the Mason-Dixon line. President Wilson, the first Southern-born president since the war, consented to speak at the reunion.[44] The *Times* of London hailed this as a great sign of reunification: "The celebrations are receiving an extreme amount of detailed attention from the Press, which hails the fraternizing of the North and South on the bloodiest and most important battlefield of the war as a signal sign of the disappearance of sectionalism."[45] Another editorial noted, "It is because the cause on both sides was such as good men may fight for and die for that the victors and vanquished have long since become brothers again." The newspaper stated that Stonewall Jackson's frequent comments about honor spoke for the South, and "[t]he voice of the North is heard in those wonderful words which Lincoln spoke on this same field of Gettysburg when, a few months after the battle, it was made sacred to the dead. They are amongst the simplest in modern oratory, and they are perhaps the most impressive."[46]

The event's organizers probably expected Wilson to invoke the Gettysburg Address. In addition to his political career, Wilson was a professionally trained historian who in 1902 wrote a multivolume history of the United States. In the section dealing with the Civil War, he included a facsimile of the Gettysburg Address but made no comment on the speech. However, Wilson once told a dinner guest that he rated the Gettysburg Address *"very very high,"* and after winning reelection in 1916, Wilson said, "This, then, to repeat that beautiful phrase of Lincoln's in his Gettysburg Address, 'is not a time of congratulation but a time of rededication.'" Although botching the wording, his sentiment rang true.[47]

At Gettysburg in 1913, Wilson chose to focus on reconciliation. Rather than talk about the lynching of thousands of African Americans in the preceding decades or their continued disenfranchisement, Wilson commented, "[H]ow wholesome and healing the peace has been! We have found one another again as brothers and comrades in arm, enemies no longer, generous friends rather, our battles long past, the quarrel forgotten." Wilson did not mention the Gettysburg Address, an odd omission given his particular message and that he was in Gettysburg. Then again, a focus on battlefield valor was typically unifying, whereas invoking the Gettysburg Address could have divided those present by calling into consideration the causes and results of the war. The editor of the *Philadelphia Age* referred to the event as a "mock love fest" and said, "The truth of history was smothered." Similarly, many of the fifty-three thousand veterans, most of whom were reluctant reunionists, were upset that Wilson equated their patriotic defense of the flag with the Confederates' treason. Wilson, however, appealed to the younger generation that had been born and came of age after the Civil War and looked for reunification, even reconciliation.[48]

Wilson's omission of the Gettysburg Address is even more surprising in light of the two nearly brand-new monuments in the town to Lincoln's speech. In 1910, the Commonwealth of Pennsylvania included a statue of a standing Lincoln on its massive battlefield monument. While most of the states with participants in the battle have monuments on the field, Pennsylvania is unique in listing the name of each of its soldiers in bronze plaques around the base, with generals' names etched largely on the upper walls, and eight statues ringing the portico of the monument. Lincoln is the only non-Pennsylvanian to be honored with a statue, a fitting gesture given his importance in both the Civil War and

in ensuring that all Americans would remember that particular battlefield. Another monument to Lincoln and his most famous speech, this
one in the Soldiers' National Cemetery, had just gone in a year earlier,
in 1912. The 1895 act that established the Gettysburg National Military
Park appropriated $5,000 for the erection of "a suitable bronze tablet,
containing on it the address delivered by Abraham Lincoln, President of
the United States, at Gettysburg on the 19th day of November 1863 . . .
and such tablet, having on it besides the address a medallion likeness of
President Lincoln."[49] The Lincoln Speech Memorial contains a bust of
Lincoln by Henry K. Bush-Brown and is flanked on the left by David
Wills's invitation to Lincoln to speak and on the right by the text of the
Bliss version of the Gettysburg Address.

Rather than being anomalies, these statues were part of a larger movement. Before the 1910s, Lincoln was most often portrayed as "the Great
Emancipator," but as the semi-centennial approached, there was a shift
with more emphasizing Lincoln's words at Gettysburg. East Orange,
New Jersey, broke ground on November 19, 1910, for a Frank Elwell
sculpture of Abraham Lincoln, and when the work was finished a year
later, the final words of the Gettysburg Address were on the pedestal. In
1912, the Leonard Volk bust of Lincoln in Boston's Beacon Hill neighbor-
hood, which had previously been displayed by itself, was retrofitted and
placed above a bronze tablet with the text of the Gettysburg Address.
The same year, Lincoln, Nebraska, installed a statue of its namesake and
the text of his Gettysburg Address on the front steps of the state capitol.
It was the Kansas-Nebraska Act of 1854 that had brought Lincoln out
of a period of relative political inactivity and provoked some of his early
statements on equality that he would refine in the Gettysburg Address.
Lincoln is portrayed at the moment he finished speaking and with bowed
head gazes solemnly at the ground (see fig. 3.2). Daniel Chester French
sculpted the statue, and Henry Bacon designed the setting, a duo that
would also work together to bring to fruition the Lincoln Memorial in
Washington, D.C.[50]

In addition to these explicitly Lincoln statues, nearly every Northern
town in the nation had a monument to its Civil War soldiers, and as
historian Thomas Brown relates, "Of the texts quoted exclusively on
Union monuments, the Gettysburg Address appeared most often."[51] If an
excerpt of the speech appeared rather than the entire text, it was the final
line that adorned the nation's monuments. As Kirk Savage comments,

Figure 3.2. *Abraham Lincoln*, Lincoln, Nebraska. Sculpted by Daniel Chester French, 1909–12. Photograph, Wikipedia, by Ammodramus.

"At the very time, therefore, that a resurgent nationality was sparking a new monumental era, the meaning of nationality was changing in dramatic and unpredictable ways. . . . The process of commemoration was in fact reciprocal: the monument manufactured its own public, but that public in turn had opinions about what constituted proper commemoration."[52] The final line of the Gettysburg Address did important work in this era when unity and nationalism were required in order for America to step out on the grand stage, and that work was advanced by these monuments. For a time, anyway, the nation would seek to forget about the divisiveness that emancipation-themed statues would keep alive and seek unification around the notion that a "government of the people, by the people, for the people, shall not perish from the earth."

Reunification in the era was not just between sections but also between nations. The United States and Great Britain had alternated between enemies and allies since 1775 and had very nearly opened hostilities during the American Civil War. But in 1913, British leaders were much more concerned with Germany than America. As an island nation dependent upon control of the seas, or at least the free transit of them, Britain was worried by the increasing number of battleships Germany built starting in the 1890s. The alliance with France in 1904 did something to allay these fears, but the British felt the United States could provide the tipping point.

But how could Britain convince the Americans to ally with them rather than the Germans? One step was to give up British claims to Hawaii and allow those islands to come under American control. The same was true of their share of the future isthmian (eventually Panamanian) canal. And lastly, Earl George Curzon took the lead on an eleventh-hour attempt to convince Americans that their cultural connections with Britain outweighed those with Germany.

On November 6, 1913, less than two weeks before the semi-centennial of the Address and, as it turned out, just nine months before World War I began, Curzon offered the Rede Lecture at the University of Cambridge. Then chancellor of Oxford University, Curzon had also served as the Viceroy of India (1899–1905) and would later be the foreign secretary (1919–24). In addition to his distinguished career in government service, Curzon published a number of books, mostly dealing with his travels through regions in Asia with which Britain was particularly concerned in the first decades of the twentieth century.

Curzon's lecture, "Modern Parliamentary Eloquence," evaluated many orators and their finest efforts of the preceding decades. Curzon concluded, "In this long review of the Parliamentary achievements of the past, the question may be asked whether any speech or speeches appear to stand out as the best and most perfect examples of the art whose many phases I have examined." After qualifying his forthcoming response by indicating its difficulty, Curzon admitted, "Three speeches, however, in the English language have always appeared to me to emerge with a superiority which if not indisputable, will perhaps not be seriously disputed—much in the same way as the Funeral Oration of Pericles was generally allowed to be the masterpiece of the ancient world."[53]

Curzon quickly moved past the first contender, William Pitt the Younger's 1805 response to a toast to his health, noting, "Abraham

Lincoln was the author of both the other speeches. Everyone knows them, they are part of the intellectual patrimony of the English-speaking race." This particular phrasing reflects Britain's fear of the eventual outbreak of war with Germany and resulting desire to cement its relationship with the United States. Curzon quoted the entire Address, offering a version that closely but not exactly conformed to the final draft Lincoln had written in 1864. Comparing the Briton and American, Curzon asked, "Pitt's speech occupied only a few seconds in delivery, Lincoln's less than three minutes: and yet where are the world-famed pages, the crowded hours of rhetoric, compared with these?" Curzon deemed Lincoln's Second Inaugural Address, specifically its phrase identifying slavery as the cause of the war, the other challenger. Curzon concluded by calling Lincoln's offerings "the purest gold of human eloquence" and that they belonged "among the glories and the treasures of mankind." Curzon resisted ranking one over the other: "I escape the task of deciding which is the masterpiece of modern English eloquence by awarding the prize to an American."[54] In the very late nineteenth century, conservatives had found in Lincoln a defender of national unity and had joined their liberal opposition in embracing him and his Gettysburg Address.[55]

The next day, the *Times* of London summarized Curzon's speech, and, soon, the American papers did as well. Both the *New York Herald* and *New York Evening Post* took note of Curzon's speech, on November 19 and 24, respectively, thereby helping cement the fond feelings between England and the United States, or at least the Northern portion.

In 1916, Lord Charnwood, a liberal politician and writer, penned a biography of Lincoln. Too old to serve in the military, Charnwood considered the task a wartime duty. Of the Gettysburg Address, Charnwood said simply but tellingly, "The few words of Abraham Lincoln were such as perhaps sank deep, but left his audience unaware that a classic had been spoken which would endure with the English language."[56] The thirty-fifth printing of the book came out in 1940, a testament to its reach and influence.[57] In her biography that same year, Edith Elias, a professional author and British citizen who wrote on a range of topics, declared that Lincoln's speech "has become immortal" and offered the complete text of the Address. In conclusion, Elias posited, "Lincoln felt a slight stir of disappointment among the listeners. . . . But Time has completely changed the verdict of the disappointed listeners. The little speech, so simple yet so nobly befitting the occasion, has been given a high place among the finest prose literature in the world, and as long as the English tongue is spoken it will never be forgotten."[58]

Although Englishmen largely ignored the Gettysburg Address in 1863, instead focusing on the words of Seward or Everett, by 1913 they no longer mentioned Seward's role at Gettysburg and only invoked Everett as a lesson against making long speeches. In 1863, there was the possibility of war between Britain and the United States, and as such, the provocations offered by Seward and Everett caught Englishmen's attention more than the nonspecific language Lincoln employed in his brief speech. But, by 1913, Britain sought closer ties with the United States, necessitating a glossing over of past troubles, such as those alluded to by Everett at Gettysburg. By emphasizing the Gettysburg Address as one of the greatest in the *English* language, Englishmen suggested that Lincoln himself, and an appreciation for the man's greatest speech, connected America and Britain in a way that America and Germany could never be united. The reunification spirit of the era did not end at the borders of the United States but also included an ongoing effort to cement the Anglo-American alliance.

On November 19, 1913, just thirteen days after Curzon's speech, citizens in Gettysburg gathered to commemorate the fiftieth anniversary of the speech. By the early 1900s, a large percentage of the town's residents made their living through the patronage of the 150,000 tourists who visited the battlefield, meaning that many of the townspeople literally owed their livelihoods to the Gettysburg Address and its subject, the great battle. Whereas Gettysburg had three hotels in 1863, there were eight by 1885. That growth was solely due to tourism, as the *Star and Banner* lamented in 1900, noting that the dedication of so much of the town's land to the nontaxable battlefield "has prevented the location of factories here and has retarded the growth of the few we have." Instead, most people who lived in Gettysburg were employed either directly or indirectly by the tourist industry. In a single week in 1904, tourists purchased a hundred thousand postcards in the town, and over a hundred residents made their living by guiding visitors around the battlefield. In short, tourism was "the goose that lays the golden egg for Gettysburg," as one local paper stated.[59] Even the local institution of higher learning, Pennsylvania College, changed its name in this era to Gettysburg College in order to take advantage of the town's name recognition. Any threat to that "golden goose" was taken quite seriously by the townspeople, who came to view safeguarding the legacy of the Address as crucial to the vitality of their town and personal futures. The increasingly frequent invocations of snippets of the Gettysburg Address that divorced Lincoln's words from their town caused concern and led to local attempts to reassert authority over the remembrances and uses of the Gettysburg Address. As a town supported by tourists from all parts of the United States and even other countries, Gettysburgians were concerned with presenting a Gettysburg Address that was acceptable to all and that would stimulate people from all parts of the nation to come to their town. Local resident Luther Minnigh's 1892 guidebook *Gettysburg—What They Did Here* reproduces a line from the Address—"The world will little note nor long remember what we say here, but it can never forget what they did here"—on both the front cover and first page and offered the entire text in a section about the cemetery but avoided emphasizing any part of the speech that might be controversial.[60]

The commemorative event came during the Fifty-Ninth Annual Adams County Teachers' Institute scheduled for November 17–21. On the opening day of the institute, the *Gettysburg Times* outlined the upcoming program: "William McSherry Esq. will tell the history of the Soldiers' National Cemetery; four short addresses will be made by Prof. Calvin Hamilton, Hon. Wm. McClean, Dr. T. C. Billheimer and Dr. P. M. Bikle, telling of their memories of Lincoln's visit to Gettysburg; Judge S. McC. Swope will read the Lincoln Speech and the oration will be delivered by Rev. J. B. Baker. Dr. A. E. Wagner will make the prayer and there will be special music." The selection of four educators to share their reminiscences of the Address indicates the role the Adams County Teachers' Institute played in organizing the celebration. As for those who heard Lincoln speak but did not have a spot on the program, the newspaper noted, "Chairs will be provided on the stage for all those who were present in Gettysburg on November 19, 1863." That was a dangerous promise to make: If all the people who claimed to have sat on or under the speakers' platform at Gettysburg while Lincoln spoke had ever gathered in one place, the Earth would have shifted on its axis.[61]

One of those who probably was on the stage that day was Hugh Paxton Bigham, a local man who served in the 21st Pennsylvania Cavalry during the war and stood guard outside Lincoln's room at the Wills home the night before he gave his speech. The *Star and Sentinel* reported, "Mr.

Bigham recalls that during the evening Mr. Lincoln desired to visit Secretary Seward at his stopping place and that he made way through the crowd for the parly." Lincoln frequently asked Seward to read and recommend changes to his public addresses (the First Inaugural Address, for example), and it seems likely he visited Seward with this end in mind. By illustrating the role of a local man in this drama, the Gettysburg papers of 1913 tightened the connections between the town and the Address.[62]

All three of the local papers then publishing, the *Star and Sentinel* (1867–1961), *Compiler* (1818–1953), and *Gettysburg Times* (1909–), extensively covered the event. The daily *Gettysburg Times* carried its account on November 20; the *Star and Sentinel* and *Compiler*, both weeklies, had to wait until November 26. The *Compiler* also published the proceedings in a pamphlet *Lincoln Anniversary Souvenir*. The text offered in the *Souvenir* and *Compiler* is the same as that appearing in the *Star and Sentinel* of November 26, indicating some sort of cooperative effort. Both the *Star and Sentinel*'s article and the *Compiler*'s pamphlet published the speakers' full orations; the *Gettysburg Times* summarized the speeches more briefly. Additionally, the *Star and Sentinel* reprinted the entire coverage of the original 1863 dedication ceremonies that had appeared in the November 24, 1863, edition of the *Adams Sentinel*, the predecessor to the *Star and Sentinel*.

In reviewing the day's events, the *Gettysburg Times* declared that the ceremony "was one of the most successful events of the kind which the town has ever enjoyed. . . . [O]n the platform were a hundred men and women who heard Lincoln."[63] In the words of the *Star and Sentinel*, "The gaze of the younger persons of the audience fastened on those silver heads and furrowed features, listening to the reminiscences of participants in the older scenes, enabled them without the aid of much imagination to consider themselves a part of, and witnesses to, the soul-stirring scene of fifty years ago." Those on stage linked the greatness of the Gettysburg Address and the man who had authored it to the present day, ensuring their own place in the town's history.[64]

After a musical selection from local teachers and an invocation from Rev. Dr. A. E. Wagner, William McSherry, a local lawyer, offered a history of the National Cemetery beginning with the battle and continuing up to the moment of his address. McSherry affirmed local pride in the cemetery, calling it "the most beautiful national cemetery in all the civilized world." Generally, McSherry's address recounted the various dates and people involved in establishing and maintaining the cemetery. The one exception was in his categorization of the Gettysburg Address as "[t]hat wonderful address of about twenty lines, which is recognized as one of the literary gems of the world, and is remembered and known and admired wherever the English language is spoken." Although the *Star and Sentinel* reprinted McSherry's comments about the Address, the summary of his remarks in the *Gettysburg Times* ignored that part of his speech. The omission is puzzling as the title of the column indicated that it was about Lincoln's speech but could reflect the fact that McSherry did not hear Lincoln's Address, while those who followed him did. The elimination of his comments suggests a safeguarding of the legacy of the Address: Only those present in 1863 could express an opinion on Lincoln's words.[65]

Calvin Hamilton followed McSherry, the first of four to speak that day who had attended the 1863 dedication. Hamilton served with Company K of the 30th Pennsylvania (a company from Gettysburg) during the Civil War and suffered a wound during the battle in his hometown. Left behind to recover, he was still in Gettysburg in November and "present that day on crutches, with an open wound" when Lincoln gave his Address. Hamilton served as the president of the local school board for some time and as the fifth superintendent of the National Cemetery, a position he held in 1913. All the local papers merely summarized Hamilton's speech, suggesting that it was given extemporaneously. The *Gettysburg Times* reported that Hamilton "could scarcely give an unbiased account of what occurred here on the day of dedication" as "4000 dead, many of them killed by his side and one of them a school mate" surrounded him. Hamilton's encounter with Lincoln at Gettysburg was his third, following previous meetings at the Executive Mansion in 1861 and during the President's review of the army after Antietam in 1862. "I was thrilled each time and at Gettysburg possibly more by his presence than by anything he said," Hamilton recollected.[66]

The coverage in the *Star and Sentinel* and *Compiler* focused on Hamilton's personal experiences that day, noting that he had been on crutches. Like the coverage in the *Gettysburg Times*, this pamphlet recorded Hamilton's assertion that he had not formed an impression of the Gettysburg Address, but the *Star and Sentinel* offered an explanation as to why: "As he stood there that day the memories of the fields of [c]arnage of the previous two years covering his service and particularly the impressive thought that the preparation of a last rest of the martyred dead of Gettysburg would provide an everlasting memorial for his bosom friend, so filled his mind that he received little impression from the spoken words." Hamilton's implication is that the overwhelming emotion the ceremonies brought forth rendered him incapable of properly evaluating Lincoln's speech, something others likely felt as well.[67]

However, in a letter to New York collector John E. Boos just nine days later, Hamilton offered almost a complete refutation of his reminiscences at the fiftieth-anniversary celebration: "I remember how his presence and words thrilled me, but do not recall applause, though there may have been." These contradictions are not easily sorted out. It is possible that Hamilton opened up more with fellow Gettysburgians than with strangers.[68]

Hamilton's ambiguous remarks contrast sharply with the praise of Judge McClean, who noted that Lincoln "[s]tood in all the gravity of his mien and manner as a Seer with a message, and as a prophet with a vision." Like McSherry, McClean offered substantial background information on the invitation to both Everett and Lincoln to speak at the dedication ceremonies. James A. Rebert, a local man serving in the 21st Pennsylvania Cavalry and assigned to guard duty at the Wills house, relayed to McClean that Lincoln stated at 9 A.M. on November 19 that he had just then finished his remarks. While the date and place where Lincoln penned the Gettysburg Address may seem trivial, it mattered a great deal to these Gettysburgians. If Lincoln wrote the Address while actually in Gettysburg, it linked the town even more closely to his speech than if he had composed it in Washington, D.C., or on the train en route to Gettysburg. McClean's mention of this incident reveals, again, the interpretation of a national issue through a local lens.[69]

Whereas the account in the *Gettysburg Times* implies that McClean had said little about Lincoln's actual speech, the *Star and Sentinel* rectifies that misconception. McClean noted that Lincoln's speech consisted of a mere 267 words while Everett's oration exceeded twenty-seven and a half printed pages. McClean took as his source for this comparison the transcriptions of the speeches offered in Pennsylvania's official report of the dedication ceremonies. McClean claimed to have stood "about eight feet from and facing Mr. Lincoln" and said he had "very little recollection of the President meeting with applause" other than that due to a man in his high position regardless of the occasion or performance.

McClean broke Lincoln's Address into three distinct parts and offered his opinion on each. In the opening paragraph, McClean said that Lincoln affirmed that "all men are created equal, a principle that was heard and accepted and acted upon, not only by the thirteen colonies, but elsewhere throughout the world, by a Lafayette, a Kosciusko, Baron Steuben and others." Lincoln used the word *nation* five times in the speech, McClean observed, though he attributed no significance to that choice in words other than Lincoln's love for his country. In concluding, McClean stated that Lincoln's call for "a new birth of freedom" garnered an audience "in our own country, in France, Cuba, Philippines, Portugal, and on the other side of the world in China."[70] In his speech, McClean discussed all three of the major issues then surrounding the Gettysburg Address: which version to accept, the reception by the audience, and the meaning of the speech.

The exact text of Lincoln's speech as delivered remained a mystery, and fascination with identifying an official version intensified in the early 1900s. Congress printed many conflicting versions of the Address, and with more and more monuments, including the proposed Lincoln Memorial, looking to etch Lincoln's words in marble and stone, it only made sense to establish a definitive version. A 1909 proposal to place a marker containing the text of the Gettysburg Address in each of the country's national cemeteries prompted a major consideration of the various copies of the Address then circulating. The extent of this issue is evidenced by the scrapbook on the matter kept by Colonel John P. Nicholson, the chairman of the Gettysburg National Park Commission, between 1909 and 1920. The scrapbook stretches almost a hundred pages, many with multiple clippings.[71]

Much of this confusion originated with Lincoln himself. In the four months after the ceremonies, Lincoln wrote out and distributed five different versions of the Gettysburg Address. Lincoln wrote the first draft partly on Executive Mansion stationery and partly on regular paper, and the second draft on the same type of paper as the second page of the first draft. The early histories of the first two copies are somewhat murky, but it seems likely John Nicolay had both until 1901, when they passed from his estate to John Hay. In 1916, the Hay family donated both manuscripts to the Library of Congress, where they reside today.

In early 1864, Everett asked Lincoln for a copy so that he might auction it off to raise money for the New York Sanitary Fair. The copy remained in private hands until the 1940s, at which time the estate of James C. Ames generously offered the document to the Illinois State Historical Library for the sum of $60,000, much less than Ames's original purchase price. Schoolchildren raised the lion's share of the money by donating their pennies. When they fell short, Chicago millionaire Marshall Field III stepped in and contributed the balance. This copy, frequently referenced as either the Everett or the Illinois version, is now in the collection of the Abraham Lincoln Presidential Library.

In 1864, historian George Bancroft requested a copy for a collection to be bound and reproduced for sale at the Baltimore Sanitary Fair. The original version remained in the possession of Bancroft's family until 1929. In 1949, a benefactor purchased the document and donated it to Cornell University, where it remains.

The Bliss copy, the final version and the one now commonly accepted and reprinted, came about as a result of an accident. When Lincoln produced the copy for Bancroft, he wrote on both sides of a single sheet of paper, something that made reproducing the item in the desired format impossible. Bancroft's stepson, Alexander Bliss, requested another copy. The President complied, and the original remained in the hands of the Bliss family until 1949. The Bliss version—sometimes called the Baltimore Sanitary Version II—was also a "mistake" in that it consists of three pages, not the desired two. Cuban Oscar Cintas purchased the draft in 1949 and willed that it pass on to the American people upon his death, which occurred in 1957. It is now located in the White House's Lincoln Bedroom. There could be no better spot: In 1862, this room was where the cabinet met and where Lincoln both announced and signed the Emancipation Proclamation.[72]

Unfortunately, each version differs. Lincoln continued to edit the Address in ways that did not greatly change the meaning of what he had said but certainly changed the look. There are convincing arguments for each of the first three copies being closest to what Lincoln *actually* said, while the Bliss version is probably closest to what Lincoln *wanted* to say. Robert Todd Lincoln, Lincoln's only surviving son, certainly thought so. In a May 5, 1909, letter, Robert said, "The Baltimore Fair [Bliss] version represents my father's last and best thought as to the address, and the corrections in it were legitimate for the author, and I think there is no doubt they improve the version as written out for Col. Hay,—and as I said to you before, I earnestly hope that the Baltimore Fair version will be used."[73]

In addition to these texts, there are various transcriptions of the Address recorded by those present, most notably by Joseph Gilbert. However, the *Chicago Times, Cincinnati Daily Gazette*, and *Philadelphia Inquirer*, among others, offered competing transcriptions. Some are fairly close to Gilbert's transcription and the various copies in Lincoln's hand; others seem almost a different speech. In 1917, Gilbert insisted, "Before the dedication ceremonies closed the President's manuscript was copied, with his permission; and as the press report was made from the copy no transcription from shorthand notes was necessary." The version Gilbert submitted for the Associated Press does not correlate to any of the five in Lincoln's hand, making it *possible* that a sixth copy exists or at least existed. Wills also requested a copy, but none exists in his papers. Perhaps he ended up with Lincoln's reading copy.[74]

On February 20, 1913, the U.S. Senate adopted a joint resolution stating, "Protests having been made that there are many different versions of Lincoln's Gettysburg speech, which it is proposed to inscribe on the Lincoln Memorial to be built [in Washington, D.C.], the Senate adopted Senator Root's joint resolution to-day, authorizing a committee to report the correct version."[75] The twelve-year-old plan to build a memorial to Lincoln in Washington, D.C., was finally showing some progress, but before construction could start the designers had to know which version of Lincoln's speech to reproduce on the south wall. By this time, more than one hundred published versions of the Address existed, making the confusion understandable.[76]

Following the lead of the national press, a local Gettysburg paper weighed in on the issue, urging the acceptance of the version printed in its pages in 1863. On November 19, 1913, the *Star and Sentinel* carried a two-column-wide picture of Lincoln taken just eleven days before his speech at Gettysburg in 1863 and a transcript of the Address on the front page. The version featured was an "Exact Reprint From the 'Adams Sentinel' of November 24, 1863." On the second page, the editor noted that the transcript from 1863 "varies somewhat from the version now in popular use" but contended, "There are many reasons that incline us to the belief that the Sentinel reported this speech as it was spoken by Mr. Lincoln, and received by the audience." Most conclusive, the paper's editor in 1863, Robert G. Harper, lived next to Wills, Lincoln's host on the night preceding the dedication ceremonies. Secretary of State William Seward lodged with Harper on November 18, and Lincoln visited the residence to meet with his most trusted cabinet member, making it "practically certain that Mr. Harper came in personal contact with Mr. Lincoln during his staying in Gettysburg." Given that likelihood, the *Star and Sentinel* contended that Harper "could with all propriety, have secured his original copy from the President or his secretary. . . . We believe he did this; that the Lincoln speech printed on the first page is the Lincoln speech that was actually delivered, and that the inserted marks of applause were the observations of a trained newspaper man." Having built a case for the acceptance of Harper's version of the Gettysburg Address, the *Star and Sentinel* asked, "Is it not reasonable to conclude that the impression of the newspaper man, set down less than three days after the occurrences can be accepted as the record of what actually occurred that day?" But as the preceding chapter discusses, the account printed in the *Adams Sentinel* of November 24, 1863, came from Gilbert of the Associated Press, not Harper.

Regardless of who authored the text of the Gettysburg Address appearing in the November 24, 1863, *Adams Sentinel*, the 1913 discussion in the *Star and Sentinel* reveals the way local considerations shaped responses to a national issue. Gettysburgians supported the move for a single, authoritative version of the Gettysburg Address but showed their parochialism by calling for the adoption of a locally authored version of the speech, despite the multiple copies of the speech in Lincoln's own hand.

In its call to accept Harper's putative version of the Gettysburg Address, the *Star and Sentinel* also referred to another national debate: whether the audience had applauded during and after Lincoln's address. Gettysburgians considered the issue very significant. In 1863, many newspapers implicitly or explicitly contended that the audience did not applaud and thought little of Lincoln's effort. Gettysburg's own Democratic paper, the *Compiler*, reprinted the text of Lincoln's address on November 23, 1863, but did not note applause either during the speech or at its conclusion. By 1913, when most Americans proclaimed the greatness and immortality of the speech, battle lines formed around the applause issue. One explanation for the divisiveness of this issue is that Gettysburgians feared that those who contended the audience had not applauded implied they lacked the sophistication to recognize the greatness of Lincoln's words in 1863. The publication of two works in 1906 heightened Gettysburgians' feeling of persecution. Clark Carr's *Lincoln at Gettysburg* said of the crowd, "They could not possibly, in so short a time, mentally grasp the ideas that were conveyed, nor even their substance. Time and again expressions of disappointment were made to me."[77] Gettysburgians found the implicit statement that Lincoln's words soared over the heads of the audience highly offensive and sought to prove Carr wrong.

In "The Perfect Tribute," also published in 1906, Mary Raymond Shipman Andrews asserts, "[T]here was no sound from the silent, vast assembly" when Lincoln finished his oration. "He stared at them a moment with sad eyes full of greatness, of resignation, and in the deep quiet they stared at him. Not a hand was lifted in applause. . . . [T]here was no sound of approval, of recognition from the audience." To Gettysburgians, the suggestion that they saddened Lincoln and that it took a Confederate to heal the wound they created was a serious charge. The audience's reception of the Address, and the related applause issue, occupied a central role in reminiscences of the Address in the early twentieth century. The *Star and Sentinel* articulated the two sides of the applause controversy: "The recollections of men now living in Gettysburg are at variance. Some remember the liberal applause that the Sentinel's report indicates. Others with equal certainty deny that there was any outward expression of approval. They were all young men. Their presence on that occasion was prompted by curiosity alone, and their present recollection is clouded by a lapse of fifty years of time."[78]

In this passage, the *Star and Sentinel* refers to the applause in the original transcription of Lincoln's speech by Gilbert. That version contains four breaks for applause and a notation of sustained applause at the end. But in a speech delivered at the annual meeting of the National Shorthand Reporters' Association in 1917, Gilbert asserted, "It was not a demonstrative nor even an appreciative audience. Narratives of the scene have described tumultuous outbursts of enthusiasm accompanying the President's utterances. I heard none. There were no outward manifestations of feeling." This was a remarkable statement from the man who had convinced many in 1863 that the audience enthusiastically and loudly received the President's speech. Like the controversy over which text should be accepted, the question of whether the audience applauded remains to this day.[79]

Gettysburg's Judge McClean addressed all of these controversies in his comments at the fiftieth-anniversary commemoration. First, he urged the adoption of the version of the Address that appeared in the local *Adams Sentinel* and a host of other places. His comment that he remembered little applause is enigmatic as McClean offered no thoughts as to what that signified. The third issue, the meaning of the Address, provoked considerable debate.

In their writings in the late 1800s, the Populists asserted that the Gettysburg Address affirmed the principle of democratic governance: "government of the people, by the people, and for the people." But McClean offered the counterpoint: The Address remained significant due to its discussion of equality and freedom rather than proper forms of government. The differences between these two viewpoints are substantial: An interpretation without equality left room for segregation and Jim Crow laws, which were then taking hold in both North and South. In McClean's world, where a new birth of freedom meant equality for all, there was no place or justification for the racial apartheid taking hold in the nation.

T. C. Billheimer, another Pennsylvania College student who had participated in the parade to the cemetery in 1863 and ended up close to the speakers' platform, followed McClean and also spoke extemporaneously. He noted that Everett's oration tired him out and that the people did not expect much of Lincoln as his only other public speech, on the East Coast, "was a failure." According to Billheimer, "There was tremendous applause when [Lincoln] appeared, but with the conclusion came a feeling of awe that was not dispelled until the time for applause had passed."[80] Billheimer concluded, "There will never be another Lincoln—such a scene, such a speech, such a cause! It was an occasion of a man's lifetime. I have seen it. I am proud of it." Like Hamilton, Billheimer attributed the lack of applause to the overwhelming emotion of both the occasion and the oration. Billheimer's explanation differs, though, in that it implies the crowd expected a poor performance out of the President and that his eloquence shocked them.[81] Two weeks later, Billheimer wrote to Boos and completely contradicted what he said at the fiftieth-anniversary ceremonies. In that letter, Billheimer contends, "There was applause when he finished."[82] As with Hamilton, one can only speculate as to why Billheimer offered divergent opinions on the issue. Perhaps, the two men were conscious of their town's reputation: A lack of applause might suggest to outsiders that they had not recognized the speech's greatness, a charge they wished to avoid at all costs even while acknowledging a different story when in the company of their townsmen.

Philip Biklé, a former schoolmate of Billheimer's, took the podium next. Of all those who spoke on the fiftieth anniversary, Biklé alone admitted he did not fully appreciate Lincoln's speech at the time: "His short speech impressed me, a mere school boy, as very simple and very appropriate but nothing remarkable . . . but I have long since seen why it has been regarded also as a most remarkable speech." In this comment, Biklé was one of the few, particularly in Gettysburg, to admit that he had not instantaneously recognized the greatness of the speech. While the *Star and Sentinel* provided Biklé's full oration, the *Gettysburg Times* contained just a summary, leaving out entirely his evaluation of the speech and subsequent change of heart. As with the McSherry portion of the article, the *Gettysburg Times* ignored the aspect of the reminiscence dealing with the Gettysburg Address, possibly because Biklé had not offered a positive review.[83]

Reverend Joseph B. Baker gave the main oration, the text of which the *Star and Sentinel* fully reprinted. After a long prelude on the souls and immortality of those who had fallen in the battle, and of Lincoln himself, Baker began his commentary on the Gettysburg Address by incorporating some of its very lines into an evaluation: "While the world will little note nor long remember what we do here it can never forget what he said here." Baker especially emphasized the town's connection to Lincoln: "It is not given to many towns to be visited by the immortals; fewer yet have the privilege of entertaining them while they make themselves immortal." Indirectly, Baker also offered his thoughts on the audience's reception of Lincoln, "When Lincoln arose in Gettysburg the multitude saw him transfigured," suggesting that the crowd understood they witnessed a masterpiece. The bulk of Baker's speech put Lincoln in the context of his Greek, Roman, and biblical predecessors and, finally, into the American narrative. Despite his long soliloquy, Baker offered little evaluation of the speech's meaning, choosing instead to state its greatness and focus his attention on placing the man, rather than his speech, in historical perspective.

Judge Samuel McCurdy Swope, a local man present at the dedication ceremonies as a thirteen-year-old boy, recited the Gettysburg Address. It is likely he used the Associated Press–*Adams Sentinel* transcription, Gettysburg's favored choice at the time. The crowd sang "America" and then dispersed following a benediction.[84] While the day had all the makings of a joyous celebration, at least a few people found their wallets missing. In this sense, little had changed since 1863, for pickpockets also worked that crowd.[85]

When the speakers at the fiftieth-anniversary celebration of Lincoln's Gettysburg Address took center stage, they were aware of several national controversies surrounding the great speech: the selection of a correct version of the Address, the debate over whether applause followed the oration—or in other words, whether those present instantly recognized the speech's significance—and, finally, the greater meaning of the speech. The reminiscences presented in Gettysburg on the fiftieth anniversary reveal how local considerations shaped the answers each participant offered to these national questions. The Gettysburg Address came from Abraham Lincoln, but it discussed events that occurred in their town and was delivered (even partially written) in their town and, consequently, belonged to them. When asked for their recollections of the events by outsiders, Gettysburgians presented a rosy picture of applause and acceptance while privately acknowledging a different story. At the same time, because the tourism industry was so essential to the town, and tourists came from all over, the townspeople—except perhaps McClean—presented a Gettysburg Address that all could accept. The controversies they engaged in, the exact wording of the speech and the amount of applause at its conclusion, if any, were not ones that would offend their neighbors to the south. While some considered the larger meaning of the Address, most Gettysburgians avoided it in their reminiscences for fear of alienating some listeners. Though impossible to foresee in 1913, the Gettysburg Address would grow even more revered in the coming years. On the other hand, it also slipped the bonds of the local town that had once been its home, eventually becoming the intellectual property of the world.

The story of the 1913 celebration is not complete without a brief consideration of who was not there: the nation's African Americans. Since the 1880s, the Baltimore chapter of the Grand Army of the Republic, or GAR—a Union veterans' organization—had yearly come to Gettysburg in September to commemorate the issuance of the preliminary Emancipation Proclamation. The number of visitors, 7,094 in 1894 alone, was staggering. The linking of the date of emancipation with the location of the Gettysburg Address shows how connected those documents were in the minds of some. Like many day-trippers of all races, these black

Baltimoreans spent most of their time at Round Top Park, an amuse-
ment park on the south end of the battlefield. To avoid racial conflict,
the GAR and Round Top Park arranged these visits for off days when
the park was normally closed. Even so, as historian Jim Weeks observes,
"The town's Democratic paper continually stirred racial animosity, and
townspeople showed little sympathy for black equality." The visitors
from Baltimore, and other locales, were undeterred: Lincoln had used
Gettysburg to offer the nation's African Americans freedom from oppression in 1863, and in the early twentieth century, black visitors came
to escape the oppression of urban and industrial America despite their
shabby treatment by some townspeople.[86]

Despite these trips to Gettysburg, there were few African American
comments on the Gettysburg Address during this era. Sociologist Barry
Schwartz comments, "Most black editors, commentators, and spokesmen
respected Lincoln, but many doubted that his opposition to slavery was
based on a desire to make America a racially integrated society." In his
1882 *History of the Negro Race in America from 1619 to 1880*, the first such
work, former soldier and fellow African American George Washington
Williams had neglected the Gettysburg Address entirely and wrote of the
Emancipation Proclamation, "Even this proclamation—not a measure of
humanity—to save the Union, not the slave—left slaves in many counties
and States at the South. It was a war measure, plain and simple." In 1985,
historian Ira Berlin said, "Williams was forever turning on those who
supported him." It would be tempting to apply that statement to explain
Williams's passing over the Gettysburg Address and his appraisal of
Lincoln's motives in the Emancipation Proclamation, except that so
many other prominent members of his race shared his outlook.[87] On
November 22, 1913, the *Chicago Defender*, an African American weekly
newspaper, offered an admonishment to the Appomattox Club, a group
of prominent African Americans from Chicago, for not properly marking the semi-centennial of Lincoln's address. The paper said, "There is
nothing in the life of Lincoln that we should overlook," but the inclusion of such an admonition suggests that readers must not have agreed.
Richmond, Virginia's African American paper, the *Richmond Planet*,
carried a large picture of Lincoln with the caption "Fiftieth Anniversary
of Lincoln's Gettysburg Address" and reprinted the speech along with
a short explanation of the cemetery dedication in 1863. However, there
was no editorial comment or consideration of the place of the speech,

indicating that the editors did not see a role for the Gettysburg Address in their struggle against segregation and discrimination.[88]

In the interwar period, African American historian Carter G. Woodson called Lincoln "overrated as the savior of the race. . . . At best Lincoln was a gradual emancipationist and colonizationist." The era's most influential African American leader and thinker, W. E. B. DuBois, used the pages of the magazine the *Crisis* of the National Association for the Advancement of Colored People (NAACP) to offer his evaluation of Lincoln as "big enough to be inconsistent . . . despising Negroes and letting them fight and vote." Historian Merrill Peterson offers an explanation: "DuBois came to believe it was important to 'demythicize' the Great Emancipator in order to improve the Negro's own self-confidence and clear sightedness. . . . Some negroes were beginning to wonder if it was not [the image of Lincoln the Man of the People] they needed emancipation from." James Weldon Johnson, NAACP secretary, engaged in an act of re-created self-emancipation under a statue of Lincoln in New York City's Union Square in 1925. Johnson wrapped himself in a chain of flowers and then broke the chain, symbolizing both the end of slavery and the end of Lincoln's image as the Great Emancipator.[89]

Taken together, these African American evaluations of Lincoln's thoughts on emancipation and equality help explain the lack of a substantial black commentary on the Gettysburg Address in the early part of the twentieth century. If leading African Americans doubted that Lincoln really even desired emancipation other than as a war measure, they surely could not have believed that he truly desired "a new birth of freedom" that would ensure "that all men are created equal." Schwartz notes, "African-American experience has moved back and for the between assertiveness and accommodation," depending on whether white society was in a racist or accepting mood.[90] For most of this period, white society fell into the former camp, and, thus, many African American leaders counseled a new form of self-emancipation that did not rely on invoking Lincoln's Gettysburg Address.

As in 1863, the Gettysburg Address in 1913 received much more attention and coverage locally than nationally or internationally, and coverage patterns in 1913 did not differ dramatically from those in 1863. In New York, the *Masses* and *New York Call*, both socialist or workers' journals, ignored the speech, as did the *New York Evening Telegram* and the *New York World*. This is a curious omission, as Lincoln's assertion that government should be "of the people, by the people, for the people" certainly appeals to socialists. The *New York Times* printed the Bliss version of the speech and a very short introduction noting that Lincoln "strengthened the foundations of the 'government of the people, by the people, for the people' to which he was devoted." The *New York Herald* of November 19, 1913, also reprinted the Bliss version, a picture of Lincoln, and an excerpt from Curzon's speech. The *New York Sun* and *New York Tribune* of November 20 both offered brief accounts, likely from the Associated Press, of the commemoration activities in Gettysburg. The *New York Evening Post* of November 24 carried a long review of Curzon's speech.

The *New York Evening Mail* offered by far the most extensive coverage of the fiftieth anniversary of the Gettysburg Address. The paper's November 19, 1913, edition carried an account of the commemoration as well as a brief article noting that students throughout Illinois had memorized the Gettysburg Address and recited it at the same time of day that Lincoln had offered the original fifty years earlier as part of an organized statewide initiative. A long column, "Lincoln's Masterpieces: Which Is the Greatest?" also appeared. Lastly, the paper printed the full text of Lincoln's Gettysburg Address, his letter to Mrs. Bixby consoling her on the loss of her sons in the war, and his Second Inaugural Address. Similar to columns in several other New York papers, this one mentioned Curzon's remarks about the Address, and it seems probable they may have inspired this article. The *Post*'s final column on the Address came on November 21. "Unappreciated in Its Day" noted that a popular collection of Lincoln's works in the 1860s left out the Address and that the speech had only recently come to hold such an exalted place. The writer concluded that the Bixby letter and Second Inaugural Address were superior to the Gettysburg Address in literary terms.

Thus, New York's coverage of the Gettysburg Address in 1913 mirrors that of 1863. Editors often reprinted the speech, but while most evaluations asserted the immortality and magnificence of the speech, they did not say what made it so. By 1913, most had completely forgotten the other speeches delivered at Gettysburg, namely those by Seward and Everett. The specific issues related to the war that these men discussed no longer mattered to average readers, and several book-length works on the Battle of Gettysburg made Everett's oration obsolete. The very factors that made their speeches noteworthy in 1863 now condemned them to obscurity.

Richmond offered far less coverage. On November 25, 1913, under the section "Fifty Years Ago," the *Richmond Times-Dispatch* reprinted its account from the November 24, 1863, *Richmond Dispatch*. By reprinting this article without commenting on the mistakes and omissions from the 1863 piece, the *Richmond Times-Dispatch* clung to that flawed report long after the newspaper editors knew of its inaccuracies. Just as in 1863, the editors omitted the actual text of Lincoln's Gettysburg Address. The paper had no additional coverage of the Gettysburg Address during its fiftieth anniversary, but on November 23 in "Our Confederate Column," it did run the story "The Faithful Slave of the Older South: Some Memories of Negroes Who Cared for Their Master and Their Master's Family—A Tribute to Those Who Served 'Little Massie.'" The following day, in a flashback to news from fifty years ago, the *Times-Dispatch* reminded readers that in 1863, "Wendell Phillips said that Lincoln admitted to him that the greatest folly of his life was in issuing his emancipation proclamation." The dearth of coverage of the Gettysburg Address contrasts sharply with these two other pieces but does follow the same pattern of the Southern textbooks of the era of at least refraining from denigrating the speech, emphasizing that while the North and South had reunified, they had not necessarily reconciled.

Many of London's papers ignored the Address on its actual anniversary. The *London Spectator*, a weekly journal, offered no stories on the Address, instead focusing on the two major events of the day, the Home Rule Crisis in Ireland and the Mexican Revolution. Perhaps, they felt their comment on Curzon's speech a fortnight earlier made further articles superfluous. And perhaps, like the biographies of Lincoln published around this time in London, they accepted the Address as magnificent but had little prolonged thought on its significance. The world wars would change that paucity of responses to the great American speech.

During World War I, many on both sides of the Atlantic found cause to invoke Lincoln's speech. However, responses to the Address in this era differ from those that came before, during the semi-centennial in 1913, and after, with the dedication of the Lincoln Memorial in 1922. The dedication of the Lincoln Memorial on May 30, 1922, culminated a twenty-one-year project begun in earnest in 1901 when the Senate Park Commission, or McMillan Commission, proposed placing a statue of

Lincoln at the end of the Mall in Washington, D.C. Even before that, an 1867 plan called for a monument to Lincoln on the grounds of the Capitol. In the interim, a number of smaller statues to Lincoln were erected throughout the city, but many believed that none exhibited the majesty that a man of Lincoln's stature warranted.

A mixture of factors came together in 1902 to urge reconsideration of a Lincoln monument. American victory over Spain in the War of 1898 reduced North-South tension, making such a monument more tolerable to Southerners. Then again, the origination of the Monument Avenue project in Richmond and the construction of a major statue to Robert E. Lee in 1890, soon to be followed by similarly grand memorials to General J. E. B. Stuart, Confederate president Jefferson Davis, General Thomas Jonathan "Stonewall" Jackson, and Commander Matthew Fontaine Maury, signaled the throwing down of the gauntlet of commemoration. Finally, after a series of weak executives, William McKinley returned the presidency to a position of power, reminding his fellow Americans of the last man to exhibit such leadership.[91]

Despite the plan in 1902, it was a torturous road before a Lincoln Memorial became a reality. For one, there was no general agreement on what form the memorial should take. This decade saw the rise of the automobile and the inauguration of "Good Roads" projects around the country, and many thought a Lincoln memorial highway the most fitting tribute, linking the nation's past and future while also advancing the country's infrastructure, something Lincoln had always championed. Others who accepted the desirability of a monument or statue debated the location. For nearly a decade, there was little real progress toward the memorial.

The 1910 Congressional elections turned the tide. Since 1896, the Republicans had controlled Congress, but in 1910, they lost major ground, making it apparent that the 1912 elections would sweep them from power. Partisanship surrounded the Lincoln memorial project from the start, with Republicans pushing the project and Democrats holding back, and now its champions hastened to inaugurate the project before it was too late. Just three days before Lincoln's birthday in 1911, Congress passed a bill creating a commission "to procure and determine upon a location, plan, and design for a monument or memorial." A competition between architects Henry Bacon and Charles McKim resulted in the eventual approval of Bacon's design in January 1913. Building began immediately, but problems with drainage around the site and the outbreak of World War I slowed construction.[92]

As Christopher Thomas argues in his excellent overview of the subject, "Lincoln's Memorial was built to foster consensus and reconciliation." Its location, symbolically linking the Capitol in Washington, D.C., with Arlington, Virginia, proved that. So did the inscription above Lincoln's head:

IN THIS TEMPLE

AS IN THE HEARTS OF THE PEOPLE

FOR WHOM HE SAVED THE UNION

THE MEMORY OF ABRAHAM LINCOLN

IS ENSHRINED FOREVER

Lincoln's saving the Union, not his role in ending slavery, justified the memorial. The author of that inscription, art historian and critic Royal Cortissoz, explains, "By emphasizing his saving the union you appeal to both sections. By saying nothing about slavery you avoid the rubbing of old sores." Indeed, every Southern congressman voted for the bill to fund the memorial's construction. But the memorial features Lincoln's two most famous speeches, the Gettysburg Address and Second Inaugural Address, both of which suggest Lincoln's legacy as the Great Emancipator.[93]

On May 30, 1922, an estimated thirty-five thousand citizens attended the dedication of the Lincoln Memorial. The program emphasized national unity, and in a sign of how far sectional relations had come, former Confederate soldiers, dressed in gray, attended the ceremony. Schwartz contends that the memorial purposely appealed to Southerners: "On the Southern wall, [is the] Gettysburg Address, which Southerners took to refer to Southern as well as Northern soldiers." Indeed, the reunificationist spirit of 1922 led to a recently constructed interpretation that Lincoln had surely meant his words to be applicable to all Americans.[94]

At the same time, Robert Moton, the president of both Tuskegee Institute and the National Negro Business League, was invited to speak at the dedication. Moton subscribed to Booker T. Washington's idea that African Americans should strive for economic gain rather than political and social equality and, thus, was considered a fairly conservative black leader. Even so, event planners feared what Moton might say and rejected the draft of his remarks submitted two weeks before the ceremony. Moton toned down the comments but was still positioned early in the program so that Chief Justice William Howard Taft and President Warren G. Harding, both slated to speak later, could counter or downplay any controversial statements Moton might make.[95]

After an invocation and the presentation of the colors, Moton rose to speak. The following day, the *New York Times* headlined its coverage "Morton [*sic*] Says Negroes Are Loyal" and reprinted three short paragraphs. In those paragraphs, Moton mused, "Upon us, more perhaps than upon any group of the nation, rests the immediate obligation to justify so dear a price for our emancipation." After quoting Moton's review of the loyalty and sensibility shown by African Americans since emancipation, the paper included Moton's assertion, "A race that produced a Frederick Douglass, in the midst of slavery, and a Booker Washington, in the aftermath of reconstruction, has gone far to justify its emancipation." The coverage of Moton's speech in the *New York Times* advanced the notion of unity and reunification and downplayed any racial divisions on the country.

Moton's delivered speech was far more divisive. Beginning with the story of the Mayflower sailing for Massachusetts at the same time the first ship bringing slaves to Jamestown made its way to that port, Moton noted that the forces that brought the descendants of Pilgrims and these first slave owners met on the battlefield, suggesting that the North was the moral actor in the drama. In explaining his race's devotion to Lincoln, Moton acknowledged, "There is no question that Abraham Lincoln died to save the Union." But continuing, Moton invoked the Gettysburg Address to explain Lincoln's greatest achievement: "The claim of greatness for Abraham Lincoln lies in this, that amid doubt and distrust, against the counsel of chosen advisors, in the hour of the Nation's utter peril, he put his trust in God and spoke the word that gave freedom to a race and vindicated the honor of a Nation conceived in liberty and dedicated to the proposition that all men are created equal." Moton reminded listeners again of Lincoln's words at Gettysburg: "Lincoln has not died in vain. . . . [T]o-day are found black men and white in increasing numbers who are working together in the spirit of Abraham Lincoln to establish . . . that a nation conceived in liberty and dedicated to the proposition that all men are created equal can endure and prosper and serve mankind."[96]

This was Moton's delivered speech, but his initial draft differed in substantial ways. Moton had written more directly on the horrors of slavery, "A bondage degrading alike to body, mind, and spirit," and to the insidious nature of slave owners, "They who for themselves sought liberty and paid the price thereof in precious blood and priceless treasure, somehow still found it possible while defending its eternal principles for themselves, to deny that same precious boon to others." In another excised passage, Moton used the Gettysburg Address to make clear how far the nation had to go: "Upon the field of Gettysburg [Lincoln] dedicated the nation to the great unfinished work of making sure that 'government of the people, for the people and by the people shall not perish from earth.' And this means ALL the people. So long as any group is denied the full protection of the law; that task is still unfinished. So long as any group within the nation is denied an equal opportunity for life, liberty and the pursuit of happiness, that task is still unfinished. . . . This memorial which we erect in token of our veneration is but a hollow mockery, a symbol of hypocrisy, unless we together can make real in our national life, in every state and in every section, the things for which he died."[97]

In his delivered speech, Moton, instead, concluded, "I somehow believe that all of us, black and white, both North and South, are going to strive on to finish the work which he so nobly began to make America an example for the world of equal justice and equal opportunity for all who strive and are willing to serve under the flag that makes men free." Both contained references to the Gettysburg Address, one of the only such public invocations by an African American leader in this era, but carried totally different messages. In 1922, Moton wanted to remind his listeners, white and black, that, as in 1863, much work remained to ensure equality for all. Indeed, for in 1922 the second Ku Klux Klan was ascendant, and around fifty African Americans were lynched each year. A variety of laws made it impossible for African American men to vote, and Congress had no black members. Moton's censors ensured that the call for "increased devotion" would apply only to African Americans expected to sacrifice for their nation, shifting the onus to make good on the promises of the Declaration of Independence and Lincoln's Gettysburg Address away from white people. Unfortunately, it would take forty-one more years before an African American could stand at the Lincoln Memorial and call for equality.[98]

Moton was followed by Chief Justice Taft, who, in his role as a member of the Lincoln Memorial Commission since 1902, conveyed the memorial from the commission to President Harding as the representative of the American people. Noting that the location of the memorial bridged the North and South, Taft asserted, "It marks the restoration of the brotherly love of the two sections in this memorial of one who is as dear to the hearts of the South as to those of the North. . . . [H]ere a sacred religious refuge in which those who love country and love God can find inspiration and repose." Taft's triumphant comments about national unity, in contrast with those of Moton, aligned with the dominant theme of the era and represented Republicans' deepest desertion of minority rights.[99]

President Harding's speech in accepting the memorial for the American people further played up reunification while downplaying emancipation. Harding noted, "The supreme chapter in history is not emancipation, though that achievement would have exalted Lincoln throughout all the ages. . . . Emancipation was a means to the great end—maintained union and nationality. Here was the great purpose, here the towering hope, here the supreme faith." Harding's exclusive focus on union is surprising: He had supported an antilynching law and in 1921 gave a speech in Birmingham, Alabama, advocating full legal—though not social—equality for African Americans. Harding could just as easily have thrown his support behind Moton as Taft. Perhaps, the Senate filibuster and ultimate rejection of that antilynching law just a few months earlier had given the affable Harding pause and exposed just how fragmented the nation remained. Regardless, Harding's words at the dedication of the memorial are those of a man who understood Lincoln's purpose at Gettysburg but, nonetheless, shied away from further antagonizing the South. Harding admitted that one of the main functions of the monument was to foster a sense of union in the present: "This monument, matchless tribute that it is, is less for Abraham Lincoln than for those of us today, and for those who follow after."[100]

Newspaper coverage of the dedication of the Lincoln Memorial varies tremendously. Gettysburg newspapers virtually ignored the ceremonies. As they had in 1913, Gettysburgians vigilantly tried to keep their town tied to the Gettysburg Address. The inscription of Lincoln's words on the walls of the Lincoln Memorial further eroded any control Gettysburgians once had over the speech and, as such, made them uneasy. In this context, the articles printed in Gettysburg papers after Memorial

Day bemoaning the small turnout that year carried an implicit warning of what the Lincoln Memorial might mean for the future of the town and its connection to Lincoln's speech. That a large percentage of the Memorial Day celebrations around Gettysburg featured recitations of Lincoln's Address furthers the notion that Gettysburgians sought to remind anyone who would listen of their town's role in the birth of the nation's greatest speech.

New York offered more extensive coverage of the Lincoln Memorial dedication and embraced the reconciliation narrative. The *New York World* carried a massive front-page article on the event that ran onto the second. On the fourth page, an editor endorsed Harding's focus on unity: "Lincoln realized so clearly how much more important in the long run is the maintenance of union to the abolition of any particular evil."[101]

In Richmond, both of the major papers, the *Richmond Times-Dispatch* and *Richmond News Leader*, offered fairly scant coverage of the Lincoln Memorial dedication. Richmond's African American paper, the *Planet*, ran a brief editorial on the Memorial dedication and specifically focused on the segregated seating at the ceremony, a great irony given the bent of the words in the Gettysburg Address and Second Inaugural Address staring down at those in attendance. African Americans had to sit nearly a block away and among weeds. Furthermore, a contingent of hostile U.S. Marines made the experience far from pleasant.[102]

While Taft, Harding, and others, such as the editors from the *New York World* and *New York Times*, played up the theme of unity and reconciliation, others saw the monument as problematic. For one, architectural critic Lewis Mumford wondered just what that unity would mean for the rest of the world: "The America that Lincoln was bred in, the homespun and humane and humorous America that he wished to preserve, has nothing in common with the sedulously classic monument that was erected to his memory. Who lives in that shrine, I wonder—Lincoln, or the men who conceived it: the leader who beheld the mournful victory of the Civil War, or the generation that took pleasure in the mean triumph of the Spanish-American exploit, and laced the imperial standard in the Philippines and the Caribbean?"[103] Indeed, Americans in 1922 constructed a Lincoln who advanced their agendas and their worldview and now commemorated that iconic image as if it had been real. From Gettysburg to Richmond, New York to London, people saw in Lincoln what they wanted to see in him, discarded the rest, and cited the great man's words to support their every action, justified or not.

In 1863, people around the world focused less on Lincoln's now-immortal words than on one of the other speeches at Gettysburg, feeling that the others contained more that demanded comment. But, by 1901, those speeches had faded away, with no one remembering Seward's brief comments and only a few recalling that Everett had spoken. But the same thing that had made the Gettysburg Address so easy to pass over in 1863 now made it impossible to ignore. Questions of liberty, equality, and democracy still reverberated, whereas the specifics of secession and the debate over the legality of the Confederates building warships in England had long since faded.

Between 1901 and 1922, the nation tried to move past the sectional tensions of the nineteenth century and reunify. From Andrews's fictional account of the speech, to the careful crafting of Northern appraisals of the Address to only talk about the parts acceptable to Southerners, to a regionally unifying Lincoln Memorial, the Gettysburg Address garnered a starring role in that reunification. While these invocations are instructive, the silences reveal almost as much. Former Confederates—or sitting presidents—who could not praise the speech because of its assertions of equality and freedom at least refrained from commenting negatively, censoring themselves as a way of advancing sectional peace.

The reunification of the late nineteenth and early twentieth centuries, a process accelerated by the passing of the Civil War generation and their memories of the war, was one based on shared notions of the preeminence of America and undergirded by Social Darwinism, the White Man's Burden, and Manifest Destiny. Broad acceptance of these notions brought a unity to the nation that allowed America to step out onto the international stage, initially with World War I and peaking with the Cold War, and along the way led to the idea of the American Century. There is no better symbol of that reunification and the function it served than the Lincoln Memorial, a monument simultaneously honoring its subject and its builders.

The Gettysburg Address was also a powerful weapon for those who posited that there were major issues to work through before there could be a real reunification, not to mention reconciliation. Ironically, the two groups pushing this agenda were diametrically opposed: the die-hard

Confederates and their ancestors on the one side and African Americans on the other. Confederate sympathizers, such as Mildred Rutherford, denigrated the Gettysburg Address because it was Lincoln's most eloquent argument for keeping the Union together and denying the Confederacy independence. On the other extreme, African Americans used Lincoln's statement that "all men are created equal" and promise of "a new birth of freedom" to voice their frustration with the current government's unwillingness to enforce the Fourteenth and Fifteenth Amendments to the Constitution guaranteeing equal protection under the laws and the right to vote for all races.

This was the darkest hour for the Gettysburg Address. Held hostage by a dominant majority who sought sectional reunification and an increased role on the international stage, even those who printed or read the speech in its entirety did not consider it in that way but rather cherry picked a line or two ("shall not perish," "government of the people, by the people, for the people") that advanced concepts of reconciliation, unity, or democracy and passed over those that argued for placing equality at the nation's core. This parsing of relevant lines was a practice that began in this era but continued for the next half century as a way for constituents to advance their own interests even though many were in direct conflict with Lincoln's true meaning.

Baum's recollection of the Gettysburg Address, closing the preceding chapter, did note that the audience met Lincoln's speech with profound silence. But there was more. Baum remembered "profound silence, followed by hearty applause." Unfortunately, two people standing next to each other could be applauding for opposing reasons, and, likely, neither one would have earned Lincoln's endorsement.[104]

4

For That Cause They Will Fight to the Death: Wartime Usages of the Gettysburg Address

> These . . . words will arouse the hearts of his countrymen
> to purer patriotic purposes in generation[s] to come.
> —Reverend Thomas Field, 1865, *Funeral*
> *Observances at New London, Connecticut*

In June 1917, as the first American soldiers landed in France to join the fight against the Central Powers, the *Times* of London assured its readers, "The men in these ships, and the millions they left behind them, know well what is the cause for which they are ready to sacrifice their all. It was defined for them and for the kindred democracies of the world once for all in the cemetery of Gettysburg. They are fighting that this world 'under God shall have a new birth of freedom, and that government of the people, by the people, for the people, shall not perish from the earth.' And for that cause they will fight to the death."[1] The *Times* editorial was perhaps more hopeful than accurate. Would Americans in 1917, and later in 1941, really fight and die for the ideals Lincoln put forth in the Gettysburg Address? *All* Americans? *All* the ideals?

From 1914 to 1918 and 1939 to 1945, the Gettysburg Address was invoked more often and for greater purposes than ever before. As the *Times* editorial suggests, these invocations took three main forms. First, the document was used within the United States to encourage Americans to sacrifice their bodies and pocketbooks in defense of the ideals to which Lincoln dedicated the nation at Gettysburg. Second, Lincoln's words were cited by those trying to explain to international audiences why the United States fought alongside the Allies. Last, foreigners praised the speech to make common cause with the United States by showing their appreciation for the most succinct expression of what America stood for or to suggest a model for reforming their own government as the postwar period neared in both eras. Despite frequent references to Lincoln's words, how and by whom the speech was invoked reveal the deep cultural divide that remained in the nation and an interpretation of the Gettysburg Address that had far to go before reclaiming Lincoln's full message.

The United States avoided any serious foreign entanglements in the generation after the Civil War. During the War of 1898, former Confederate and Union officers became brothers-in-arms once again, and feelings of sectionalism ebbed slightly. While some prominent anti-imperialists, including Mark Twain and William Jennings Bryan, questioned what a democracy was doing inaugurating such wars, a full wartime consideration of the meaning of democracy was still two decades in the future.

While European powers mobilized their armies in 1914 following the assassination of Austria's Archduke Franz Ferdinand, the United States attempted to stay out of the war. It was not a foregone conclusion that the United States would support the Allies over the Central Powers at first; though the United States was culturally closest to Great Britain, German Americans made up a considerable slice of the population, and two hundred thousand Germans had fought for the North during the Civil War. Germans admired and praised Lincoln as much as Britons, evidenced by the nine German-language biographies of the American president published between 1865 and 1914, a number greater than that produced in Britain.[2]

The shift toward considering the Gettysburg Address as a philosophy of government that might apply abroad as well as at home did not take place overnight. During the years of neutrality, most Americans responded to the Gettysburg Address as they had over the preceding fifty years. In 1914, Gettysburg again held a substantial commemorative ceremony. Whereas the event in 1913 addressed questions such as an official version of the speech and whether or not there was applause—issues of national attention—the 1914 observation was more overtly local. The focus of the event was the placement of three bronze tablets on the pew at Gettysburg's Presbyterian Church occupied by Lincoln and John Burns on the evening of November 19, 1863.

As in 1913, somewhere around fifty people who attended the original ceremony in 1863 found their way back to the cemetery again in 1914. Several men delivered their reminiscences both of John Burns's actions during the battle and his visit with Lincoln. The local newspapers all covered the event, and the *Compiler* published a pamphlet of the day's speeches. Demonstrating the continued impact of the Civil War on

Gettysburg, the November 21 edition of the *Star and Sentinel* reporting the celebration also carried a story about the unearthing of two Civil War skeletons on the southern side of town.[3]

The following year, the celebration was more subdued, consisting of a brief speech by Dr. O. T. Corson, the Ohio State Superintendent of Public Instruction, and the recitation of the Address by those present.[4] In November 1917, historical lecturer and memorabilia dealer John White Johnston of Rochester, New York, asked those who heard Lincoln's famous speech to congregate around the monument in the cemetery, where he then made a photograph of all present. Forty-two people appear in the photograph, and Johnson soon mailed them a letter asking for their recollections of that momentous day fifty-four years earlier.[5]

Neither Richmond's primary paper, the *Richmond Times-Dispatch*, nor the city's lone black paper, the *Richmond Planet*, offered a single thought on the Address during its various anniversaries from November 1914 through November 1918. The *Dallas Morning News* ran one article commenting at considerable length on the Address during those years, a story about a funeral oration in Scarborough, England, by the Archbishop of York, Cosmo Gordon Lang, that was so eloquent as to measure up to Lincoln's famous address.[6]

Even the *New York Times* offered few stories mentioning the speech in the years before the U.S. entry into the Great War. One exception was a 1915 article that called Lincoln's oration "the noblest monument of American literature, a classic of the world." After alleging that the speech "produced nothing like the impression which might have been expected," the author considered a recent assertion that Lincoln's final line (the source of which was discussed in chapter 1), in fact, originated with Maximilien Robespierre. The anonymous writer concludes that no matter who first uttered the phrase, it was Lincoln who said it best and, therefore, deserved credit for the line.[7]

In February 1916, Nicholas Murray Butler, the president of Columbia University, told seven hundred members of the American Bankers' Association, "Hamilton's writings in the Federalist, Webster's reply to Hayne, and Lincoln's Gettysburg address and second inaugural . . . [were] the crystallization of the essential ideals of Americanism of the past, a message which Americans could give to the world in the present crisis, and a foundation for the foreign policy of the republic."[8] Butler's comment was one of the first by an American that began to situate the Gettysburg Address as an American gift to the world, and one with continued significance, but it differed little from comments typically made in the nineteenth century in that it did not explain the "message" of the "American past." Did Butler mean democracy, equality, or a combination of both? While this type of general statement probably offended no one, it also failed to unify the nation, for Butler's evaluation offered nothing to unite around.

Commemorations of Lincoln's birthday in 1917 were more widespread than in previous years and more explicitly tied to the terrible conflict in Europe. Congress did not adjourn for the day but rather listened to a variety of speeches. Illinois Senator J. Hamilton Lewis noted, "Today in the crisis pending between the United States and the lands of Europe, the issue before the world is the issue which Lincoln gave to America—the right of man to exercise liberty of action, freedom of intercourse, and to enjoy justice from all." In both 1918 and 1919, Congress held similar observations and always featured a recitation of Lincoln's speech.[9]

The actions of the German kaiser and military soon shifted any popular sentiment away from the Central Powers and firmly toward the Allies. Former President Theodore Roosevelt reflected a popular view:

> As things actually are at this moment, it is Germany which has offended against civilization and humanity—some of the offences, of a very grave kind, being at our own expense. It is the Allies who are dedicated to the cause and are fighting for the principles set forth as fundamental in the speech of Abraham Lincoln at Gettysburg. It is they who have highly resolved that their dead shall not have died in vain, and that government of the people, by the people, and for the people shall not perish from the face of the earth. And we have stood aside and, as a nation, have not ventured even to say one word, far less to take any action, for the right or against the wrong.

With the dash of a pen, Roosevelt turned the Allies into democracies, which would have been news to most of them. At the same time, he said nothing of the powers' various stances on equality, implying that such considerations should not determine which side the United States join.[10]

For almost three years, the United States stayed out of the war. In 1916, President Woodrow Wilson, himself a great admirer of Lincoln, campaigned for reelection on the slogan "He kept us out of war." But when the Zimmerman Telegram, the German proposal to Mexico to invade the United States, became public, the United States could no longer remain neutral and declared war on Germany on April 6, 1917. While the outbreak of war united the country in some ways, it also led to a rash of anti-German literature that often compared militant Germans to Southern slave-owners. These analogies brought a backlash, the most virulent by Virginia's Lyon Gardiner Tyler, the son of President John Tyler and one of the most outspoken critics of Lincoln in the early twentieth century. John Tyler died less than a year into the Civil War—as a member of the Confederate Congress—and young Lyon spent the war years in exile on Staten Island with his mother, Julia. The origins of Lyon Tyler's hatred of Lincoln likely dated to this period. At different times during the war, Lincoln refused to issue passes that would have allowed the Tylers to travel between New York and Virginia, and in 1864 federal authorities seized some of the Tylers' employees and property in Virginia. Lincoln refused to act expeditiously in restoring these things to the Tylers, and in the interim, the family estate was sacked by former slaves in the region.[11]

When the Civil War ended, Lyon Tyler returned to his native state and in 1870 entered the University of Virginia. He graduated with a masters of arts in history in 1875. A year as a professor at the College of William & Mary was followed by four years as a high-school principal in Memphis, and then six as a lawyer in Richmond before Tyler returned to William & Mary as the school's president in 1888. In 1892, he began publication of the *William and Mary College Quarterly Historical Magazine*.[12]

In 1880, Julia began lobbying for a pension as the widow of an ex-president. Mrs. Lincoln, who struggled for five years after her husband's death before receiving a pension, was incensed, writing to a confidant, "I observed a little paragraph recently in the papers that Mrs John Tyler, was applying very vigorously for a Pension, from OUR Government. A woman, who was so bitter against our cause during the War, with much Northern property & money—as well as the South—but so *fearful* a Secessionist—Our Republican leaders will, I am sure, remember ALL THIS—& the Country will not have fallen upon such 'evil times,' as to grant her impudent request."[13] Though Mrs. Tyler was eventually awarded a pension, the vote was far from unanimous, and it seems likely that both the congressmen considering the issue and the Tylers knew Mrs. Lincoln's position on the matter.

One of Lyon Tyler's first notable attacks on Lincoln came in July 1917, in response to several recent articles comparing the South of 1861 with the Germany of 1917. Most of Tyler's attention was devoted to rebutting "[t]he

Hohenzollerns and the Slave Power," an anonymous piece in the *New York Times*. That article declared, "There is an essential analogy between the spirit of the Hohenzollerns and that of the slave power with which the nation came to grips in 1861. The slave power was arbitrary, aggressive, and oppressive . . . The Hohenzollern leaders are fighting in the same way, equally obstinate and more savage."[14] Responding in the *William and Mary College Quarterly Historical Magazine*, Tyler lashed out, "At a moment when union and cooperation on all lines of action are highly expedient, there seems to be a concerted effort by Northern writers and speakers to cast slurs upon the old South by drawing analogies between it and Germany." By responding to the piece, however, Tyler also posed a threat to "union and cooperation," and his subsequent argument that the South did not desire to extend slavery in 1861 suggests that Tyler's real purpose in writing was to relitigate the war, not to advance unity in the 1910s. Tyler was one of the leaders of the Lost Cause movement in Virginia that sought to exonerate the South for its part in the Civil War and simultaneously to create and maintain a Jim Crow society that privileged whiteness.[15]

Toward that end, Tyler also critiqued another piece, "America in the Battle Line of Democracy," which he cited to the February 1917 edition of *World's Work*. Unfortunately, the citation was incorrect, and the origin of the piece unknown, forcing one to rely on Tyler's description: "The writer in pointing the moral to his story quotes Lincoln's Gettysburg address and states that these last words of his speech, 'That the nation shall under God have a new birth of freedom and that government of the people, by the people, and for the people shall not perish from the earth,' described the great cause for which Lincoln sent armies into the field. Here is the same lack of logical and historical accuracy. The North had been antagonistic to the South from the first days of union, but it was really the jealousy of a rival nation."[16]

In the following paragraph, Tyler tried to deconstruct the Gettysburg Address, contending that if Lincoln announced in 1861 that he was raising an army to fight "for a 'new birth of freedom' and to keep popular government 'from perishing from the earth,' he would have been laughed at." Moreover, "[i]n his Gettysburg speech Lincoln talked about popular rule, but this was a kind of oratory in which South and North had both indulged for one hundred years, and we are told that the speech made no particular impression at the time. It was not until long afterwards that its literary merits were recognized, and from praise for its sentiments the Northerners have passed to regarding it as presenting a historical concept of the war." Tyler's tacit admission that the "literary merits" of the speech were "recognized" suggested he did not recognize them, a conclusion supported by a footnote in which he commented, "In his work, 'Some Information Respecting America,' published in 1794, Thomas Cooper, the celebrated philosopher, writes on page 53, referring to the United States: 'The government is the government *of* the people and *for* the people.'"[17] In this implicit charge of unoriginality, Tyler had much company, then and now, but whereas most others paint this borrowing of phraseology in benign terms, Tyler's footnote smacks of a college professor tongue-lashing a red-faced student for plagiarism. The attack on Lincoln's writings was not limited to this instance; at other times, Tyler referred to Lincoln as a "word juggler" and the Gettysburg Address as a "gilded fraud."[18]

Tyler's statement that at Gettysburg, Lincoln asserted a number of falsities was more serious. So was his contention that the demise of the Union would have *increased* popular governments by creating an additional nation based on that notion. Tyler's explicit assertion that the nation was *not* dedicated to "a new birth of freedom" revealed his feelings on that matter. The ideology of the Gettysburg Address was a complete sham, Tyler implied, for the war was not about "a new birth of freedom," and its result would not affect the future of popular gov-ernments worldwide. The Virginian was careful not to engage Lincoln's opening line and, thereby, avoided contradicting that other Virginian, Thomas Jefferson. The article was reprinted in the popular magazine *Confederate Veteran*, giving it a wide circulation.

Tyler's vitriol extended to Lincoln supporters. In the 1920s, Lincoln scholar William E. Barton (who in 1930 wrote *Lincoln at Gettysburg*, the most comprehensive book on the subject until Louis Warren's 1964 study) began arguing that Lincoln and Lee descended from the same family lineage. While Barton may have been looking for a way to further not just reunification but also reconciliation, Tyler had other thoughts and responded with a pamphlet, *Barton and the Lineage of Lincoln*, that sought simultaneously to refute Barton's claims and cast aspersions upon the author. In an ensuing exchange of letters, Tyler wrote to Barton, "I have nothing but contempt for a man who when his errors are called to his attention seeks to find his defense in the errors of other people. My errors are immaterial and inconsequential as far as they relate to the issue in controversy. But yours go to the very essence. You ought to be ashamed of yourself to impose upon the public such a rotten statement of Lincoln's descent."[19] Barton responded, "My correspondents mainly use the language which gentlemen employ in addressing each other. I am at a disadvantage in answering a man whose abuse is so virulent and unprovoked. I implore you, sir, in sheer self-respect, to exercise some degree of self-control."[20] Tyler continued to denigrate Lincoln until Tyler's death on February 12, 1935, Lincoln's birthday.

A *Saturday Evening Post* article written by Pennsylvanian George Pepper that appeared on May 5, 1917, prompted another attack by a Virginian. Pepper, later a Republican senator, suggested, "In the Gettysburg Speech Lincoln expressed our idea of popular government in words that may become immortal. Every school child can now speak glibly about 'government of the people, by the people, and for the people.' Possibly the words are so familiar that we forget to consider their meaning." Lloyd T. Everett, of Ballston, Virginia, took exception with this comparison between the Civil War era and World War I and responded with an article in the *Confederate Veteran*. In Everett's estimation, both Lincoln and Pepper got it wrong: "The true meaning of this phrase ["government of the people, by the people, for the people"] is not so easily grasped and retained, especially as applied to a 'confederated republic,' as Washington termed the United States under the Constitution of 1789 . . . All powers not granted to the newly formed central government . . . necessarily belonged to these several free, creating States." It is difficult to discern whether Everett blamed this perceived misinterpretation of the phrase "government of the people, by the people, for the people" on twentieth-century Northerners who sought to twist the martyred president's words for their own gain, or on Lincoln himself. The tone of Everett's response, however, condemns the man who originally uttered the phrase and those who sought to interpret it as increasing federal power at the expense of state power. Like Lyon Tyler, Everett focused solely on the aspects of the Gettysburg Address dealing with government, not those concerning equality.[21]

Pepper's comment that few considered the meaning of Lincoln's words got to the heart of the matter, for, in the 1910s, most people focused on the eloquence of Lincoln's words rather than his message. Ironically, some of the fullest considerations of the speech's significance came from the South. Men like Tyler and Everett understood that that the Gettysburg

Address was a powerful argument for the necessity of equality within a democracy, and, thus, they rejected and tried to dismiss Lincoln's speech. In the North, Pepper and his contemporaries bemoaned the lack of full consideration most gave the Gettysburg Address, while missing its main point themselves.

Despite all of this, after the United States entered the war, references to the Gettysburg Address became even more common. In a January 27, 1918, *New York Times* article, the former wife of President Grover Cleveland, Mrs. Frances Preston, discussed her efforts as a member of the Patriotism through Education Committee:

> We are planning a nation-wide Lincoln celebration. In this we are getting the co-operation of the schools, neighborhood clubs, and other educational institutions. The program of the day will consist of the study of Lincoln's work and its bearing upon present-day needs and problems. One of the features of the celebration will be the pledging of every individual to the spirit embodied in the closing lines of Lincoln's Gettysburg Address: "We here highly resolve that these dead shall not have died in vain, and that this Government of the people, by the people, and for the people shall not perish from the earth."[22]

This was a safe line to choose, for it left out both lines that demanded a reconsideration of equality. At the same time, by including the first part of the phrase, "We here highly resolve that these dead shall not have died in vain," Preston related the words specifically to the context of the ongoing war and to honoring the conflict's fallen soldiers. No patriotic American, North or South, could disavow this part of Lincoln's address.

Before April 1917, references to the Gettysburg Address in the context of the world war were of an unofficial nature. But once the war machine cranked up in the spring of 1917, the federal government added its voice to those invoking Lincoln's Gettysburg Address. President Wilson, who held a PhD in history from Johns Hopkins University, understood history's potential as a wartime tool. In an 1885 letter, Wilson said, "I should be complete if I could inspire a great movement of opinion, if I could read the experiences of the past into the practical life of men today."[23] By the outbreak of World War I, five hundred Americans held an advanced degree in history, and the managing editor of the *American Historical Review*, Wilson's former professor J. Franklin Jameson, used his position to encourage historians to contribute to the cause of democracy during World War I.[24]

Perhaps the most pervasive outreach programs were the recruiting and propaganda posters that soon cropped up around the nation. Sociologist Barry Schwartz notes, "All belligerent nations convened their past heroes to mobilize wartime motivation, but not as often as America convened Lincoln," a result both of the chronological closeness of Lincoln to the 1910s and the similarity of the issues in the 1860s and 1910s. Government-produced patriotic posters featured Lincoln steadying Wilson's hand as he signed the declaration of war, Lincoln and Wilson facing the proverbial storm together, a woman asking Lincoln, "What would you do?" and more.[25]

On several occasions, posters urging Americans to purchase Liberty Bonds invoked Lincoln's words. An advertisement for the second Liberty Loan featured Lincoln's speech, with the caption "The Hand of Abraham Lincoln" and the phrase "It is . . . for us here to be dedicated to the great task remaining before us . . . that government of the people, by the people, for the people, shall not perish from the earth." The poster encouraged the purchase of Liberty Bonds with the promise, "Yours is the most wonderful privilege that has been reserved for any man—for, as your hand signs the application for one of these Bonds, *it becomes the hand of Abraham Lincoln*, helping to guard your own hearthstone, to wipe away the agonies of Nations, and to preserve for all time the liberties of the Peoples of the World."[26]

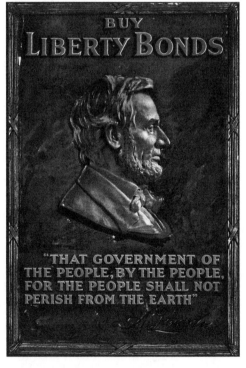

Figure 4.1. *Buy Liberty Bonds*, 1917. Third Liberty Loan. Created by the American Lithographic Company. Prints and Photographs Division, Library of Congress.

A *New York Times* article on March 10, 1918, announced the issuance of nine million posters advertising the third Liberty Loan: "The Lincoln poster has attracted much attention in advance of its general publication." Produced by the American Lithographic Company, the poster featured a bust of Lincoln with "Buy Liberty Bonds" above and "That government of the people, by the people, for the people shall not perish from the earth" below (see fig. 4.1). The poster's popularity led Joseph Pennell to create another one featuring Lincoln and the Gettysburg Address for the issuance of the fourth Liberty Loan later in 1918. That poster featured the Statue of Liberty and the phrase "That liberty shall not perish from the earth" (see fig. 4.2).

In 1918, the Havoline Oil Company encouraged the purchase of Liberty Bonds, urging Americans to be "Warriors All!" and featuring Lincoln's final line from the Gettysburg Address: "That government of the people, by the people, for the people shall not perish from the earth."[27] In all these posters, the common theme is twofold: first, that the value of America was that it was a government of, by, and for the people and, second, that it must not perish. The creators of these posters ignored Lincoln's other assertions about equality and freedom, choosing to fight one war at a time. The government-produced posters carefully utilized phrases that would unify the nation, not divide it and reopen sectional wounds from generations past that could harm the current war effort.

Figure 4.2. *That Liberty Shall Not Perish from the Earth*, 1918. Fourth Liberty Loan. Created by Joseph Pennell. Prints and Photographs Division, Library of Congress.

Some privately produced posters struck a different

tune. In 1918, Charles Gustrine created a beautifully illustrated poster captioned "True Sons of Freedom," which features a unit of African American soldiers fighting against Germany. An explanatory phrase on the poster reads, "Colored Men—The First Americans Who Planted Our Flag on the Firing Line." Looking down on the men is Abraham Lincoln, and next to him is the Gettysburg Address–inspired line, "Liberty and Freedom Shall not Perish" (see fig. 4.3). Gustrine was a white man in his late twenties who worked as a printer for a publishing company in Chicago.[28] This image stands out when compared with others, for Gustrine's image is the only one suggesting that equality, or the lack of, was a major issue. In a not-so-subtle image, Gustrine reminds viewers that fighting for an abstract notion of democracy alone is not enough, equality needs its defenders, too, and that the African American soldiers in France more than held up their end of the bargain. Gustrine's image recaptures Lincoln's message but was part of small counternarrative that never found wide acceptance in the world wars period.

Overseas, Americans soldiers saw a steady stream of material on the Gettysburg Address. In its inaugural issue, *Stars and Stripes*, a magazine for the American forces in France, considered "Father Abraham" and explained Lincoln's success in terms of his great personal patience. In concluding, the author exclaimed, "To-day a united nation, united because he made it possible to be so, stands in battle array to vindicate the principle which he held most dear: 'That government of the people, by the people, for the people shall not perish from the earth.' It is our privilege, and our glory, as members of America's vanguard of liberty, so to fight, so to strive, that we may rightly be called the fellow countrymen of Father Abraham." Three months later, the Memorial Day edition featured a cartoon of Lincoln standing over Uncle Sam and Lady Liberty, who together hold a wreath with the years 1861–65 on one side and 1917–18 on the other. Beneath the cartoon is the entire text of the Gettysburg Address.[29]

Reflections on the larger purpose of the war and of the future of the country were often built around the Gettysburg Address. In the issue published before Christmas in 1918, a writer explained some of the ways the war had changed the soldiers: "The war has mixed us all together. Alabama and Iowa have joined to form in a single brigade, and what a brigade!" The war made them all better citizens, the soldier continued.

Figure 4.3. *True Sons of Freedom*, 1918. Created by Charles Gustrine. Prints and Photographs Division, Library of Congress.

We of this generation had come to take our country for granted. We had come to take our liberty as a matter of course, like the air we breathed and the unfailing sun. It was not so with the generation that wrung the first homesteads from the wilderness. It was not so with the generation that conceived the nation in liberty and dedicated it to the proposition that all men are created equal. It was not so with the generation that fought a civil war to prove whether that nation, or any nation, so conceived and so dedicated, could long endure. But we—we of the easy spring of 1917—were like the idle sons of some rich man, inheritors of a fortune which only he could value who had by toil and sacrifice amassed it. Now we have done more than inherit the treasure. We have earned it. We were children of a great estate. We have added to it.[30]

The refrain was a common one. During the War of 1898, those supporting the conflict frequently decried their generation's easy upbringing and openly hoped that a war would literally toughen them up, create leaders for the new century, and remind Americans of the nation's ideals.[31] In this passage, the author holds up the Civil War generation as the best example of dedication to a cause and the Gettysburg Address as the perfect summation of that dedication. What this analysis lacks is the role African Americans were to play.

Perhaps, the best illustration of the pervasiveness of the Gettysburg Address appeared in an advertisement in the *Stars and Stripes*. On Valentine's Day in 1919, the paper ran an ad from Society Brand Clothes, a store with branches in Chicago, New York, and Montreal, Canada. The spread featured two dapper young men standing in front of the Augustus Saint-Gaudens statue of Lincoln in Chicago's Lincoln Park. Below the image is the line, "That Government of the People Shall Not Perish from the Earth." The advertisers proclaim, "The whole world subscribes to Lincoln's ideals now." While the connections between the speech and the wartime effort are fairly obvious, that advertisers believed the speech so well-known and meaningful as to help sell their clothes indicates a more popular dispersion of the speech than in previous eras.

If the response in London was any measure, the Society Brand Clothes advertisement might not have overstated too drastically in proclaiming the whole world was aware of and adhered to the Gettysburg Address. The praise that Earl George Curzon offered the Address in 1913 was echoed many times over by his countrymen during World War I. On April 16, 1915, the day after the fiftieth anniversary of Lincoln's death, the *Times* of London ran a story titled "A Great Example." The piece begins, "In the throes of the fiercest and the most fateful struggle the English people have ever fought for liberty and for right, they cannot but recall the day, now fifty years ago, when the greatest and noblest leader whom democracy has yet given the world perished by the knife of an assassin." This last phrase, of course, is incorrect as Lincoln was shot, not stabbed. Regardless, the article followed in Curzon's footsteps in attempting to bind the fates of Britain and America together by recognizing Lincoln as a common hero. Making sure the connection between past and present was firmly entrenched, the editorial continues, "The struggle in which the greatness of LINCOLN was gradually revealed to others, and perhaps to himself, resembled in other respects as well as in its righteousness that in which we are engaged to-day." After quoting the final sentence of the Gettysburg Address, the writer reflects, "His words are familiar to us all, but they are so noble and they seem so apt to our present circumstances that all Englishmen, and, as we believe, all true Americans, will thank us for repeating them . . . We are firmly convinced that we ourselves are fighting for this same cause to-day."[32]

During the World War I, Americans began to see the Gettysburg Address in the context of a world document. It was not just a tool to critique domestic issues but a charge to ally with democracy and its supporters across the globe and to do all that one could to promote free government. With rare exceptions, such as the one poster featuring African American soldiers, the Gettysburg Address of World War I was a speech whose significance was in that final line: "that government of the people, by the people, for the people shall not perish from the earth." Americans sought to spread democracy across the globe, but domestic crises, such as the Red Scare and rise of the Second Ku Klux Klan, highlighted that there were many different interpretations of who exactly Lincoln was, referring to when he used the term *people*. In this way, the invocations of the World War I era mirror those of the 1901–22 period. Unlike the peacetime period, however, the counternarratives during the war, though few and far between, presaged changes to come later in the century.

When the Treaty of Versailles brought World War I to a close in 1919, France's great military hero Ferdinand Foch prophesized, "This is not a peace. It is an armistice for twenty years." Although Foch would ultimately be proved correct to the very year, it was not so obvious in the immediate aftermath of World War I that the United States would again find itself allied with the British and French against the Germans. As with the pre–World War I era, both Britain and Germany in the interwar period rushed to celebrate the great American president.

Shortly after the war, an 1893 Lincoln statue in Edinburgh by Wallace Bruce commemorating emancipation and the role played by soldiers of Scottish descent in the Civil War was joined by two more. On September 15, 1919, a copy of the Cincinnati George Barnard Lincoln statue was unveiled in Manchester. Mr. and Mrs. Charles Phelps Taft, the half-brother and sister-in-law of President Taft, commissioned Barnard to make the casting and intended to present it to Britain as a gift for Parliament Square to celebrate the century of peace between the United States and Great Britain since the Treaty of Ghent ended the War of 1812. But some, including Robert Todd Lincoln, saw Barnard's lifelike depiction of Lincoln's features and stature as grotesque and opposed placing such a monument in London. Manchester, one of the centers of Britain's pro-Emancipation meetings in 1862 and 1863, requested and received the Barnard statue in May 1919.[33]

London instead received a Saint-Gaudens statue of Lincoln in 1920. Like the Barnard statue, this is a recast, with the original residing in Chicago's Lincoln Park.[34] Elihu Root, former secretary of state and Nobel Peace Prize laureate, gave the dedicatory address. Root emphasized the links between Britain and the United States, noting that the Lincoln who composed the Gettysburg Address learned to write such beautiful language by reading "the English Bible and English Shakespeare."[35]

It was not just Britain that celebrated Lincoln during the interwar period. Germany also rediscovered the Great Emancipator. In announcing the Weimar Republic in 1918, Social Democrat Philipp Scheidemann stated that it was "all for the people and by the people." During the years of the Weimar Republic from 1919 to 1933, Germans wrote six biographies of Lincoln. In 1930, the author of one of those biographies, Emil Ludwig, wrote a piece, "A New Lincoln: A World Figure," for the *New York Times* comparing the American to Germany's unifier, Otto von Bismarck. While noting that Bismarck possessed superior "genius," Ludwig determined that Lincoln had greater character. Observing that many Europeans knew little of Lincoln, Ludwig believed that this was because in the nineteenth century Europe was mostly concerned with power, whereas Lincoln promoted democracy, two notions often in conflict with each other. But in the 1930s, with many European nations becoming more democratic, Ludwig believed Lincoln's reputation would rise. If Lincoln had lived, Ludwig contended, he would have expended his energies on internal projects, such as the railroad and shipping improvements on the Great Lakes, a path that Ludwig felt proper: "This is the road which today leads to enduring fame, as neither the winning of battles nor the conquering of provinces does." But the Weimar Republic was not to last, and when Adolph Hitler and the Nazi party rose to power, one of the books they banned was Ludwig's biography of Lincoln. The ban was no doubt due to Ludwig's Jewish ancestry, but the Lincoln he presented also concerned Nazi leaders, who disavowed any notion of racial equality. Fortunately, Ludwig left Germany for Switzerland in 1932 and avoided the Holocaust.[36]

An anxious world looked on as the Nazis concentrated their power in Germany in the 1930s. The German invasion of Poland in September 1939 ensured that should the United States again enter a war on the European continent, it would do so on the side of the Allies, including old brethren Britain and France. As in World War I, Americans generally wished to avoid war, and the president, this time Franklin Delano Roosevelt, tried to steer a path of neutrality while supporting the Allies. Such a plan was workable until December 7, 1941.

When the Japanese attacked the American base at Pearl Harbor in Hawaii on December 7, 1941, the U.S. government quickly put the lessons from World War I to work. The government used notions of America's role as the "city upon a hill" the need to live up to the legacy of past generations to garner support, sell bonds to fund the war, and encourage devotion from the nation's citizen-soldiers. Images of World War II soldiers marching alongside the patriots of 1776 or 1861 are common and powerful. The major difference between World War I and World War II is the speed with which the government incorporated the Gettysburg Address into the "arsenal of democracy." In 1917, Americans were thinking about Lincoln's speech as an example for other nations for the first time, consequently references to it on the international stage were limited. But, by 1941, Americans were accustomed to thinking about the Address as an internationally significant document. From the very beginning, Americans invoked the speech to recommend to the Allies the proper form of government and to chastise the Axis Powers for not adhering to Lincoln's ideals. That message was apparently effective, for it was during this era that large numbers of foreign nations first began talking about the speech as setting an ideal for governments to strive toward.[37]

A week after the attack on Pearl Harbor, the *New York Times Magazine* ran a two-page spread featuring photographs of America's shrines, including the Lincoln Memorial, Independence Hall, Valley Forge, Monticello, Fort McHenry, and the Tomb of the Unknown Soldier. Beneath the photograph of the Lincoln Memorial is the final sentence of the Gettysburg Address; across the top of the pages is the phrase "Shall Not Perish From the Earth."[38] Soon thereafter, artist Allen Saalburg created a poster commemorating the attack for the Office of War Information, imploring Americans to "Remember Dec. 7th," and featuring the phrase, "we here highly resolve that these dead shall not have died in vain" (see fig. 4.4). Another poster, this one created by John Falter, encourages Americans to "Remember Last December!" and enlist in the Navy so "that free peoples may not perish from this earth" (see fig. 4.5). This phrase, irrelevant during peacetime, once again took on great significance, particularly in light of the surprise attack and sudden and unexpected deaths of over two thousand Americans.

Robert Penn Warren said in 1961, "We can remember that during World War II, the Civil War, not the Revolution, was characteristically used in our propaganda, and that it was the image of Lincoln, not that of Washington or Jefferson, that flashed ritualistically on the silver screen after the double feature." At the height of that war, *Lincoln Lore*, a magazine devoted to the sixteenth president, commented, "The Gettysburg Address has been given a new emphasis in view of the war effort. Its timely phrases spoken on a famous battlefield find a sympathetic response during a contest where liberty again seems to be a motivating factor." After the attack on

Figure 4.4. *Remember Dec. 7th!* 1942. Created by Allen Saalburg for the U.S. Office of War Information. Prints and Photographs Division, Library of Congress.

Pearl Harbor, the Library of Congress dispatched nearly five thousand cases of materials to five secret locations for safekeeping, including its copies of Lincoln's Address. In October 1944, the pieces finally returned to Washington, D.C., where U.S. Marines guarded them for the rest of the war.[39]

As the war continued, references to the Address became almost ubiquitous. The parades, concerts, and funeral ceremonies that invoked the Address defy enumeration. Similarly, the number of casual references to the Address in newspaper stories is astounding. The assertion in a *New York Times* editorial on April 16, 1942, that Americans "have never strayed far or long from the principles of the Declaration, the Bill of Rights and the Gettysburg Address" is notable for its similarity to dozens of other statements, not for its uniqueness. Indeed, the Address was becoming so pervasive that Wendell Wilkie, Republican nominee in the 1940 presidential race, even proposed part of the speech as a key component of the Republican platform for the 1944 elections. During dark hours when the war was not going well, columnists reminded their readers that simply because Lincoln proclaimed the value of a democratic government did not mean one would prevail in a contest of arms and that Allied victory required redoubled efforts. Others thought that the Gettysburg Address would, in fact, help them win the war. During New York's celebration of Lincoln's birthday in 1943, Henry Williams, the oldest alumnus of New York University, touted the Gettysburg Address as "combating foreign propaganda endeavoring to poison the minds of our people."[40]

Figure 4.5. *Remember Last December!* 1942. Created by John Falter. Prints and Photographs Division, Library of Congress.

As much as anything, the government needed funds in order to fight the war, and as in World War I, it turned to the Gettysburg Address to help sell bonds. A 1943 poster features Daniel Chester French's statue from the Lincoln Memorial above the corpse of a dead World War II soldier, with the line, "That we here highly resolve that these dead shall not have died in vain," on the side. A defense-bond and savings-stamp advertisement featuring the bust of Lincoln and the line, "That government of the people, by the people, for the people, shall not perish from the earth," appeared in the *New York Times* three days before Lincoln's birthday in 1942 and, evidently, was effective because another poster, this one featuring a bust of Lincoln and that same line, ran almost exactly two years later. If that hint was too subtle, a three-page article encouraging Americans to purchase the bonds less than a week after the invasion of Normandy concludes, "War bonds remain on a voluntary basis. The program is of the people, by the people, for the people." Despite his assertion to the contrary, the writer wanted the readers to believe the program was not voluntary but rather necessary to the preservation and promotion of democracy at home and abroad.[41]

War posters helped raise funds and motivate the older generation, and the nation's leaders also sought to reach millions of schoolchildren. With the outbreak of war in Europe in 1939 and even more so after the beginnings of American involvement in 1941, the United States quickly reoriented the nation's public-school education toward civic education. Whereas only 17 percent of seventeen-year-olds graduated from school at the end of World War I, by the outbreak of World War II, that number had jumped to 51 percent, making schools an efficient venue for such programs.[42] Nearly all the education associations, from the National Education Association to the National Council for the Social Studies, identified the need among young people for a greater understanding of the nation's past and its values as a means of building support for the war effort. During World War I, schools had adapted their curriculum to the new realities, but the lack of a national education infrastructure precluded any massive attempts at coordinating wartime programs. In fact, the federal government largely stayed out of school affairs in the 1910s, setting standards for health within the schools but leaving issues of curriculum up to state and local officials.[43] Rather than encouraging the role of schools in promoting democracy and civic education during

World War I, the government restricted textbook production to 50 percent of the prewar levels, allocating those cut resources to the war effort.[44]

The interwar period saw great advances in education, particularly related to social studies. The National Education Association was founded in 1857, but its growth mirrored that of the public schools and did not really take off until after World War I. In 1921, the National Council for the Social Studies was founded, signaling the rising emphasis on that subject. The term *social studies* is a telling choice; in the aftermath of a world war, the nation's leaders wanted to ensure greater knowledge not just of the United States but also of the world's other countries. America did not know her allies or enemies well enough, educational leaders thought, and feared that parochialism would lead to future wars.[45]

By 1941, social studies was an integral part of the school curriculum. This time around, rather than seeing textbooks and programs of study as a burden on the nation's resources, the country's leaders saw them as necessary tools to remind Americans for what they fought and whom they should support. Just months after the outbreak of war, educators began modifying their curricula in ways that brought greater visibility to the Gettysburg Address.

In 1941, the Federal Security Agency and U.S. Office of Education published A. Laura McGregor's *Living Democracy in Secondary Schools*, showing the integral part education played in national defense. In the very first line of her work, McGregor established the centrality of the Gettysburg Address to the American experiment: "The people of the United States believe in government of the people, by the people, for the people." That same year, the National Education Association's Educational Policies Commission produced a report *Our Democracy*. Under a section "What We Mean by Democracy," the authors noted, "The idea of democracy is well summarized by Lincoln's famous phrase, 'Government of the people, by the people, for the people.'" The commission members came from Maryland, Massachusetts, Michigan, Missouri, Ohio, Pennsylvania, and Washington, D.C., all either Northern or Border States during the Civil War.[46]

This distribution is not surprising. Robert Cook argues that "popular interest in the Civil War waned in the 1920s as a consequence of the mass killing on the western front during World War I" before a comeback in the 1930s. In that decade, the Pulitzer Prize was awarded to three works that dealt with the Civil War: Margaret Mitchell's fictional *Gone with*

the Wind, Douglas Southall Freeman's *R. E. Lee*, and Carl Sandburg's
Abraham Lincoln. The movie adaptation of *Gone with the Wind* sparked
even more interest. In 1940, the nation's first Civil War Roundtable, a
discussion group for enthusiasts, was founded in Chicago, and by 1958,
there were over forty in the nation.[47] This growth in interest in the Civil
War should not, however, be confused with a convergence in views on
the conflict. In regards to the causes of the war, generally speaking, both
Northerners and Southerners still blamed one another and thought their
side had been in the right, even while agreeing that history had shown
it fortunate that the nation had remained unified and strong enough to
be a world presence in the twentieth century. African Americans sided
with the Northern interpretation of the origins and causes of the war
and simultaneously argued that the promises of equality offered at the
end of the war and in Reconstruction had, thus far, been largely ignored.
Those wishing to invoke the memory of the Civil War as a weapon in
World War II had a complicated task.

In September 1942, the National Council for the Social Studies created
a commission on wartime policy. At the national meeting two months
later, the commission presented its report, *The Social Studies Mobilize for
Victory*, noting, "The war requires that American citizens learn about many
topics of new or increased importance. Among these are: the meaning
of democracy, its history, its practice, and its continuing development,
together with the alternatives posed to totalitarianism." Under a heading
of "The Democratic Way of Life Must Be Understood and Appreciated by
All Citizens of Democracy," the council recommended, "In the elementary
and secondary schools pupils should study the great documents of our
national democratic tradition and present crisis such as the Declaration
of Independence, the Constitution, the Gettysburg Address, Wilson's
Fourteen Points, the Atlantic Charter, and the Four Freedoms . . . Schools
should make arrangements for representatives of minority groups within
the community to serve as resource persons for acquainting teachers and
pupils with the points of view, cultural contributions, and problems of their
groups." Although that suggestion went largely unheeded during the war,
it presaged the postwar dialogues on the place of minorities within the
community and the appropriateness of segregated schooling.[48]

By far the biggest link between the Gettysburg Address and World
War II–era education, however, came from Chicago. When James

C. Ames, the owner of the third, or Everett, copy of the Gettysburg Address, died in 1943, his heirs offered their copy of the speech to the Illinois State Historical Library. On October 12, 1943, Vernon L. Nickell, Illinois Superintendent of Public Instruction, announced a campaign for the state's schoolchildren to donate their pennies, $60,000 worth, to purchase the manuscript. In the midst of a war consuming every national resource, the outlay of schoolchildren's pennies symbolized both how much the Gettysburg Address meant to Americans of all ages and a wartime sacrifice. The program was portrayed as something these children could do to make a contribution to their nation during the war despite being too young to serve in the armed forces or a crucial wartime industry. Over the ensuing five months, the children raised $50,000, and when it appeared they might fall short, department-store magnate Marshall Field III donated the final $10,000.[49] Field could well afford his generosity: On his fiftieth birthday, in 1943, he inherited approximately $75 million, and that stood in addition to an estimated $93 million he received on earlier birthdays.[50]

On March 24, 1944, the Columbia Broadcasting System (CBS) affiliate in Chicago, WLS, aired a fifteen-minute radio program celebrating the schoolchildren's purchase of the Address. The announcer, WLS educational director Jerry Walker, commented, "The immortal words of this address belong to all Freedom-loving Americans. And now that we are again 'engaged in a great war, testing whether that nation or any nation so conceived and so dedicated can long endure . . .' we pause to pay tribute to the Great Emancipator, Abraham Lincoln." Oliver Barrett, the chairman of the board of trustees of the Illinois State Historical Library, spoke at length about the speech in its day: "The youth of America are trustees for the security of its future. And the school boys and school girls of Illinois—representatives of awakened youth—by their gift to the State have conveyed a promise and a pledge that they are, and ever will be, worthy of that trust." Nickell explained the role of schoolchildren in the project: "From the very first, the boys and girls have demonstrated a high degree of patriotism and enthusiasm. In this national crisis when our young men are dying on the battle fronts around the globe in defense of our free institutions, the school children have demonstrated that they have the spirit of sacrifice and devotion to the end that the American Way of Life may 'long endure.'"[51]

Though World War II would last for another seventeen months, this event was, in many ways, the culminating experience of schoolchildren's interactions with the speech during the war. Invoked throughout the war in America's schools, the Address reminded everyone of what the country stood for and what it fought for from 1941 to 1945. As in other venues, however, the public-school invocations of the speech focused on Lincoln's final line and continually ignored Lincoln's call for equality.

During World War II, the annual commemoration of the Address in Gettysburg was spearheaded by the Lincoln Fellowship of Pennsylvania, a group organized upon the seventy-fifth anniversary of the speech in 1938. In 1942, the ceremony was highlighted by the presence of three very old men who had heard Lincoln deliver the Address as very young children. In both 1943 and 1944, two of these three, William C. Storrick and Edward Trostle, attended the ceremonies. Storrick made somewhat of a career as a professional "rememberer" of the Gettysburg Address, as did a number of his townsmen in the early part of the twentieth century. Wartime rationing of gasoline curtailed these celebrations and precluded the Lincoln Fellowship's organizing large events with a national draw, ensuring that the ceremonies resembled the local affairs of the 1910s.[52]

A ceremony at Gettysburg on Memorial Day in 1944 suggests that fighting a common enemy allowed Americans from both sections to proclaim a shared vision of the Gettysburg Address. The two main speakers that day, Republican Governor Leverett Saltonstall of Massachusetts and Democratic Governor J. Melville Broughton of North Carolina, represented states that had opposed each other on the battlefield eighty years earlier. Broughton said, "Evil forces—Nazi, fascist and pagan—tauntingly have flouted democracy in all the earth and plotted its destruction" and that Gettysburg "is a memorial to American ideals as symbolized by two of the Greatest Americans of all time—Abraham Lincoln and Robert E. Lee . . . North and South stand united today."[53]

But Southern perspectives on the Gettysburg Address were not so generous as Broughton indicated. From 1939 to 1945, neither of Richmond's major white papers, the *Richmond Times-Dispatch* or *Richmond News Leader*, made any mention of the Address during the week surrounding its anniversary. The *Richmond News Leader* did make two allusions to the Address during the world war, both merely in passing. The first came on December 21, 1943: "Churchill knows what Lincoln never learned—that his supreme words have stirred and strengthened the soul of a generation." A few months later, the paper ran "Too Short to Be Taken Seriously," referencing a story in a recent issue of *Lincoln Lore* that mentioned tremendous applause during Lincoln's Gettysburg Address: "It begins to look as if unappreciated authors will have to abandon their reference to Lincoln's Gettysburg Address as an example of the public's failure to accept great literary art." But Richmond papers offered no additional references. Other Southern papers in Norfolk, Atlanta, and Dallas, for example, regularly cited the Address during the war, but, oftentimes, these columns came courtesy of the Associated Press and did not originate in Southern locales.[54]

For example, on Lincoln's birthday in 1943, the *Dothan (AL) Eagle* carried an image featuring World War II GIs marching, French's statue from the Lincoln Memorial, and the line, "It is for us the living to be dedicated here to the unfinished work which they who fought here have thus far so nobly advanced. It is for us to be here dedicated to the great task remaining before us." The caption reads, "On this 134th anniversary of his birth, Abraham Lincoln is a guiding force in the fighting for the freedoms he championed. As at Gettysburg in 1863, Lincoln's words apply in 1943 at Guadalcanal and on other world fronts where Americans are dedicated to the completion of an 'unfinished work.'" This would be remarkable if the image originated in Dothan, but, in fact, it was a national image reproduced in papers across the country.[55]

In the absence of real Southern admiration of the Address, a writer, once again, sought to create one. During the first year of the war, Alexander Woollcott published a brief pamphlet, "For Us the Living: A Footnote to the Gettysburg Address." Woollcott was a *New York Times* critic who had served in World War I and written for *Stars and Stripes*. In the pamphlet, Woollcott posited a Southern connection to Lincoln's most famous speech. Woollcott claimed that a friend of his, Colonel John W. Thomason of the U.S. Marine Corps, recently found a letter written by a young Confederate captain wounded at Gettysburg. The soldier wrote to his father, "Pop, we've got to stop fighting that man," implying that Lincoln's true audience was south of the Mason-Dixon line.[56] But Union authorities removed the Confederate prisoners from Gettysburg long before November 1863, making his story a work of fiction along the lines of Mary Raymond Shipman Andrews's *Perfect Tribute*, a piece Woollcott criticized for its inaccuracies. Like Andrews, Woollcott probably invented a positive Southern reaction to the Address because he could not find an authentic one.

Although the Address was still ignored in large parts of the old Confederacy, such was far from the case in Britain. *Words for Battle*, a 1941 film released by Britain's Ministry of Information, features scenes from the English countryside and the hustle and bustle of a small town, culminating with the statue of Lincoln in Parliament Square, across from the Houses of Parliament, and narrator Laurence Olivier reciting the final line of the Gettysburg Address. Significantly, the writers subtly altered Lincoln's wording from "this nation" to "the nation" to make the speech applicable to Britain.[57]

Perhaps more consequential, Winston Churchill, himself a writer of note, greatly admired Lincoln and his Gettysburg Address. On December 26, 1941, less than three weeks after Pearl Harbor, Churchill addressed the U.S. Congress, seeking to strengthen the Anglo-American alliance. Noting his past service in the House of Commons, not the House of Lords, Churchill painted himself as democratically minded: "I have been in full harmony all my life with the tides which have flowed on both sides of the Atlantic against privilege and monopoly, and I have steered confidently towards the Gettysburg ideal of 'government of the people by the people for the people.'" In January 1945, Churchill addressed the House of Commons, regarding Britain's responsibilities as the war ended, particularly in regards to ensuring that the Eastern European countries become "government[s] of the people, by the people, and for the people, set up on the basis of free universal suffrage, election with secrecy of the ballot, and no intimidation." On August 17, 1945, shortly after the Japanese surrender, Churchill reiterated, "Our idea is government of the people, by the people, for the people." In 1863, the idea of democracy had been radical in Britain; by the 1940s, it, and Lincoln, had become mainstream. Much as Curzon tried to cement the Anglo-American alliance in the years leading up to World War I by praising the Gettysburg Address and linking it to Britain, Churchill throughout World War II subtly reinforced the alliance by invoking Lincoln's speech. The tactic was effective; in 1941, the *New York World-Telegram* reported that many in America compared Churchill's speeches to the Gettysburg Address.[58]

Other Britons also drew on the Gettysburg Address during the war. In September 1941, the Duke and Duchess of Windsor came to Washington, D.C., primarily to discuss the defense of the Bahamas, the islands the duke governed. After visiting the war and navy departments, the duke visited the Lincoln Memorial, where he read the entire Gettysburg Address inscribed on the south wall. Two years later, the duke was bested when Lord Victor Bulwer Lytton declared that the Gettysburg Address "has an appeal all the greater today because its application is wider . . . If the world is to have a new birth of freedom after this war it must be secured by nations that are good neighbors." That members of the British aristocracy had such positive assessments of the Gettysburg Address reveals both how much that nation had changed in the preceding century and also the near universal application of the Gettysburg Address at a time of acute national crisis. In a final sign of Britons' respect for Lincoln, on his birthday in 1944, his ancestral home in Norfolk, England, was made a historic memorial. The move, in addition to strengthening ties with the United States, was also the final step toward appropriating Lincoln as an international figure, no longer the citizen of just one country.[59] In 1863, British papers had passed over the Gettysburg Address as not worthy of mention; now, they clung to it like a life raft.

Other nations also saw the Gettysburg Address's democratic principles as transcendent. In 1912, Sun Yat-sen based the new government of the Republic of China on the "Three Principles of the People." In his writings, Sun explicitly acknowledged Lincoln as his inspiration: "The Three Principles of the People correspond with the principles stated by President Lincoln—government of the people, by the people, for the people. I translated them into min yu (the people to have), min chih (the people to govern), and min hsiang (the people to enjoy)."[60] In 1942, the United States and China jointly issued stamps to commemorate both the fifth year of Chinese resistance to Japanese aggression and the founding of China's government on Lincoln's principles (see fig. 4.6). In the United States, the stamp was debuted in Denver, a city where Sun Yat-sen spent considerable time. As World War II drew to a close and now-liberated peoples sought to develop democratic governments, a number cited the Gettysburg Address as their guiding principle, following the route China took thirty years earlier.

Figure 4.6. Chinese commemorative stamp, 1942.

Greece was one of the first countries to take this path. From 1936 until 1942, a dictatorship ruled the country. Greece's secret police, trained by Hitler's men, suppressed the Boy Scouts, persecuted Jews, and forbade schoolchildren from learning Pericles's funeral oration and the Gettysburg Address. Pericles's oration, which, Gary Wills convincingly argues, inspired Lincoln, identified Athens's freedom of government and opportunity for advancement as its central traits, two characteristics the Greek government of the 1940s specifically disavowed. But with the end of the dictatorship in 1942, Greece sought to return to the glory days of Athens and lifted the bans on Lincoln and Pericles.[61]

In the United States, author Upton Sinclair wrote in a 1943 editorial of his fear that post–World War II Germany would resemble post–World War I Germany, allowing for the rise of another Hitler. To guard against this possibility, Sinclair proposed a comprehensive plan centered around the idea of a "Freestate" cooperative without tariffs that would replace Germany. The Allies would establish and initially administer the area but, eventually, would turn it back over to the native inhabitants. Sinclair cautioned, "But if Freestate is to endure it must become a government of the people, by the people and for the people."[62] At least one European agreed with Sinclair. Just three days after the appearance of Sinclair's editorial in the *New York Times*, Eugene Reffi, formerly of the Republic of San Marino, claimed in a letter to the editor that his previous country "[h]as no arms and no warriors, but has survived because of a government of the people, by the people, and from a past lived honestly and Christianlike."[63]

In late 1943 in a *New York Times* article, "Balkan Sentiment Seen Cool to Kings," correspondent Joseph Levy reported, "All the peoples of south, east and central Europe are staunchly republican and vehemently opposed to royalty. They are aiming for government of the people, by the people and for the people—government that will endeavor to raise the standards of living of workers and peasants." A year later, Bulgaria's communist Minister of Interior Anton Yugoff asserted, "The Government's aim is to help the people and establish a Government of the people, by the people, for the people."[64] Yugoff's comment further illustrates that Lincoln's general language meant everyone could claim to draw support and legitimacy from the speech, even diametrically opposing entities.

The calls for "government of the people, by the people, for the people" stretched past Europe to South America. In 1945, Brazilian officials called for general elections, the first since 1937. In response, former Foreign Minister Oswaldo Aranha commented that he hoped the country's politicians would implement "a system of government of the people, by the people and for the people." Peru followed suit and allowed all political parties to participate in the presidential election of 1945 for the first time in fourteen years. The *New York Times* reported that the leftist candidate, Dr. Luis Bustamante Rivero, "[p]romises a government founded on the late President Roosevelt's Four Freedoms and on Abraham Lincoln's rule of the people, by the people and for the people."[65]

As the war came to a conclusion and the rebuilding began, citizens throughout the world found inspiration in the Gettysburg Address. Whether it was by reciting the Address over the graves of the fallen or by pointing to the democratic ideals Lincoln spelled out as offering a better system for the future, people throughout the world kept Lincoln's most famous words near to their hearts as they stood in 1945 and looked both at their past and future.

One of the few African Americans to take this view was artist William H. Johnson in his *Lincoln at Gettysburg III*, likely painted between 1939 and 1942 as a study for a potential mural (see fig. 4.7). Johnson, a native South Carolinian born of a white father and a mother of both African and Sioux Indian ancestry, began drawing in the dirt with a stick as a

young man before entering New York's National Academy of Design at
age twenty. Realizing there were few opportunities in America for a black
painter, Johnson left for Paris in 1926 and did not return permanently until 1938. Those around him were often unsure of Johnson's racial identity,
but his "unswerving sense of allegiance to his race," as one biographer
has termed it, led Johnson to proudly claim his race rather than "pass"
for another. Not long after arriving in Paris, Johnson married a Danish
woman fifteen years his senior named Holcha Krake. In November 1938,
with war on the horizon, the couple moved to the United States despite
concerns over the discrimination they would face.[66]

Figure 4.7. *Lincoln at Gettysburg III*, 1939–42. Created by William H. Johnson. Acces-
sion no. 1967.59.177R-V, Smithsonian American Art Museum; gift of the Harmon Foundation.

With his return to the United States, Johnson moved away from his familiar subject of landscapes and began painting figures, including many persons of historical significance from both races. With the outbreak of World War II, he offered a series of military- and war-themed paintings as a way, art historian Richard Powell argues, "[h]e could participate in the struggle against fascism." These paintings offer a glimpse into the proper interpretation of his *Lincoln at Gettysburg III*, for Powell explains, "In the military-inspired works, Johnson's conscious depictions of the soldiers, commanding officers, and other military personnel as African-Americans transform these paintings into social statements . . . [H]is World War II paintings, taken as a whole, are compelling visual arguments against racism in armed services."[67]

Lincoln at Gettysburg III blends the historic figures Johnson had been painting with his World War II–themed antiracism offerings. The image shows a towering Lincoln on the stage at Gettysburg. Lincoln is protected by an African American soldier in Yankee blue, the only person in the scene armed. Ironically, the only African American known to be in the cemetery was Lincoln's valet, also a man named William Johnson, but there were certainly no African American soldiers present, and none on stage. But Johnson is clearly crossing between the World War II and Civil War eras in more ways than one: The clothing of those present is quite obviously that of the twentieth century, and the soldier reminds viewers that the nation's African Americans were doing their part in the armed forces. Upon second glance, it is not quite clear who is the protector and who the protected in this image: It is the African-American soldier who is armed, but Lincoln stands between that man and the rest of those present, and given the immense size Johnson has assigned to Lincoln, one suspects Johnson conceives of this as a mutualistic relationship. The Gettysburg Address is less a promise from Lincoln to the African American community, Johnson seems to be saying, and more a contract between the two sides to each work towards "a new birth of freedom."

On the other hand, some African Americans implied that Lincoln's finest speech now simply reminded them of how bad their situation had become. In back-to-back issues in the summer of 1943, two editorials in the *Chicago Defender* invoked the Gettysburg Address to point out the nation's hypocrisy. The first suggested that the African American community was not fooled by the Roosevelt administration's invocation of Lincoln's most famous words: "We have never succeeded in mustering the same enthusiasm that others have exhibited when administration cohorts began waving the Gettysburg address with a minimum benefit to Negroes and a maximum benefit to themselves." The second, a letter by Corporal James Johnson, exhorted, "This country is supposed to be the greatest democracy of the universe, and my conception of the word is as Lincoln expressed in his immortal Gettysburg address, 'All men are created equal.' We are now giving everything to save the same democratic way of life that Lincoln cherished. But I ask myself, why sacrifice everything that we hold dear for something we have never fully shared? If the colored soldier has to make the supreme sacrifice, let it not be in vain."[68] For these African Americans, the Gettysburg Address had come to represent not a promise but a false promise. That his intent was so misconstrued by so many surely would have saddened Lincoln.

Between 1914 and 1917 and 1939 and 1945, constituencies official and private, domestic and international invoked the Gettysburg Address on countless occasions. The speech, commemorating and memorializing sacrifices made for democracy and ensuring that those who fought would never be forgotten, seemed perfectly suited to unify and inspire the nation to join the fight against those totalitarian regimes seeking global domination. However, where those references originated and which lines they emphasized reveal a less-than-unanimous agreement that the Gettysburg Address provided an ideal model for democratic government.

The dominant narrative, originating in the northern United States and including the federal government, suggested that the Gettysburg Address summed up the ideal of democracy as a "government of the people, by the people, for the people" and that the United States should support like-minded nations around the world. With the increasing dispersal of this message in the World War II–era, foreign nations from Bulgaria to Brazil picked up and largely bought into this narrative, loudly proclaiming the Gettysburg Address as a model by which they could base their own governments in the postwar period. This Northern-international alliance largely backfired at home, however.

Those suggesting that the Gettysburg Address represented the country's ideals overstepped in Southern eyes, for that region refused to agree that a document with racial equality at its center defined the nation, even though invocations of the speech rarely emphasized Lincoln's reaffirmation of Jefferson's principle "that all men are created equal." The comparison of the Germany of 1914 to the South of 1861–65 with articles carrying titles such as "The Hohenzollerns and the Slave Power" or "The South and Germany" further increased the regional divide. For nearly fifty years after the Civil War, the South quietly put aside the Gettysburg Address rather than trying to explain why Lincoln erred in connecting democracy and equality. During the world wars, the increasingly frequent invocations of the Address and the North's use of familiar tropes about slavery and secession reopened the old regional divides. During a time when Curzon called the Gettysburg Address "part of the intellectual patrimony of the English-speaking race," Southerners felt increasingly isolated. While the majority remained silent, as they had in the 1901–22 period, others like Lyon Tyler rose to the challenge and painted Lincoln's words at Gettysburg a sham.[69]

The other, nearly silent, counternarrative comes from Charles Gustrine's image of African American soldiers fighting in World War I. Had not the time come, Gustrine seemed to ask, when we should live up to the ideal expressed in the *first* line of Lincoln's speech? As in the larger 1901–22 period, the two competing counternarratives, one from the white South and one from the African American community, both vied against the dominant reunificationist narrative of a Gettysburg Address solely concerned with "government of the people, by the people, for the people." In World War II, a similar counternarrative came to the fore with the *Pittsburgh Courier's* advocacy of a "Double V" campaign: victory over fascism abroad and racism at home. While these counternarratives added an important voice, in neither case did they offer a serious challenge to the dominant narrative.[70]

When the world wars' generations invoked the Gettysburg Address, they did so in a far-reaching but limited sense, far-reaching because it was during this era that the speech became global and all pervasive but limited because it was used by the dominant constituency solely to encourage democracy, not equality. In so doing, they strayed from the ideal Lincoln established in 1863. It was the rising counternarrative in this era that advanced the march toward Lincoln's true meaning by bringing into the debate, slowly and almost imperceptibly, a consideration of that first line declaring "all men are created equal." Strange bedfellows, Lyon Tyler and William H. Johnson, but together, they had started the recovery. In 1945, no one would have guessed it would take an unintentional collaboration of the Soviets and the nation's African Americans for the majority to finally rediscover Lincoln's message in the mid-1960s.

5

The Very Core of America's Creed: 1959–63

> The central commitments of the American experi-
> ment are probably known to more people in other lands
> through the words of the Gettysburg Address than
> through those of the Declaration of Independence.
> —Dean Rusk, November 17, 1963

In the dozen years after World War II, the United States continued to deploy the Gettysburg Address worldwide for propagandistic purposes. In 1950, General Dwight David Eisenhower oversaw a campaign by the Crusade for Freedom, the fund-raising arm of Radio Free Europe, to honor West Berlin's fight against communism with the presentation of a replica of Philadelphia's Liberty Bell. Not content to simply reproduce the original bell, the designers added the line, "That this world under God shall have a new birth of freedom." West Berliners enthusiastically embraced the bell and immediately put its image on a stamp that just a few years earlier had carried the likeness of Adolf Hitler (see fig. 5.1). Literally as well as metaphorically, West Berlin replaced Hitler with Abraham Lincoln and totalitarianism with "a new birth of freedom." As the Cold War replaced World War II, the Gettysburg Address seemed more applicable than at any previous time.

By the late 1950s, the decade-old Cold War seemed interminable. The United States and the Soviet Union competed for influence with the nonaligned countries around the globe, with the Americans promoting capitalism and the Soviets making the case for communism. As historian Charles Evans Hughes said in the interwar period, "We are seeking to establish a *Pax Americana* maintained not by arms but by mutual respect and good will and the tranquilizing process of reason." Throughout the Cold War, the U.S. government invoked the Gettysburg Address often to inspire that "mutual respect and good will" but continued the earlier theme of focusing almost exclusively on the final line advocating a "government of the people, by the people, for the people."[1]

Figure 5.1. German "freedom bell" stamp, 1951.

In 1963, uses of the speech were of a different nature, reflecting a nation with a shifting perspective. Historian Penny Von Eschen notes that the early Cold War presidents "saw racial discrimination in America as its Achilles' heel in a propaganda battle with the Soviet Union to win the allegiance of Africa and Asia," and, thus, the Department of State sponsored programs ranging from jazz tours by the great Louis Armstrong to speeches by public intellectual Carl Rowan and even distributed copies of the Gettysburg Address. But Von Eschen concludes that such actions "represented the triumph of a politics of symbolism over a genuine commitment on the part of the U.S. government to protect the rights of its black citizens" as the actions "replaced, rather than complemented, commitments on the part of the Truman and Eisenhower administrations to civil rights at home."[2] Just as ensuring equality was central to Lincoln's plan to preserve the United States in 1863, a century later, civil rights reform—or at least the appearance of reform—was crucial to the nation's ultimate triumph in the Cold War. Consequently, while invocations of Lincoln's greatest speech in 1959 focused on the line dealing with democracy, a shift by 1963 was perceptible in the dominant narrative, with most discussions of the Address considering both Lincoln's first line reminding listeners that the nation was founded on the principle "that all men are created equal" and the final line that the United States was a "government of the people, by the people, for the people." After nearly a decade of nonviolent protests, the Civil Rights Movement was making progress with the dominant majority and forcing a change in opinions. A shift that at first may have been for outward appearances only soon became part of the national fabric, even became ensconced in law with the Twenty-Fourth Amendment, Civil Rights Act of 1964, Voting Rights Act of 1965, and Equal Employment Opportunity Act of 1967. After a century, the nation had come to grips with and was beginning to live up to Lincoln's message in the Gettysburg Address.

In April 1957, the Lincoln Group of the District of Columbia asked Congress to create a national commission to organize the sesquicentennial commemoration of Abraham Lincoln's birth.[3] The request could not have come at a better time. In 1956, the Soviet Union had done more to celebrate the 250th anniversary of Benjamin Franklin's birth than the Americans, and the U.S. government was determined to not let that happen again.[4] President Eisenhower, an admirer of Lincoln, owned a home in Gettysburg and had already seen that both Lincoln and his Gettysburg Address were tremendous Cold War weapons.

Government use of propaganda was fairly new in the Eisenhower years. Although the United States has tried to sway foreign public opinion since the days of Benjamin Franklin, it was not until the 1920s that nations began formalizing their propaganda efforts under central ministries or departments. In the United States, the agencies created during the world wars were soon disbanded, though the experiences of mobilizing audiences at home and abroad to support the war efforts would later prove valuable. The ease with which people were manipulated to despise the enemy showed the effectiveness of wartime propaganda. Under Eisenhower's leadership, the Allies dropped eight billion propaganda pamphlets over the Europe Theater of war. In 1945, Eisenhower declared of the recent Allied victory, "I am convinced that the expenditure of men and money in wielding the spoken and written word was an important contributing factor in undermining the enemy's will to resist and supporting the fighting morale of our potential Allies in the Occupied Countries."[5]

In the postwar period, President Harry S. Truman recognized, "The nature of present-day foreign relations makes it essential for the United States to maintain informational activities abroad as an integral part of the conduct of our foreign affairs," but under his leadership, the efforts were diffuse strands. It was Eisenhower who pulled those strands together to form a coherent and functioning propaganda machine to operate domestically and internationally.[6]

As president, Eisenhower engaged in what historian Kenneth Osgood calls a "secret propaganda battle at home and abroad. . . . Far from being a peripheral aspect of the U.S.-Soviet struggle, the competition for hearts and minds—the cold war of words and of deeds—was one of its principal battlegrounds."[7] In the Cold War, America's greatest military leader of the twentieth century saw culture, not weapons, as his best tool against the forces of communism. In his campaign, Eisenhower promised to wage psychological warfare against communism, and one of his first actions as president was to create the United States Information Agency (USIA), an organization intended "to provide real unity and greater efficiency" in the dissemination of information abroad.[8] The nearly one thousand propaganda specialists in this organization worked with a budget of over $100 million by decade's end. Eisenhower placed such value on this organization that he made the director a regular participant in cabinet meetings and gave him a seat on the National Security Council.[9]

Early on, the Eisenhower administration and USIA realized that their propaganda programs needed to be more subtle and that the most effective were both truthful and verifiable.[10] As its motto, the USIA took "Telling America's Story to the World" and looked for ways to portray the United States in the best possible light. In the late 1950s, that story was not flattering. The 1954 Supreme Court ruling in *Brown vs. Board of Education of Topeka* disallowing racial segregation in the nation's public schools brought regional and racial antagonism to the surface. The Montgomery Bus Boycott in 1955–56, the murder of Emmett Till in 1955, and the forced integration of Little Rock's Central High School in 1957 provided further fodder for the country's enemies. In Japan, one man asked, "If Americans can regard Negroes as inferior, how do they really regard Asians?"[11] The upcoming Lincoln Birth Sesquicentennial offered another, more favorable narrative. As USIA officer Manning Williams suggested, a commemoration of Lincoln would "demonstrate that the democratic and humanitarian ideals of Lincoln are revered in the America of today, but overlooked in the Soviet Union."[12]

Eisenhower was happy to bring Lincoln into the public eye, at home and abroad, and, on September 2, 1957, authorized the appointment of an Abraham Lincoln Sesquicentennial Commission (ALSC). Eisenhower saw domestic and international propaganda as two sides of a single coin, so in addition to the positive impact he hoped the commemoration would have on uncommitted foreign audiences in danger of sliding towards communism, he believed that Lincoln would help remind Americans of the nation's values. Although Eisenhower had publicly mentioned Lincoln many times previously, and the government had invoked the Gettysburg Address for a variety of purposes, the use of Lincoln's words as Cold War propaganda truly began during the sesquicentennial.[13]

In its final report, the ALSC noted, "The nonpartisan character of the Sesquicentennial was pointed up by composition of the Commission whose members were chosen without regard to political affiliation and by the activities of the Commission which have been devoid of partisanship." But, in fact, the commission *did* have a serious bias; only Texan Ralph Yarborough hailed from a former Confederate state. Similarly, of the nineteen states to establish Lincoln commissions, only Louisiana's came from the South. While the commission hoped to project an image of national reverence for Lincoln, it was still largely a regional phenomenon.[14]

On February 12, 1959, President Eisenhower spoke to those at the National Lincoln Sesquicentennial dinner about Lincoln as "A World Figure." After noting the establishment of a Lincoln Society in New Delhi, India, Eisenhower observed, "The first President of modern China, Sun Yat-sen, found his three basic principles of government in Lincoln's Gettysburg Address." At the height of the Cold War, Eisenhower sought to use Lincoln to illustrate the United States' role as a global leader, even amongst countries antagonistic to it, and did so by portraying the Gettysburg Address as a statement on democracy. To close the event, actor Fredric March read the Gettysburg Address for those assembled. Eisenhower's speech was part of a coordinated effort, for that day, the Common Council for American Unity sent a press release to six hundred foreign newspapers and seven hundred foreign radio stations, covering the same ground as Eisenhower—the international significance of the speech.[15]

Domestically, the Lincoln Fellowship of Pennsylvania (founded in 1938) continued to host a major commemoration in the cemetery on November 19 each year. Pulitzer Prize–winning author and poet Carl Sandburg dazzled the audience of four thousand in 1959 with his recitation of Lincoln's words and comments of his own. While Sandburg certainly had a flair for the dramatic—Edmund Wilson commented in 1962, "The cruelest thing that has happened to Lincoln since he was shot by Booth has been to fall into the hands of Carl Sandburg"—in quoting three of Lincoln's speeches in which the President affirmed a commitment to equality, Sandburg came closest to recapturing Lincoln's intent at Gettysburg. However, this counternarrative was from a private citizen, not a government official, and was quickly followed by Secretary of Health, Education, and Welfare Arthur Flemming, who noted his "concern that we in our day will make the maximum possible contribution to a 'new birth of freedom.' . . . Are we willing, for example, to make sacrifices in order to strengthen the foundation on which our form of government rests? . . . Are we willing to make sacrifices in order to 'provide for the common defense' and thus 'secure the blessings of liberty to ourselves and to our posterity'?" While Flemming invoked "a new birth of freedom," he did so in a way that emphasized democracy, not equality.[16]

These domestic celebrations paled in comparison to the effort put forth on the international stage, mostly by the USIA. Five years earlier, the National Security Council had decreed, "The purpose of the U.S. Information Agency shall be to submit evidence to the peoples of other nations by means of communication techniques that the objectives and policies of the United States are in harmony with and will advance their legitimate aspirations for freedom, progress and peace."[17] On June 17, 1959, the ALSC, chaired by Senator John Cooper of Kentucky, presented the Vatican with a Latin translation of the Address. Cooper stuck to the Cold War theme of democracy, referring to just one line from the speech, "These words of Lincoln, which speak of government by the people." Edwin Ryan, the translator and a participant in the event and a man, like Sandburg, without an official position, saw a different meaning in the speech: "Lincoln has expressed succinctly the truth that human freedom is based upon human equality." In accepting the document, Edigio Vagnozzi, the Vatican's apostolic delegate to the United States, noted, "The address is one of the greatest documents ever issued by man. It is a great American document; it is a great human document, and I might truly say that it is a great Christian document."[18] The U.S. government fostered this international attention whenever possible. In addition to sending historians abroad to lecture on Lincoln, the Department of State mailed out fifty thousand reproductions of the Address "to State Department grantees and other exchange visitors to the United States who had returned to their home countries."[19]

After the communist takeover of China in 1949 and North Korea in 1950, Southeast Asia became an area of concern for the United States, with the USIA spending a third of its budget in Japan and Indochina in the late 1950s. The agency flooded the region with propaganda, sending fifty million items to South Vietnam in 1956 alone. While the agency translated and distributed books that circulated in America, it also commissioned and published over one hundred original books annually in the late 1950s and over thirty periodicals in seventeen languages. Representative of these efforts, in 1950 and 1951, the agency published and disseminated half a million copies of *Herblock Looks at Communism* in English, Chinese, German, Indonesian, Malay, Telugu, Spanish, Tamil, Thai, and Vietnamese.[20]

In a similar vein, in 1959, the USIA, in conjunction with the ALSC, produced a comic book on the life of Lincoln for distribution throughout Southeast Asia. This medium reflected the USIA's 1958 decision to target young people, both because it was they who were most ardently anti-U.S. and because they would soon be in leadership positions.[21] The USIA used the story of Lincoln's life to showcase American values and featured the Gettysburg Address on the inside cover with the explanation that Lincoln's words "will endure forever as an expression of the spirit of the United States of America." The work equally emphasizes Lincoln's "two purposes in life—reunite his torn Nation and free the slaves." When it came to 1863, the comic book dedicated an entire page on the Gettysburg Address, declaring it "the speech that has become one of the most famous in history" and the one "which so classically expresses the democratic ideal" (for an illustration of Lincoln giving the Address, see fig. 5.2).

สุนทรพจน์ที่เก็ตติสเบอร์ก – ต่อมาใน พ.ศ. ๒๔๐๖ นั่นเอง ลินคอล์นก็ได้กล่าวสุนทะพจน์อันเป็นที่
เลื่องลือที่สุดในประวัติศาสตร์ ในพิธี อุทิศสมรภูมิเก็ตติสเบอร์กส่วนหนึ่งให้เป็นสุสานทหาร   เขาได้กล่าว
ข้อความแสดงถึงอุดมคติของประชาธิปไตย ซึ่งคำรงคงอยู่ชั่วกัลปาวสาน เป็นใจความว่า "ระบอบการปกครอง
ของราษฎร โดยราษฎร และเพื่อราษฎร จะต้องไม่สูญไปจากโลกนี้เป็นอันขาด"

Figure 5.2. *Abraham Lincoln, 1809–1865*, 1959. Thai translation. Comic
book produced by the U.S. Information Agency and Abraham Lincoln Sesquicentennial
Commission. Abraham Lincoln Presidential Library and Museum, Springfield, Illinois.

The final page, "Heritage," reveals why foreign nations should study Lincoln: "To Americans and to the peoples of many nations, Abraham Lincoln is the beloved symbol of humanity and democracy. His faith in people, in freedom, in the goodness of man is the very core of America's creed. To study the life of Lincoln is to reach out and touch the soul of a nation." The Lincoln Memorial graces the following page. With the exception of one line from his Second Inaugural Address, no other Lincoln speech but the Gettysburg Address is quoted. The message is clear: Foreign nations must come to know America through Lincoln, and the way to know Lincoln is through the Gettysburg Address. The USIA translated over a hundred thousand copies into a variety of foreign languages and distributed them throughout southeast Asia; thirty-two thousand into Vietnamese, twenty thousand into Thai, twenty-five thousand into Urdu, five thousand into Nepalese, eight thousand into Marathi, eight thousand into Gujerati, an unknown number into Arabic, five thousand into Tamil, and ten thousand into Singalese, though the last two omitted the Gettysburg Address. One authority concludes, "It is safe to say that the USIA *Abraham Lincoln* reached millions of readers across the globe."[22]

It is difficult to judge the impact of these comic books in encouraging democracy and pro-Americanism in Southeast Asia. However, a 1983 work published in Korea by Donggill Kim, *Abraham Lincoln: An Oriental Interpretation*, is suggestive. Kim says Lincoln's "enormous popularity" in Asia is "often baffling and sometimes enigmatic" but "is associated with two important fundamentals—the concept of democracy and the spirit of *jen*. . . . In the minds of the Orientals, Abraham Lincoln is the champion of democracy." Noting that Sun Yat-sen drew on the Gettysburg Address in writing the Three Principles of the People for the Republic of China, Kim states, "For millions of Asians, Lincoln is, then, the 'symbol of the free man' and the personification of democratic ideals." The principle of *jen* is one of love, which Kim contends Lincoln exhibited toward his fellow man throughout his life. The author concludes, "Abraham Lincoln transcends his own race, nationality, and age. Examined from an Oriental viewpoint, Lincoln emerges as an Oriental sage, a secular saint."[23]

More evidence comes from China, where Jiang Zemin recited the Gettysburg Address during student protests in the 1980s before becoming the General Secretary of the Communist Party in 1989 and

President of China in 1993. During a 1989 visit with former President Richard Nixon, Jiang interrupted the American to recite the Address from memory and did so again upon meeting President Bill Clinton. It would appear those comic books resonated with their audience. Jiang's recitations are not surprising, for while others frequently invoked Lincoln's call for "government of the people, by the people, for the people," to counter communism, that phrase can be interpreted to support the ideology.[24]

A subtle yet massive dispersion of the Address came via the U.S. Postal Service. Customers desiring to send mail abroad could do so with a stamp featuring the image of Lincoln surrounded by his famous phrase from the Gettysburg Address: "of the people, by the people, for the people" (see fig. 5.3). The government intended to use Lincoln to promote American democracy during the 1960s and what better way than by reminding everyone who received a letter from the United States of Lincoln's most famous discourse on popular government.

Figure 5.3. Abraham Lincoln airmail stamp, 1960–65.

The dialogue on the Gettysburg Address ran in both directions, as ninety countries around the globe commemorated Abraham Lincoln in 1959, many via his words at Gettysburg. On November 19, Prime Minister Harold MacMillan of Great Britain, Prime Minister Jawaharlal Nehru of India, Chancellor Konrad Adenauer of Germany, President Juscelino Kubitschek of Brazil, Prime Minister Kwame Nkrumah of Ghana, Prime Minister Tunku Abdul Rahman of the Federation of Malaya, President Ngo Dinh Diem of the Republic of Vietnam, and Speaker Ryōgorō Katō of Japan all offered tributes to Lincoln's words. Lincoln, Argentina, named for the President after his assassination in 1865, erected four large plaques inscribed, "Of the People, by the People, and for the People." El Salvador concluded a year-long celebration of Lincoln with a ceremony on November 19, 1959, marking the Gettysburg Address. In Rome, a capacity crowd at the Embassy Theater viewed a program on the speech. Morocco produced a souvenir pamphlet celebrating the life of Lincoln that features an Arabic translation of the Address on one cover and an English translation on the other. Honduras produced stamps with six different scenes from Lincoln's life, including one of him delivering the Address at Gettysburg (see fig. 5.4). Taiwan produced a stamp with the dual images of Sun Yat-sen and Lincoln "of the people, by the people, for the people" written in English under Lincoln and the Chinese equivalent under Sun Yat-sen (see fig. 5.5).[25]

Figure 5.4. Honduran stamp commemorating the 150th anniversary of Lincoln's birth, 1959.

Figure 5.5. Taiwan's Sun Yat-sen and Abraham Lincoln stamp, 1959.

These nations commemorated Lincoln and his Gettysburg Address for many reasons. In 1958, President Eisenhower said, "In his writing and speaking Lincoln described the nature of American democracy—'of the people, by the people, for the people'—with such clarity and splendor that it became the inspiration for movements toward free and responsible government the world over." Thus, one reason is because these respondents genuinely appreciated Lincoln and his philosophy of government.[26] Another is that many nations simply took their cue from the United States, saw that Americans believed Lincoln to be their best representative and his Gettysburg Address to be the best American speech, and parroted that appreciation back for self-serving reasons.

The case of Honduras, which commemorated Lincoln with the issuance of six stamps, one featuring the Gettysburg Address, and another "special booklet on Abraham Lincoln," is instructive and perhaps suggestive of Latin America in general.[27] The United States and Honduras have a long history of interaction, dating most ignominiously to the invasion of the country by the American filibuster William Walker in 1860. In the early twentieth century, the nation was again host to American outsiders with parasitic designs: the United Fruit Company. In the early 1950s, the United States government was far more concerned with matters in Europe, but the election of Jacobo Arbenz in Guatemala, a man many feared was a Marxist, refocused attention on Latin America. In 1950, George Kennan, American diplomat and architect of the Containment Theory, noted, "It is better to have a strong regime in power than a liberal government if it is indulgent and relaxed and penetrated by communists."[28] A region that the United States had long considered part of its sphere of influence and part of the "free world" was no longer so secure.

In 1951, the United States provided funds to Latin America via the Mutual Security Program, with Honduras receiving a chunk in 1954 as a part of the deal to help overthrow, with U.S. assistance, Guatemala's Arbenz. The U.S.-Honduras Bilateral Treaty of Military Assistance, signed that year, furthered entrenched the military oligarchy and tied that nation to the United States. Over the course of the 1950s and 1960s, the United States provided approximately $120 million in aid to Honduras, a large sum considering that Honduras's GDP in 1960 was $335 million.[29]

In the United States, the phrase "government of the people, by the people, for the people" was and is viewed as a single ideal, but in Latin America, those were three separate possibilities; whereas only a democracy could be of, by, and for the people, a host of other government types could satisfy one of those criteria. In 1954, the Honduran military seized control and disavowed the election of Ramón Villeda Morales, declaring, essentially, that while the government would be for the people, it would not be of or by the people. Many had feared that Villeda Morales was a communist sympathizer, but during two years in exile, he became a hero to the Honduran people, and following another overthrow and the drafting of a new constitution in 1957, Villeda Morales was installed as president by a military junta. Surprisingly, given his support from the military, Villeda Morales in temperament was a liberal dedicated to uplifting the lower classes while modernizing the education, medical, and social welfare systems. Consequently, he had ideological reasons to support commemorations of Lincoln and his conception of a nation for the people. As historian Paul Drake shows, Latin American constitutions often articulated an ideal rather than a reality. Perhaps, in this vein, the Gettysburg Address was the ideal for which Villeda Morales and Honduras strove. On the other hand, Villeda Morales served at the pleasure of the military junta (and would be removed by it in 1963) and understood that the junta's funds and support came from the United States. In feting Lincoln and his most famous speech, Honduras indicated its understanding of U.S. Secretary of State Dean Acheson's comment after

World War II, "We are willing to help people who believe the way we do," giving many a reason to claim a kindred outlook.[30] The issuance of these stamps was a case of a single action serving multiple purposes.

Across the Atlantic Ocean in Italy, the situation was similar. The ALSC reported that a full crowd attended a program on the speech at Rome's Embassy Theater, but that country had been the second-largest recipient of Marshall Plan funds, was a recent inductee into NATO, and continued to receive significant economic aid from the United States in 1959. Further, the Christian Democratic Party had received "bags of money" from the United States in 1948 that helped secure its place as the country's dominant party, a run that would continue until the 1990s.[31] Were that not enough, in January 1959, the United States made clear what it expected of Italy by delivering five hundred copies of a sixty-six-page press kit on Lincoln to the Roman media. Consequently, according to the *Lincoln Sesquicentennial Intelligencer*, "Beginning 12 February a flood of Lincoln material appeared in the Italian press. Incomplete check shows 31 daily newspapers carried items on Lincoln."[32] Eisenhower embraced overt and covert propaganda, and as illustrated by the preceding anecdote, one of the USIA's favorite tactics was to plant a story in a foreign newspaper and then clip and reprint the article so as to mask U.S. authorship and give it the appearance of coming from a foreign writer.[33] It is not hard to surmise that Italy's leaders saw a public display of appreciation for the Gettysburg Address as a way to cast aside their own recent history with fascism and appease new allies at the same time. While the individual attendees of the program may have been pure in motive, Italy's leaders had more than one reason for celebrating Lincoln's speech.

Perhaps most significant, Taiwan produced a stamp containing the dual images of Sun Yat-sen and Lincoln, with "OF THE PEOPLE, BY THE PEOPLE, FOR THE PEOPLE" written in English under Lincoln and the Chinese equivalent displayed in characters under Sun. During the Chinese Civil War of 1949, the communist People's Republic of China (PRC) led by Mao Tse-tung took over the mainland. Chiang Kai-shek and the government of the Republic of China (ROC) fled to Taiwan. Over the ensuing years, the United States protected Taiwan from the constant threat of a PRC amphibious assault, fearing the loss of another region to communism. This 1959 stamp came during both the sesquicentennial of Lincoln's birth and the ten-year anniversary of the ROC's resistance to the PRC. American support of Taiwan upset the

PRC, a wound this stamp leveraged to the advantage of Taiwan both by reminding the world of its legitimacy and by cementing the bond with America. Further, by featuring Sun, the founder of both the ROC and modern China, the ROC reasserted its place as the rightful ruling party for all of China. While Sun was sincere in his appreciation of Lincoln, his heirs a half-century later saw the sesquicentennial of Lincoln's birth as a chance to reaffirm Sun's faith in Lincoln while taking a swipe at communist China.

While the United States felt the range of programs on the Gettysburg Address sponsored by foreign nations was a sign that it had a powerful Cold War weapon in Lincoln's legacy, a more careful examination of the form of those commemorations, the context in the observing countries, and their relationships with the United States suggests that in some cases, in order to sustain the flow of economic and military aid, these foreign nations may have been simply parroting what they knew the United States wanted to hear. Eisenhower viewed the Gettysburg Address as a propaganda weapon in the Cold War, but, oftentimes, it was a propaganda weapon turned against the United States. In the United States, however, officials rarely stopped to ask why Lincoln was honored but, rather, rejoiced that it was so.

By any measure, the United States' attempt to spread the word about and literally the words of Lincoln during the sesquicentennial of his birth was a success. Eisenhower, the USIA, and the ALSC all pointed to the international outpouring of comments on the Gettysburg Address and commemorations of that speech as evidence that Lincoln was helping sway the world's neutral nations towards democracy and away from communism. The dominant and official narrative in this era, as in the world wars, was that the significance of the speech was in the final line advocating "government of the people, by the people, for the people." Although the Civil Rights Movement that would eventually urge a reconsidering of the speech was already underway, the Cold War in 1959 still held primacy. The alternative narratives urging a reconsideration of the place of equality within the speech and the nation came from unofficial and infrequent sources.

Lincoln and his most famous speech were still largely taboo in the white South, as evidenced by the presence of just one Southern congressman on the ALSC and the formation of a state commission only in Louisiana. When the ALSC held a competition for students to submit essays on Lincoln, of the seven pieces that focused on the Gettysburg Address, one each came from California, Indiana, and Minnesota, with two from Pennsylvania, and two from Emmitsburg, Maryland, a town adjacent to Gettysburg. Not a single submission came from the former Confederacy.[34] Given that Southern congressmen could easily block USIA and ALSC funding, one can see why official speakers continued to emphasize that universally embraced final line of the Address.[35] In addition to these domestic considerations, the government did not want to call attention to America's failures to live up to Lincoln's vision and give the Soviets a tool to sway nonaligned countries. In 1959, the nation still thought it could win the Cold War without addressing civil rights and that it could invoke selected phrases of the Gettysburg Address while ignoring the central message. The ensuing three years would shatter those misperceptions and lead to a radically different interpretation of the Gettysburg Address during the Civil War Centennial.

While the Abraham Lincoln Birth Sesquicentennial was primarily celebrated by Northern states and international audiences, the Civil War Centennial was a thoroughly national affair with forty-five states establishing commissions to organize commemorations of the war. Of those states not establishing commissions, four did not achieved statehood until after the war, and the fifth, Nevada, entered the Union in 1864.[36] Despite popular desire to commemorate the Civil War, many feared the paths such ceremonies could take. Virginia's commission proclaimed their "firm belief that political controversy of the 1960's should have no connection with a commemoration of the valor and sacrifice 100 years ago of Americans whose critical disagreement was whether there should be one nation or two."[37] The national commission noted its concern over whether the commemorations "could be planned in such fashion as not to reawaken memories of old sectional antagonisms and political rancors, but instead strengthen both the unity of the Nation and popular devotion to the highest purpose of the Republic."[38] Indeed, strengthening the republic in the midst of the Cold War was one of the primary reasons for, and overriding considerations of, the entire centennial commemoration. Robert Cook, author of the only full study of the centennial, states that Southerners feared that if the centennial remained in private hands, moneyed Northerners would dominate, and so the Southerners favored a national commission.[39]

In a 1959 pamphlet, *Guide for the Observance of the Centennial of the Civil War*, the U.S. Civil War Centennial Commission (USCWCC) commented, "With the limited funds Congress has authorized, it is evident the National Commission cannot conduct every commemorative exercise all over the nation. What it has in mind is the true American approach: *for each locality to plan and commemorate the chief events of its history during the great national crisis.*" The national commission "aims to serve only as a cooperating agency or clearing house to guide and coordinate the overall programming, so as to avoid costly conflicts and overlapping and to furnish helpful information." The commission remained true to its word, only organizing and hosting two events on its own: the 1962 commemoration of the Emancipation Proclamation and a 1964 symposium on the Gettysburg Address. Over three hundred local Civil War centennial commissions put on literally hundreds of events. Virginia alone boasted 116 county and local commissions.[40]

In addition to the national publications of the USCWCC already mentioned, each state produced varying quantities of written material. Most states printed early pamphlets to notify the citizens of events planned by their state commissions and also offered suggestions for activities local commissions could organize. Subsequently, after the centennial and at various times throughout, the state commissions reported their activities.

The Northern states commonly referenced the Gettysburg Address in these publications. The commissioners from Washington, D.C., offered an extensive paragraph on the Address in their 1962 booklet *The Symbol and the Sword*. Though much of the account simply tells the events of that day, the conclusion muses, "Mr. Lincoln went to Gettysburg and spoke the few words which he believed the world would little note nor long remember. When he arrived back in Washington people looked at him the same way, not knowing how tremendously he had grown." Massachusetts' history of the state's experience during the war includes a letter from Governor Endicott Peabody noting that the Civil War "was an American tragedy, but it was also 'a new birth of freedom.' And freedom needs its champions in the 1960's as in the 1860's." The volume covers the dedication ceremonies in three pages, with the conclusion, "The Gettysburg address is considered one of the greatest pieces of prose to be found in the English language." When Michigan published a list of recommended materials for school use, it suggested three films dedicated solely to Lincoln at Gettysburg and two others featuring his words there.

Two sound recordings included recitations of the speech. In its handbook on the Civil War, Pennsylvania also invoked the Gettysburg Address: "These epic events of our nation's history should be commemorated with all proper dignity and respect and with an emphasis upon the devotion of those who, in Lincoln's words, fought 'that government of the people, by the people, and for the people shall not perish from the earth.'"[41]

Among the border states, Maryland alone explicitly discussed the Gettysburg Address: "Uncounted numbers of her citizens journeyed to Gettysburg for the Dedication Day Observances of The Soldiers' National Cemetery." The Delaware Civil War Centennial Commission sponsored a performance of Aaron Copland's "Lincoln Portrait," which features a reading of the Gettysburg Address, but made no other mention of the speech.[42] Of the former Confederate states, only Florida made even a passing reference to the Gettysburg Address in any publication. In its manual for local communities, the commission comments, "Floridians will want to commemorate these epic events of our State's history with all proper dignity and respect and with an emphasis upon the devotion of those who, in Lincoln's words, fought 'That government of the people, by the people, and for the people shall not perish from the earth.'"[43]

While the Gettysburg Address played a prominent role in the centennial publications of many Northern states, the border and Southern states almost completely ignored the speech. The one Southern state that did invoke Lincoln's words, Florida, possessed a Northern tradition as well as a Southern one in 1960, as nearly one-third of the population had moved to the state within the preceding decade. Further, because these publications came at the beginning of the centennial before racial discrimination became the nation's predominant issue, they still focused on Lincoln's final line.

By 1963, the Civil War Centennial gasped for air. Most state commissions were running out of motivation and funds. New York's commission would cease to function in 1964, while many others continued in name only or with a skeleton staff. Alabama Civil War Centennial Commission Chairman Albert Moore speculated on the flagging interest in 1962: "Many no doubt feel that we should focus our attention on the exceedingly difficult problems of the present instead of studying the past."[44] The U2 incident, standoff over the Berlin Wall, the Bay of Pigs, and the Cuban Missile Crisis made the Cold War more immediate than ever. But segregationist violence at home, a response to the direct-action campaigns of the Civil Rights Movement, caused even greater concern. In Birmingham, Alabama, local police broke up a children's march protesting segregation by unleashing dogs and training high-pressure water hoses on the marchers, culminating with the jailing of over six hundred children. On June 11, 1963, Alabama Governor George Wallace physically blocked African Americans from registering at the University of Alabama. The following day, Ku Klux Klan member Byron De La Beckwith assassinated NAACP field representative Medgar Evers in Mississippi. And so the tide shifted. Throughout the period, the Cold War and Civil Rights Movement were intertwined both in reality and in many of the public orations invoking the Gettysburg Address, but whereas Americans in 1959 remained most concerned with international affairs, in 1963 domestic issues took precedence. An October 1963 *Newsweek* poll revealed a shift underway: 80 percent of white people favored equal job opportunities, 95 percent favored equal voting opportunities, and 76 percent believed black people were discriminated against.[45]

Amidst all this, Pennsylvania planned to observe the centennial of the Battle of Gettysburg and the Address. The state established a Gettysburg Centennial Commission (GCC) in April 1956, over a year before the legislation that created the U.S. Civil War Centennial Commission. In January 1957, Pennsylvania Governor George Leader appointed the state's Adjutant General, Major General A. J. Drexel Biddle Jr., chairman of the commission. In a March 30, 1961, letter to Pennsylvania Governor David Lawrence (elected in 1958), Biddle addressed how the commemorations would handle racial issues, a reaction to a recent controversy in Charleston, South Carolina.[46]

In 1961, Charleston hosted the fourth national assembly of the Civil War Centennial Commissions. Coinciding with the centennial of the firing on Fort Sumter, the 1961 event made clear the nation's regional divisions. The South Carolina Confederate War Centennial Commission handled the logistics for the assembly, and they selected the Francis Marion Hotel, which did not accept African American guests, as the headquarters. In February, the New Jersey commission notified the South Carolinians that Madaline Williams, an African American woman, would attend the assembly and expressed concern that the state's segregation policies would prevent Williams from staying with the other members of the state's assembly.[47]

When the South Carolina Commission refused to change the meeting place, California, Illinois, Michigan, New York, and Wisconsin all condemned South Carolina's intransigence, and many commissions announced plans to boycott the assembly. USCWCC executive director Karl Betts deemed the matter out of his hands. The situation gained such attention that newly inaugurated President John F. Kennedy stepped in and moved the assembly to the U.S. Naval Station in Charleston, an integrated facility.[48] Both sides remained unhappy. South Carolina Representative Mendel Rivers noted that the federal intervention in 1961, as in 1861, set "a very dangerous precedent." On the other side, California continued its boycott due to "the South Carolina people's attitude against colored people."[49] Ironically, the naval base was segregated by sex, with husbands and wives occupying different nighttime accommodations.[50]

The GCC was aware this was not the only such problem. Alabama's selection of Judge Walter Jones as one of the primary speakers at a 1961 event commemorating the centennial of Jefferson Davis's inauguration in Montgomery ruffled many feathers as Jones had outlawed the Alabama NAACP five years earlier.[51] To avoid such situations, the GCC unanimously adopted the following resolution: "[The] Commission has emphasized the theme of unity and brotherhood—the unity and brotherhood that grew out of the Civil War, and that necessarily entail equality of opportunity for all. Therefore, as far as the Pennsylvania Commission is concerned, any action that would run counter to this just principle would be prejudicial to the spirit of our policy and programming. It is the sense of the meeting that we insist upon equality of opportunity as a condition for our participation in any meetings or events, in connection with our Civil War Centennial observances."[52]

Partially due to the Charleston fiasco, the national commission forced executive director Betts out in the fall of 1961. The chairman, Ulysses Grant III, tendered his resignation at the same time. During the first two years of the centennial, many felt that Betts and Grant did not make the commemorations racially inclusive and sensitive, focused on the military aspects of the war to the exclusion of the social and political issues, and did not encourage new scholarship. Their replacements, two academic historians, fixed most of those problems.[53]

The new chairman, Allan Nevins, had recently retired from a long and distinguished career at Columbia University. With more than fifty books to his credit, two of which had won the Pulitzer Prize, he was America's most prolific living historian. No one questioned his expertise in the Civil War era as he was then in the midst of writing *Ordeal of the Union*, an eight-volume masterpiece on the conflict. Perhaps most important, President Kennedy considered him a political ally.

By the end of the month, the commission also had a new executive director. James I. Robertson Jr., born in 1930, hailed from Danville, Virginia, the last capital of the Confederacy. After an undergraduate career at Randolph Macon College and a stint in the U.S. Air Force, Robertson earned a doctorate from Emory University under renowned Civil War historian Bell Wiley. Upon graduation, Robertson accepted the editorship of the journal *Civil War History*. However, when Grant and Betts resigned, Wiley suggested that the national commission offer Robertson the executive directorship. Robertson's appointment, following that of Nevins, ensured the centennial would emphasize scholarship over reenactments.[54]

Both regions claimed victory over Robertson's appointment. The Southern commissions believed he would prevent Northerners from using the centennial for political gain, while the Northern and national commissions thought Robertson would calm anxieties about their racial and political motives, bringing greater support for events like the 1962 Emancipation Proclamation centennial. All parties were correct. Robertson, who felt the Emancipation commemoration a necessary but potentially divisive event if handled improperly, personally convinced many Southern commissions to support the ceremony, ensuring that the event did not become a commentary on the current politics of race.[55]

While Nevins set out the commission's strategic vision, Robertson handled the daily logistics and decisions. Nevins remained in residence at the Huntington Library in California working on *Ordeal of the Union* and corresponded with Robertson frequently. On January 2, 1963, Nevins wrote, "The more I reflect upon the matter, the more important it seems to me that the National Commission offer some commemoration in Washington of the Gettysburg Address. . . . [T]he Address has a broad national and international interest and . . . we may well be criticized if we pass it over unnoticed, and we can easily arrange a modest observance. . . . We would gain much from it, and lose nothing."[56]

In a response penned two days later, Robertson called the Address "slanted for the Northern side" and noted the existence of "many students who do not share . . . your enthusiasm for Lincoln in general and his Address in particular."[57] Indeed, Robertson spoke the truth, as the preceding chapters show, and a commemoration of the Address sponsored by the national commission could well alienate a number of the Southern commissions. Additionally, Pennsylvania planned to commemorate the Gettysburg Address, and an event sponsored by the national commission might compete with rather than complement the local event. But Robertson was intensely loyal to Nevins. Five years later when Nevins was crafting the introduction to the commission's final report, Robertson offered Nevins suggestions but then said, "In absolutely *no* way do I mean to imply that you must accept my suggestions. (An applicant for the knighthood never dictated policy to King Arthur!)." So on January 9, 1963, Robertson traveled to Gettysburg to discuss with the Gettysburg Centennial Commission the form its commemorations would take.[58]

Robertson spoke before the Adams County Shrine Club dinner, telling Gettysburgians, "[N]o community in the nation has such possibilities as Gettysburg for its Civil War Centennial commemoration," but warned that many feared the events would take on the character of a "carnival." Robertson also cautioned against staging a reenactment, noting that Arlington would never host one and that Gettysburg should not differ. Earlier reenactments, particularly one at Manassas in 1961, possessed tremendous popular appeal while also leaving a bitter taste in the mouths of some who felt such events made a mockery of the sanctity of those who fell in battle. Robertson implied that reenactments reopened sectional strife by portraying one side as victors and the others as the vanquished: "The consuming theme in our centennial observances must be one word—unity. The great differences of 1863 were not too great for time to heal and this centennial offers a great opportunity for cementing the bonds of unity that hold our country together."[59] Indeed, the official symbol of the commemoration at Gettysburg was the image of a Union soldier and a Confederate soldier grasping hands over the stone wall at the apex of Pickett's Charge, re-creating an iconic moment from the 1913 reunion. This theme of reunification was decided upon in the late 1950s by the Gettysburg Centennial Commission and persisted in 1963 when the nation's racial discord suggested that simple reunification was not enough.[60]

After Robertson finished, Louis Simon, the executive secretary of the state Gettysburg Centennial Commission, outlined the plans for both the July and November remembrances. Simon revealed that while the planners possessed firm ideas for the July ceremonies, those for November had received little thought. He did note that they "likely will be in the nature of the Western Maryland's 'Mr. Lincoln Comes to Gettysburg' of a decade ago."[61]

While Simon's comments about the July festivities apparently assuaged Robertson's concerns over the commemoration of the battle, his parting comment about the November plan opened another can of worms. On the centennial of its founding in 1952, the Western Maryland Railway Company sponsored a reenactment of Lincoln's trip to Gettysburg and his speech at the cemetery. The assertion that the 1952 event would serve as the model for November concerned Robertson. Two days later, Robertson wrote to Nevins:

> I confess that I am not overly enthused with the Gettysburg program as tentatively planned. There will be *no* battle reenactment, but I fear that the producers are going too much for pageantry and symbolism. The head mogul for the four-day ceremony is Mrs. Adele Nathan of New York City. . . . She produced the 1952 show, "Mr. Lincoln Goes to Gettysburg," which the Western Maryland Railway sponsored, and which was a reenactment of Lincoln's trip to Gettysburg and his Address. I understand that they plan to restage this "drama" as the commemoration of the Address on November 19, 1963. Frankly the Gettysburg Anniversary Commission has made little progress toward (or, indeed, given little thought to) the November program. All their efforts currently are going toward the July 1–4 show.[62]

Robertson knew that of which he spoke, as evidenced by Simon's later admission that not until after the battle commemoration did the commission give serious thought to the November program.[63]

As to Nevins's suggestion that the national commission should commemorate the Gettysburg Address, Robertson offered the following:

> I have conferred at length with [Iowa congressman Fred Schwengel, the commission's political patron] and Dr. Wiley regarding our sponsoring a program on the Gettysburg Address. All three of us are in agreement on two points: 1) we should not do so if it appears that the Gettysburg Commission's program seems sufficient; and

2) any program held in Washington should assuredly be under the direction of the Lincoln Group, and not us. We also feel that it might be prudent to consider working with the Gettysburg people toward a big commemoration at Gettysburg, rather than have separate programs in Washington and Gettysburg. . . . Above all, we should do nothing that would be—or even appear to be—in direct competition with the program of the Pennsylvania people."

But Nevins envisioned a different type of program, an academic consideration of the speech scheduled for early 1964 to avoid any competition with the commemoration in Gettysburg.[64]

Meanwhile, Memorial Day 1963 brought Vice-President Lyndon Baines Johnson to Gettysburg. Johnson had initially turned down the invitation before reconsidering at almost the last minute. As a senator, Johnson had voted against civil rights measures, but as a younger man, he had taught in a Mexican school, and biographer Robert Caro comments, "There had always existed within Lyndon Johnson genuine empathy and compassion for Americans of color." While Johnson's ambition had previously tempered his passion on the issue, now both were unleashed.[65]

In his speech that day, Johnson offered further evidence that America was coming to grips both with the Civil Rights Movement and Lincoln's message in the Gettysburg Address. Johnson began with a Cold War theme: "Until the world knows no aggressors, until the arms of tyranny have been laid down, until freedom has risen up in every land, we shall maintain our vigil to make sure our sons who died on foreign fields shall not have died in vain." Having established democracy as central, Johnson then included the need for equality: "As we maintain the vigil of peace, we must remember that justice is a vigil, too—a vigil we must keep in our own streets and schools and among the lives of all our people—so that those who died here on their native soil shall not have died in vain. One hundred years ago, the slave was freed. One hundred years later, the Negro remains in bondage to the color of his skin. The Negro today asks justice." Finally, Johnson noted the place of the Gettysburg Address in the national pantheon, "Our nation found its soul in honor on these fields of Gettysburg one hundred years ago. We must not lose that soul in dishonor now on the fields of hate."[66] As the second-highest ranking official in the land and a native Texan, Johnson signaled the shift that was taking place in 1963: No longer could Americans discuss the Gettysburg Address's importance to their country without mentioning equality as a central component.

Simultaneously, the Gettysburg Centennial Commission finalized its preparations for the battle anniversary. As a measure of its visibility, the governors of Alabama, Delaware, Maryland, Massachusetts, Minnesota, New Jersey, North Carolina, Pennsylvania, Rhode Island, and South Carolina all took part. But the attendance of a broad cross-section of the country's governors did not mean the various speakers shared a common view of the battle or Lincoln's speech.[67]

On June 29, the president of the University of Notre Dame, Reverend Theodore M. Hesburgh, spoke at the Eternal Peace Light Memorial on the battlefield. The *New York Times* reported that Hesburgh "said in a sermon that the Civil War was fought for the Negroes' liberty, but this remained 'unfinished business.'" Hesburgh continued, "Until every white American decides to act morally towards every Negro American, there is no end to the unfinished business." Such comments would not have surprised his listeners, as Hesburgh was a serving member of the U.S. Civil Rights Commission.[68]

The following day, former President Eisenhower officially addressed the Gettysburg Fire Company, though the crowd dwarfed that small group. Even more so than Hesburgh, Eisenhower framed his remarks around a consideration of the Gettysburg Address. The *New York Times* reported, "General Eisenhower urged that every American read Lincoln's Gettysburg Address carefully and ask himself questions regarding the state of self-government today." The former president clarified what he meant in the following passages, speaking at length about the need for citizens to do for themselves all that they could and only turn to the government when they truly could not provide for themselves. Eisenhower's use of the Gettysburg Address to encourage a greater self-reliance and the curbing of government social-service programs reveals once more the variety of ways people invoked Lincoln's speech. While most either saw Lincoln's words as applicable to race relations or the status of worldwide democracy, Eisenhower found in them a more subtle message about government handouts. But then again, Eisenhower had made dozens of speeches on Lincoln and the Gettysburg Address; perhaps on that June day, he simply sought something new to say.[69]

A ceremony dedicating the Gettysburg (Battle) Commemorative Stamp on July 1 featured Postmaster General J. Edward Day. He commented that Lincoln's "remarks were immediately recognized as an extraordinary and classic statement of the democratic purpose." With an eye to the Cold War, Day concluded, "In today's world of a divided Germany, a divided Europe, a divided China, Gettysburg provides a beacon light of hope for reunification." Assistant Secretary of the Interior John Carver considered Lincoln's invocation of equality more important:

> Lincoln compressed a decade of strife and two years of war into one declaration of faith: That the Nation dedicated to the proposition that all men are created equal should not perish from the earth. That nation has not perished from the earth—but neither have its ideals, so eloquently expressed, been fully implemented. That task remains for our generation to fulfill. For a hundred years, the equality defined on this field has been withheld from millions of our fellow citizens. . . . Thus Gettysburg is more than a historical reminder, important as that is. It is just as important that Abraham Lincoln gave voice to what must be a national objective for our generation.[70]

Richard Hughes, the Democratic governor of New Jersey, echoed Carver's sentiments: "The Civil War was not fought to preserve the Union 'lily white' or 'Jim Crow,' it was fought for liberty and justice for all." For New Jersey, racial concerns defined the centennial from the start, thanks to the segregation issue in Charleston two years earlier.[71] It is doubtful the planners of the Gettysburg commemoration envisioned that so many speakers would use the battle centennial to comment on current events or that so many would use the Gettysburg Address to do so. The planners had set aside three times as much money to commemorate the battle as the Address, but many of those who spoke at the centennial of the battle ignored this cue and framed the larger significance of Gettysburg to be in the words Lincoln delivered rather than the conflict between the two armies. Not all invocations were similar, however, and the diversity of invocations of the Gettysburg Address during that weeklong remembrance testified both to the speech's continued relevance and the shift in its meaning.

The famed March on Washington, the largest in that city since the Civil War, separated commemorations in Gettysburg of the battle and the Address. As befits a national capital, those wishing to protest government inaction frequently demonstrated there. In 1894, an "army" of men led by Jacob Coxey descended on Washington to denounce rising unemployment and encourage the government to inaugurate a public works program to provide the nation with jobs. Almost two decades later, five thousand suffragettes organized their own march on Washington to protest women's exclusion from the polls. In 1932, a group of twenty thousand veterans marched on the Capitol, demanding early payment of their service bonuses to help alleviate their plight during the Great Depression. Though not a march, when black singer Marian Anderson was denied use of Constitution Hall by the Daughters of the American Revolution, Secretary of the Interior Harold Ickes and First Lady Eleanor Roosevelt arranged for the concert to be held on the steps of the Lincoln Memorial. At that event, black and white Boy Scouts handed out a program that featured the Gettysburg Address on the cover.[72] As historian Scott Sandage writes, "In one bold stroke, the Easter concert swept away the shrine's official dedication to the 'savior of the union' and made it a stronghold of racial justice."[73]

In 1941, A. Philip Randolph, the leader of the Brotherhood of Sleeping Car Porters, proposed a march on Washington to protest segregation in wartime industries. Franklin D. Roosevelt forestalled that march by signing Executive Order 8802 forbidding discrimination within the defense industry and in any company holding a government defense contract. But the idea stuck in Randolph's head, and in 1957, on the third anniversary of *Brown vs. Board of Education*, Randolph helped lead a nonviolent demonstration called the Prayer Pilgrimage for Freedom. Around twenty-five thousand people attended the event at the Lincoln Memorial, with Martin Luther King Jr. capping off the speeches with his first major address before a national crowd.

In 1963, Randolph helped organize another march, this one to protest continued segregation. The program for August 28 included most of the leaders of the various civil rights organizations: John Lewis from the Student Non-Violent Coordinating Committee, James Farmer from the Congress of Racial Equality (though his incarceration in a Louisiana jail precluded his attendance), and King, president of the Southern Christian Leadership Conference. Organizers, also invited representatives from each of the country's six major religions to speak.

Of all the speeches that day, King's most explicitly invoked history, drawing on both the Gettysburg Address and the Emancipation Proclamation. After a brief comment noting his happiness in being part of such a demonstration, King immediately referenced the Gettysburg Address, beginning his speech, "Five score years ago." His opening seems almost obvious in retrospect: On the steps of the Lincoln Memorial, King literally stood in the shadow of the text of that great speech, its words engraved in marble just a few feet away. The opening offered another benefit. Those who disavowed Lincoln likely had little time for King to begin with, but by channeling Lincoln, King ensured that Lincoln admirers listened to his words. Literature expert Eric Sundquist notes, "King effectively recast Lincoln's words and made them his own, so that his petition to President Kennedy, the Congress, and the American people appropriated the authority of the nation's most esteemed president."[74] Indeed, when queried as to the selection of Lincoln's memorial for the march, Farmer responded, "It doesn't say anything about what we thought about Lincoln. It says something about how great the image of Lincoln was, and it was something we could use to achieve our noteworthy objectives, that's all."[75] Linguist Keith D. Miller notes that much of King's effectiveness as a speaker came from his ability, an ability learned not in his graduate classes at Boston University but in the black churches of the South, to "channel" or "create their own identities not through original language but through identifying themselves with a hallowed tradition." On that August day in 1963, King merged his voice and Lincoln's, strengthening both.[76]

References to history and Lincoln were not new with King, and, in fact, while writing the speech, he had told friends he wanted it to be "sort of a Gettysburg Address."[77] In his years as a minister, King frequently drew on Lincoln and used the man as an example in his sermons. More telling, in their initial call for the Prayer Pilgrimage for Freedom in 1957, Randolph, King, and Roy Wilkins of the NAACP reminded readers, "In the words of Abraham Lincoln, this is a nation 'conceived in liberty and dedicated to the proposition that all men are created equal.'"[78] African American leaders of an earlier era, such as George Williams and James Weldon Johnson, had preached a form of black self-emancipation from white racism and discrimination and, thus, had chosen not to call on the white president's words. But King was after legal changes to the system supporting segregation and discrimination and, thus, saw Lincoln as a powerful white advocate to invoke in speaking to largely white lawmakers.

Though the media covered the March on Washington and King's speech, the use of the Gettysburg Address slipped by unnoticed. Not even the *Gettysburg Times* pointed out to its readers that King borrowed from Lincoln's greatest speech, a remarkable oversight from a paper that took every opportunity to mention the Gettysburg Address. In Richmond, the papers focused more on the limited desegregation that would occur during the 1963–64 school year than on the march in Washington.[79]

It is difficult to discern whether King's invocation of the Gettysburg Address raised or lowered the nation's esteem for that document. Unlike their nineteenth-century predecessors, newspapers in the 1960s did not typically reprint lengthy speeches, such as the one delivered by King. In Richmond, the *Afro-American* alone printed King's speech. Gettysburg's paper did not print it, nor did many of the New York or London papers, raising the question of how many people in 1963 knew that King purposely paraphrased the Gettysburg Address.

With the battle commemoration concluded, the Gettysburg Centennial Commission turned its full attention to November. The July events cost over $100,000, leaving just $33,000 for November, a sizeable amount but not nearly enough for the pageant initially envisioned. While local planners were no doubt disappointed, Nevins and Robertson breathed a sigh of relief.

The GCC desired a high-profile event and asked the governors of Kentucky (Lincoln's birthplace) and Illinois (where he spent his adult life) to participate in the ceremonies. Pennsylvania's Republican Governor William Scranton extended an official invitation to President Kennedy, but trips to Florida on November 18 and Texas on November 20 precluded his participation in the events at Gettysburg. As the official report later noted, "Little did anyone realize how the course of our history might have been changed had President Kennedy's decision been to come to Pennsylvania rather than go to Texas during that week of November, 1963."[80]

The first events commemorating the Gettysburg Address began on Sunday, November 17, at Gettysburg College. Over two thousand people attended, with admittance by ticket only.[81] The day's event featured

Secretary of State Dean Rusk, British Minister John Chadwick, French Ambassador Hervé Alphand, and Italian Ambassador Sergio Fenoaltea offering their thoughts on the Address.[82]

Chadwick said that while Britain had not immediately grasped the significance of Lincoln's words, over time "the address which we commemorate today came to be adopted and established as one of the noblest expressions of British ideals" and helped cement the bond between the British and Americans: "For us in Britain, as for you in the United States, and for our great allies, the standard which we upheld, the standard which we must proclaim to all the world, is the moral and spiritual standard defined by Lincoln in the Gettysburg address."[83] Six days later, Chadwick wrote to the local organizers, "I am particularly honoured to have been able to commemorate one of the finest human expressions of man's aims in life that has ever been made." Writing the day after Kennedy's assassination, Chadwick identified the many similarities between Lincoln and Kennedy and commented that he was greatly saddened the same fate befell both men.[84] Though Britain was at peace in 1963, Chadwick continued to tie Lincoln to his nation. Doing so during the world wars had served an obvious purpose, but in the 1960s, Chadwick's comments were part of the larger international movement to appropriate Lincoln as a citizen of—and example for—the entire world, not just the United States.

Fenoaltea observed simply that Italy also fought the forces of separation in the 1860s and that his countrymen thought much of the speech. Alphand noted the parallels between Lincoln's speech and the French national motto: liberty, equality, fraternity. The ambassador could not resist adding that his country's phrase preceded the musings by Lincoln and concluded, "[Y]our Government is still struggling against the dark forces of discrimination."[85] In so doing, the Frenchman broached international perceptions of America's continuing racial discord, a theme that greatly concerned American officials, and prefaced the remarks of Rusk.

In keeping with the theme established by the ambassadors, Rusk titled his keynote address "International Aspects of Lincoln's Address."[86] The inclusion of Rusk, like that of the ambassadors, mirrored the 1863 program when William Seward accompanied Lincoln to Gettysburg and spoke the night before the dedication ceremonies. Rusk opened, "[Lincoln's] memory is revered by all of us who are the heirs of those who fought here—both in the blue and in gray," a dubious statement at best. However, as a native Southerner, Rusk, perhaps, was stating his personal position on the speech. As befitted the secretary of state, Rusk emphasized America's role as a model for the world, particularly through documents like the Declaration of Independence and the Gettysburg Address, and noted the major themes of Lincoln's speech: liberty, freedom, and democracy.[87]

As to the stature of the Gettysburg Address, Rusk left no doubt in the minds of his listeners: "The central commitments of the American experiment are probably known to more people in other lands through the words of the Gettysburg Address than through those of the Declaration of Independence." Rusk then echoed Eisenhower's words from four years earlier regarding the impact of the Address on Sun in China and on Indian Prime Minister Nehru—suggesting that these might have been from notes prepared by the State Department for use at appropriate moments. More so than any other speaker during the Civil War Centennial, Rusk linked the domestic and foreign policy aspects of the Gettysburg Address:

> Our commitments to freedom are the source of our foreign policy. . . . They explain also our concern about our failures here at home to live up fully to our own great commitments. . . . [W]e will not be at ease until every one of our own citizens enjoys in full the rights pledged by the Declaration of Independence and our Constitution. . . . [T]he rest of the world is watching closely the struggle for full equality in this country. Our failures distress our friends and hearten our enemies. But this is not the main reason why we must complete this task. We must complete it as a duty to ourselves. It is past time to complete the task which Lincoln began with the Emancipation Proclamation.

Rusk's participation in the event signified his appreciation of the significance of the Address as a foreign policy document. Furthermore, his comments show that he understood and accepted Lincoln's assertion of the necessity of including equality within democracy.[88] As the sitting secretary of state, the Southern-born Rusk did not speak as a private citizen but, rather, as the representative of the Kennedy administration and of the country as a whole, and his comments signaled both a major shift in American foreign policy and in the dominant narrative on the Gettysburg Address.

The audience must have agreed with Rusk's assessment of the document and of contemporary politics and foreign relations, for they offered an enthusiastic standing ovation.[89] But just as Seward's comments in 1863 upset some townspeople, some in 1963 found Rusk's statement offensive. Gettysburg College student Howard Hoffer submitted a letter to the student newspaper: "Dean Rusk nicely rationalized the economically and ideologically imperialistic policies of the U.S. on the basis of the Gettysburg Address! A hiss-boo would have been necessary had not the prayer by Rev. Vannorsdall brought an air of sensibility to the program."[90] Hoffer's implication that Rusk's speech was more concerned with current politics than historical events was perceptive and echoes historian David Blight's notion of "the theft of Lincoln in scholarship, politics, and public memory."[91] Rusk held a press conference just minutes after delivering his speech and confirmed that Adams County (which surrounds Gettysburg) was one of several locations off limits to visitors from communist-bloc countries, a measure taken "to avoid incidents." Whereas the government normally viewed foreign visits to Gettysburg as desirable, Rusk calculated that any type of pro-communist demonstration in America would likely come at a significant cultural or historical site, and in November 1963, Gettysburg topped that list.[92]

The activities on November 17 concluded with a concert featuring Civil War songs by the Gettysburg College Choir and the annual Fortenbaugh lecture by Mississippi-native David Donald, professor of history at Johns Hopkins University, who discussed "Abraham Lincoln and American Nationalism." Donald argued that while Lincoln mentioned liberty and equality, the virtues of democracy, and the need to preserve the nation, the Great Emancipator dared not offend his listeners, so his call for equality only applied to white men.[93] One wonders if Donald's own situation as a man caught between the world of his birth and that of his current residence, affected his interpretation of Lincoln's actions.

The next day, a panel considered Donald's lecture. Alistair Cooke, the *Manchester Guardian*'s legendary journalist, moderated the panel, which also featured Judge Raymond Alexander of Philadelphia, Iowa Representative Schwengel, poet Archibald MacLeish, and Gettysburg College professor Robert Bloom. The panel disagreed with Donald's main point, saying that at Gettysburg, Lincoln "rose above nationalism" and focused on the issues of liberty and equality. Cooke observed, "Lincoln's words have given the people of our country for the last three or four generations a sense of what this nation is in its noblest sense. . . . The African people feel Lincoln singlehandedly freed the slaves." Mac-Leish, who had directed American propaganda for a time during World War II, noted the great steps Lincoln took toward ensuring equality and lamented that Lincoln would be "disappointed by the lack of progress on many fronts" regarding contemporary race relations. Alexander, the only African American on the panel, asserted his belief that if Lincoln had lived, African Americans would have been "raised to full citizenship a half century or more ago." At the end, the audience of nine hundred offered what the *Gettysburg Times* characterized as "an ovation."[94]

November 19 featured two major events: the Lincoln Fellowship of Pennsylvania luncheon, highlighted by Robertson's address, and the Dedication Day observances at the Soldiers' National Cemetery. The two events present a study in contrasts. Robertson's participation in the Gettysburg Address commemorative event seems a bit odd given his earlier comments about the speech. Nevins would have been a more logical choice; he later dedicated seven pages of *The War for the Union* to the Address, calling it "immortal" and declaring that as a result of it "throughout the North, more and more men comprehended that the President was the nation's greatest single asset."[95] Robertson's starring role also meant that, thus far, the three major events in Gettysburg over the past two days had all featured Southern-born speakers.

Regardless of the rationale involved in getting him there, Robertson found himself at the speaker's podium on November 19, for a talk, "The Unwanted Speaker," a reflection of his contention that Lincoln's invitation "was an afterthought, and it was also tinged with strong misgivings." To support this statement, Robertson noted abolitionist Wendell Phillips's evaluation of Lincoln as "a first-rate, second-rate man" and Thaddeus Stevens's comment that to invite Lincoln to Gettysburg was to "let the dead bury the dead." Robertson pounded home his title: "Ironically, the immortality of that occasion stems solely from the 270-odd words uttered by a man no one really wanted in Gettysburg that Thursday morning in mid-November, 1863."[96]

Turning to Lincoln's actual words, Robertson focused on those dealing with the Union: "His dream was that the Old Union, with its many virtues and in spite of its many vices, would be preserved. But at the same time, Lincoln hoped fervently that from the smoking ashes of that terrible cataclysm would rise a New Union—a union in which the nation could enjoy a new birth of freedom, a rebirth of Liberty, and an unchallenged perpetuation of a government both of and for all people." Robertson offered a mixed evaluation of the literary merits of Lincoln's words: "Lincoln spoke ten sentences. Two-thirds of his words were mono-syllable. He was not ever original in what he had to say. He had borrowed some thoughts from Thomas Jefferson, and he leaned heavily on phrases from the Old Testament. Many in the audience were more attentive of a photographer laboriously trying to get a picture than they were of the speaker." On the other hand, he concluded that at Gettysburg, Lincoln melded together his logic and imagination for the first time, making for a powerful and immortal speech. In conclusion, Robertson observed the irony of a Virginian honoring a Midwesterner for a speech made in Pennsylvania—"proof that the wounds of the civil war were not too deep for healing—that this nation did have a new birth of freedom—that Lincoln's beloved government of the people did not perish from the earth." In declaring that Lincoln's call for "new birth of freedom" related to his vision of a democratic government, Robertson downplayed equality. Few quoted the "new birth" line, but in nearly all previous references, those using the phrase linked it to equality, not democracy.[97]

Following the luncheon, a parade formed on the square in Gettysburg, just as in 1863, but instead of horses and carriages, the dignitaries rode in automobiles, and a small plane flew overhead. Nearly ten thousand spectators awaited the parade's arrival in the cemetery. The number of people on the speakers' platform, fifty-eight, revealed just how much had changed since 1863: Despite their best efforts to mirror the original program, the event planners simply could not keep the politicians at bay.[98]

In their report, the Gettysburg Centennial Commission noted three main differences between the ceremony in 1863 and that in 1963: the use of a loudspeaker, that the audience "was spared listening to anything as lengthy as Edward Everett's two-hour oration," and, last, "Of even greater import is that in 1963 it was possible for two distinguished Americans of Negro ancestry to take an impressive part in a tribute to the man who set their race on the path toward liberty. So it was that the words of Mr. E. Washington Rhodes were listened to with rapt attention, and the exquisite singing of Miss Marian Anderson charged the atmosphere, bringing forth a deeply felt emotional response from all, and tears to the eyes of many." Indeed, Rhodes, the president of the National Newspaper

Publishers Association, delivered the opening address at the cemetery ceremonies. More than any other speaker, Rhodes asserted that Lincoln's words of 1863 remained unfulfilled. Echoing Lincoln's prediction and fear that a house divided could not stand, Rhodes declared, "Second-class citizenship with all of its attendant evils must end. Unless men of substance and creative minds take positive action, move forward with alertness and stout hearts to remove this injustice, I fear that government of the people, by the people, and for the people, will soon be endangered beyond repair." For her part, Anderson's presence was also symbolic for another reason: A quarter century earlier, she had not been allowed to sing at Constitution Hall; now, she was one of the primary participants in a ceremony commemorating the Gettysburg Address.[99]

Governor Scranton followed Rhodes. Scranton touched briefly on racial prejudice in his address: "[T]he tyranny of prejudice is doomed because the American people in their deep common sense realize it is wrong." But he focused more heavily on the raging Cold War and the need to spread democracy, noting that the United States "must never abandon the ultimate effort to free captive peoples wherever they are imprisoned in the world."[100]

As Scranton sat down, Eisenhower, Gettysburg's best-known resident, took the speaker's stand. Those in the crowd must have expected more of the same from Eisenhower, who, in previous speeches, had focused on Lincoln's invocation of democracy and downplayed the references to equality. But that day, Eisenhower reversed course, declaring that Lincoln "foresaw a birth of freedom, a freedom which, under God, would restore the purpose and meaning of America, defining a goal that challenges each of us to attain his full stature of citizenship." Furthermore, he identified Lincoln's legacy as "a nation free, with liberty, dignity, and justice for all."[101] What led to Eisenhower's dramatic shift is unclear. In quoting Lincoln, Eisenhower left out the "new" in front of "birth of freedom," perhaps indicating that Eisenhower believed the founders intended this conception of democracy with full equality all along. The following day, the *Gettysburg Times* reviewed Eisenhower's speech in a column titled "Unfinished Work of Which He Spoke Is . . . Unfinished."

The *Gettysburg Times* included two separate commemorative editions with their normal publication on November 19, featuring dozens of stories about the Gettysburg Address, Lincoln, and the Civil War in general. The paper included messages from eight Civil War Roundtables in Indiana, Michigan, Missouri, Oklahoma, Pennsylvania, and Washington, D.C., and letters from the governors of Kentucky (Bert Combs), Illinois (Otto Kerner), and Pennsylvania (Scranton). Scranton acknowledged the domestic racial discord more in his letter than he did in his speech that day: "We give thanks for the distance that we have come in human relations since the time when Americans rose against Americans in the battles of the War Between the States. But we must face the challenge of the future, the many more 'miles to go before we sleep.'" Kerner spoke at length about the "spirit" of the Address without ever describing that spirit, and Combs discussed Lincoln's years in Kentucky. Some articles reprinted early accounts of the Address; others mentioned more recent scholarly debates, such as the confusion over the various copies in Lincoln's hand.

Other papers around the country and world carried considerations of both the Address and the commemorative ceremonies. The Chicago papers paid particular attention, and the *Chicago Tribune* offered a report of Rusk's speech with the subtitle "Urges Equality in the Spirit of Gettysburg." The following day, on the actual centennial, the *Tribune* reprinted Lincoln's speech along with an article about the events surrounding Lincoln's oration. The *Times* of London carried three articles relating to the Gettysburg Address centennial. American expatriate Arthur Lehman Goodhart, who had already agreed to participate in the Gettysburg Address commemorative event that Nevins organized, wrote to the *Times* on November 19 to remind the paper what it had said about the Address a century earlier. In 1963, Goodhart, a professor of law at Oxford University for twenty years, was Master of University College. Quoting a nineteenth-century writer, he argued that in 1863, many hated the Address because of its comments about democracy, something that the elite in England, including those in charge of the *Times*, tried hard to check. But now, a century later, British thinking on both democracy and Lincoln's address had come full circle. On November 20, the paper carried a brief account of the previous day's events, emphasizing, in particular, the roles of African Americans in the ceremonies. On December 4, the centennial of when the *Times* ran the text of the original speech, it reprinted that column. On November 21, Nevins wrote to Goodhart, complimenting him on the editorial but also proclaiming his confusion at the *Times*' handling of the Gettysburg Address: "Its commentary was as eccentric as it was malevolent." Much like the *Richmond Times-Dispatch* in 1913, the *Times* printed its 1863 account without noting the inaccuracies and ways interpretations of the Address changed over the century, a choice that upset Nevins.[102]

One of the final thoughts offered about the centennial ceremony locally came from a November 22, 1963, *Gettysburgian* editorial. Student Bruce Packard questioned the lack of diversity among the college's student body, noting that only one "negro" student gained admittance each year and that campus life remained difficult for minorities who found themselves without peers. Packard concluded by urging the administration and student body both to do more to diversify the student population.

National serials, including *Life*, *Reader's Digest*, and *Time*, all offered pieces of varying length, focus, and quality on the Address. Undoubtedly, the ceremonies would have received even more press coverage had not the nation turned its attention to Dallas and the Kennedy assassination on November 22. The black *Chicago Defender*, in particular, likely would have found much to comment on had it not been for Kennedy's assassination. The *Defender* published on a weekly basis, thus the edition of November 16 came the day before the Gettysburg event and that of November 23 the day after Kennedy's assassination. For the *Defender*, the death of another president friendly to their cause raised the question of whether African Americans and their supporters would ever stand a chance in America.

Nearly every speaker from November 17 to 19 at the centennial ceremony, including Hesburgh, Carver, Alphand, Rusk, the entire panel of November 17, Rhodes, Scranton, and Eisenhower, attributed the significance of the Gettysburg Address to its assertion of the centrality of equality within democracy. National leaders had finally recaptured the central meaning of Lincoln's address, replacing a dominant narrative focused solely on democracy with one that included the necessity of equality; however, from Gettysburg to Washington, from England to France, the question remained: When would the United States make good on the Great Emancipator's vision? Eight weeks later, at another event commemorating the Gettysburg Address, a distinguished group of speakers further probed this essential question.

When Nevins and Robertson took control of the USCWCC, they emphasized scholarly contributions to the field of Civil War history. The Gettysburg Address commemorative event on January 13, 1964, illustrated this priority. Featuring five lectures on various aspects of the

Address, the symposium's academic tone offered a stark contrast to the celebratory pageantry of the Gettysburg festivities the preceding November. Despite the modest scope of the event, its mere existence is indicative of the importance Nevins placed on the Gettysburg Address. During the entire centennial, the USCWCC sponsored only two events: the Emancipation Proclamation centennial observance and the Gettysburg Address ctommemorative event. The commission had a limited budget and a small staff (five people) and carefully dispensed its economic and human resources.

In early March 1963, Nevins, seeking a broad selection of speakers, invited a politician, legal historian, poet, theologian, and literary figure to speak at a January 13, 1964, event in the 755-seat auditorium of the Department of the Interior building in Washington, D.C. The date and location assured that the event would have some distance from the Gettysburg commemoration and could handle a substantial crowd. Nevins planned to have the papers published, fulfilling his desire that the centennial leave a legacy of scholarship. In a letter to Robertson in June 1963, Nevins confessed his regret at not publishing the various speeches and poems delivered during the Emancipation Proclamation celebration, and his desire not to repeat that mistake.[103]

Nevins and Robertson planned for every eventuality, except the one thing they could not control: weather. On January 13, nine inches of snow and sleet fell on Washington, D.C., forcing the cancellation of every public event in the city *except* the symposium on the Gettysburg Address. Instead of the hundreds of anticipated guests, eighty people braved the elements to attend the lectures, a number in marked contrast to the four thousand spectators at the Emancipation Proclamation celebration and the ten thousand at the November festivities in Gettysburg.[104]

Goodhart, the legal historian from Oxford University, delivered the first speech, "Lincoln and the Law." He argued that Lincoln's political philosophy came from the Declaration of Independence, quoting Lincoln's comment in 1861 that he "never had a feeling, politically, that did not spring from the sentiments embodied in the Declaration of Independence." This was logical, Goodhart continued, as Lincoln was a lawyer by profession, and the Declaration was essentially a legal brief laying out an argument for American independence based on British wrongs. Similarly, Goodhart noted that Lincoln's construction of the Gettysburg Address drew heavily on his training as a lawyer, particularly in his "borrowing" of phrases from other authors. That he chose to pull a line from the Declaration of Independence ("all men are created equal") further evidenced his privileging of that document over the Constitution. Goodhart delineated Lincoln's many violations of the Constitution, including calling up the militia without authorization from Congress and his frequent suspension of the writ of habeas corpus. Thus, Goodhart took a more guarded view of Lincoln's adherence to the Declaration, arguing that political expediency dictated his promotion of that document over the Constitution as much as his personal philosophical convictions. Goodhart also took a guarded view of Lincoln's conception of equality, arguing that it was during the 1858 debates with Stephen Douglas that Lincoln came closest to articulating his view on equality when he said of a hypothetical African American woman, "In her natural right to eat the bread she earns with her own hands without asking leave of anyone else, she is my equal and the equal of all others." Goodhart concluded, "If he had been a less able lawyer there would probably have been no United States today." Goodhart recognized the centrality of equality to Lincoln's Gettysburg Address but downplayed the significance of that stance by failing to acknowledge how much the war had changed Lincoln's view of equality.[105]

Theologian and public intellectual Reinhold Niebuhr followed Goodhart, but his topic, "The Religion of Abraham Lincoln," allowed little room for a discussion of the Gettysburg Address. Novelist John Dos Passos followed with "Lincoln and His Almost Chosen People." The title came from Lincoln's speech to the New Jersey senate in 1861 in which he called Americans the Almighty's "almost chosen people," the modifier added because the country had not yet lived up to "the original idea for which [the American Revolution] was made"—equality. Dos Passos quoted Lincoln's supposed lament to Ward Hill Lamon that his remarks at Gettysburg had failed, but, the novelist said, "[T]he address stuck in people's minds. The more they remembered it, the more they were impressed. . . . As the years went by, memorized by every schoolchild, the Gettysburg Address became, along with the Declaration of Independence, one of the grand showpieces of the American heritage." While Dos Passos's initial remarks applied most to the domestic turmoil in the United States in 1964, his conclusion blended that theme with the Cold War and offered a pitch for democracy: "The continuing process that faces the generations alive today is the adjustment of the methods of self-government and of the aspirations of individual men for a full life to the changing shape of mass-production society. . . . The alternative is the soggy despotism that pervades two-thirds of the globe."[106] This was a more positive assessment than that offered by Goodhart and so casually intertwined equality and democracy as to suggest that he felt his comments to be so straightforward and accepted as to need little explanation.

After a poem by Robert Lowell, Democratic U.S. Senator Paul Douglas of Illinois brought the evening to a close. Speaking on "The Significance of Gettysburg," Douglas cited the legion of ways the government had let down African Americans since 1865 and called for a civil rights act that would make real the promises first set forth in the 1860s. The comprehensive desegregation bill that President Kennedy had introduced into Congress in June 1963 had stalled due to Southern filibustering, and though it would pass in the summer of 1964, its prospects in January appeared bleak. Douglas tried to remove sectionalism from his appeal, noting that slavery was located in the South due to geographic happenstance and reiterating some of the failures of both leaders in his region and of his party. The senator's appeal was urgent: "I am afraid that the Roy Wilkinses and Martin Luther Kings will be pushed aside by the mass of Negro youths who will turn to more violent leaders and methods with an incalculable loss to themselves and our country."[107] Douglas, a zealous supporter of civil rights and a man whom Martin Luther King Jr. called "the greatest of all the Senators," was one of the very few in this era to pass by the speech's comments on democracy to engage solely with its advocacy of equality.[108]

In contrast to the Emancipation Proclamation centennial and the Gettysburg Address celebration in November, the press almost completely ignored this commemorative event, possibly because no reporters made their way through the snow that night. Though Nevins had already decided to publish the papers from the symposium, the poor attendance and skimpy coverage likely further motivated him toward that end. Just a week later, he contacted the editor of the University of Illinois Press about such a possibility and soon reached an agreement, with the book coming out in the fall of 1964. Titled *Lincoln and the Gettysburg Address: Commemorative Papers*, the book presents the speeches of that night, an extensive introduction from Nevins, and a brief consideration of the nuts and bolts of the Address by David Mearns of the Library of Congress.

In his introduction, Nevins states why he felt the national commission needed to commemorate the Address with a special program: "The quintessence of much of [Lincoln's] thought and emotion is compressed into his Gettysburg Address. . . . Assuredly, among the events of the war, the Address merits remembrance as much as any battle or any act of statesmanship except the Emancipation Proclamation." The critical part of the Address was its statement about equality: "The proposition that all men are created equal was a truth for all ages, and if America under God achieved a new birth of freedom, it would stand as an object lesson to all nations."[109] Four years earlier, at the annual Lincoln Dinner in Washington, D.C., Nevins spoke at great length about democracy without once mentioning liberty or equality, suggesting that the events of the early 1960s shifted his focus. An adviser to President Kennedy, Nevins was aware firsthand of the damage America's racial problems were causing abroad.[110] The book received positive reviews, even in the Japanese monthly review of American books *Beisho Dayori*, and still boasts a wide distribution fifty years later.[111]

This changing interpretation did not just occur at scholarly symposiums but also in the most basic and widespread of sources, the school textbook. In the 1950s, the three most popular texts nationwide were Leon Canfield and Howard Wilder's *Making of Modern America* (1952), David Muzzey's *History of Our Country* (1952), and Fremont Wirth's *United States History* (1955).[112] Canfield and Wilder offered three sentences on the Address, laying out the facts of its delivery, noting its frequent invocations, and then, "In the midst of the troubles and bitterness of war, Lincoln was able to express in a few unforgettable words the highest ideals of our democracy." A picture of Daniel Chester French's statue of Lincoln in the Lincoln Memorial and the entire text of the Address are on the facing page. The brief evaluation offered makes it difficult to discern whether the authors considered equality among "the highest ideals of our democracy."[113] Muzzey did not mention the Gettysburg Address at all.[114] Wirth printed the text of the speech, calling it "a masterpiece of eloquence which is today considered one of the great pieces of literature."[115]

In the 1960s, an updated version of Canfield and Wilder remained one of the most popular books and was joined by Lewis Todd and Merle Curti's *Rise of the American Nation* (1968) and Henry Bragdon and Samuel McCutchen's *History of a Free People* (1967). Canfield and Wilder did not change the text from the 1950s; instead, they merely added chapters covering the preceding decade and left the coverage of the Gettysburg Address the same.[116] The 1961 and 1968 versions of the Todd and Curti text cover the Gettysburg Address in the same way: by printing the entire text of the speech in a box titled "Living American Documents" without offering any analysis.[117] This unchanging text was fairly common: The sixth edition of Thomas Bailey's *American Pageant* published in 1979 contains the same text on the Gettysburg Address present in the first edition from 1956, namely, a brief passage on the poor reception of the speech, including a quote from the *Times* of London, followed by a phrase suggesting the detractors got it wrong: "But the President was speaking for the ages."[118]

Given how little most textbooks in this era changed from one edition to the next, the Bragdon and McCutchen work stands as a major exception. The first edition of *History of a Free People* came out in 1954, and it remained in print into the 1990s. The original edition contains a prologue announcing, "The United States was the first large nation to attempt government of the people, by the people, and for the people." The authors do not identify the Gettysburg Address by name or mention it anywhere else in the text or in the index. The coverage in both the 1961 and 1964 editions is the same.[119] The 1967 edition, however, contains significant changes, starting with the speech's appearance in the index. More significant, an extensive section on the Declaration of Independence with a subsection "Widespread Influence of the Declaration" now offered an additional comment on the speech. In each of the previous editions, this section covered Lafayette's admiration for the document and the statement by Nehru of India that the speech marked a "landmark in human freedom." For the first time, this 1967 edition also includes the phrase, "By it the Americans made a commitment, as Lincoln said in the Gettysburg Address, 'to the proposition that all men are created equal.' As a result, the Declaration has been a continual lever for change in American society, in the direction of equal rights, equal opportunities, and equal voice in government."[120] Whereas the only mention of the Gettysburg Address in the preceding editions concerns democracy alone, this reference both explicitly and by its placement in the text comments on equality. Change generally comes slowly to textbooks, as evidenced by both the consistent text many retain despite frequently "revising" each edition and by the long time spans many remain in favor with educators. Writers like Thomas Bailey who never changed what they said about the Gettysburg Address during this period are the rule rather than the exception. That the Bragdon and McCutchen textbook explicitly updated its treatment of the Gettysburg Address to discuss in greater detail its pronouncements about equality suggests that textbooks in the late 1960s were beginning to reflect the shift in interpretations of the speech on display at Gettysburg in 1963 and 1964.

The counternarrative to Bragdon and McCutchen comes from Virginia. In 1950, the General Assembly passed a resolution calling for the creation and publication of social-studies textbooks, one each for elementary, middle, and high school, that would "instill in hearts and minds a greater love for Virginia and a perpetuation for her ideals." The resolution was a part of Virginia's resistance to the nationwide integration that had begun with the desegregation of the U.S. Navy in 1947 and would soon culminate with *Brown*. A seven-member commission oversaw the selection of the authors for each text and exercised final approval for all content. The publishers, Charles Scribner's Sons for the lower two books and McGraw-Hill for the high school text, were enticed by the stipulation that the books would be used in every school in the state. That was an ironic exertion of authority given that opposition to centralized control had led to Virginia's secession a century earlier and was a marked departure from the normal policy of allowing individual districts to pick their books.[121]

The content was a throwback to the texts from the beginning of the century. For example, the commission demanded that the Northern-born author of the high school text, Marvin Schlegel, forgo any negative comments about slavery. As a result, Schlegel noted that slaves "enjoyed what we might call comprehensive social security."[122] While the elementary school text was more balanced, the middle school work featured headings such as "Northerners Defy the Fugitive Slave Law." As had their Virginia predecessors at the beginning of the century, these works offered absolutely no mention of the Gettysburg Address. The middle school text, which had referenced Lincoln a number of times in the Civil War portion of the book, even omitted the President from the index.[123] The textbooks went into circulation in 1957, were updated in 1964–65, and remained in favor until 1972. Even after that time, many districts kept using those texts for financial reasons, extending their run until 1980 when the state officially adopted new texts that portrayed slavery as an evil.[124]

The Civil War Centennial continued for another fifteen months after the January 1964 event commemorating the Gettysburg Address, but waning interest and funds precluded further significant public commemorations. During the 1964 World's Fair, the Gettysburg Address made a brief re-emergence. Walt Disney featured an exhibit "Great Moments with Mr. Lincoln" that included an animatronic Lincoln reciting the Gettysburg Address. Additionally, the state of Illinois proudly featured its copy of the Address at its state exhibit and produced a beautiful poster featuring the text of the Address in English surrounded by translations in French, German, Greek, Hebrew, Japanese, Latin, Russian, and Spanish. The 1879 prophesy of Kentuckian Robert Owen that one day the Address would be translated into all languages was well on its way to coming true.[125]

So what, then, did the Gettysburg Address mean during this era? From 1945 until 1962, those invoking the Gettysburg Address mostly did so in terms of democracy and the Cold War. In that era, most Americans felt foreign responsibilities and entanglements to be the nation's single biggest issue and threat. No one and nothing better defended and promoted democracy than Lincoln and his call for a "government of the people, by the people, for the people," so the Address was utilized to exhibit and advocate for that institution of government. By 1963, however, civil rights stood at the fore, and in that light the Gettysburg Address served the country, too, for it offered an admonition from a Southern-born Republican to embrace the promise of the Declaration by recognizing the equality of all men. A counternarrative that either ignored the speech or solely focused on its defense of democracy persisted, but it had become largely confined to the former Confederacy, and even many of the prominent men from that region, such as Johnson and Rusk, had bought into Lincoln's message.

For a hundred years, the nation had lost Lincoln's meaning at Gettysburg, for almost no one in the ensuing century discussed or acted on Lincoln's demand that democracy *must* include equality. But, in 1963, the promise of equality made in 1776 and renewed in 1863 was finally put to the test, and the Gettysburg Address became the historic symbol of that promise. In its final report, the USCWCC said that in 1957, "[i]t had become clear that a great variety of agencies, public and private, were determined to mark the centennial of the struggle that, waged during the agonizing years 1861–65, had given a final decision not only upon the indissolubility of the Union but also upon the impossibility of reconciling the continuance of slavery with basic principles of American freedom and justice." In fact, that had not been clear in 1957, and plans for the centennial at that time emphasized Union only, not "basic principles of freedom and justice."[126] Only in retrospect in 1968 could it appear that the plan had always been to link democracy and equality as the twin victories of the Civil War and as the central message of the Gettysburg Address. A message lost for a century finally reemerged due to the interplay among the Cold War, Civil Rights Movement, Lincoln Birth Sesquicentennial, and Civil War Centennial. Change had come slowly, but, at last, many Americans accepted Lincoln's message and pledged their country to live up to its ideal.

Conclusion

There was profound silence, followed by hearty applause.
—Charles Baum, December 17, 1935

Abraham Lincoln frequently read the Richmond newspapers, the *Rich-mond Examiner* and *Richmond Dispatch*, in particular, and it is quite possible he saw their comments on his speech at the Soldiers' National Cemetery in Gettysburg. It might have amused him that they portrayed his impromptu remarks on November 18 as the only public words he spoke while in Gettysburg. Given Lincoln's appreciation of comedy, he likely would have laughed heartily upon reading editor John Daniel's assertion that the ceremonies were "the substitution of glittering foil and worthless paste for real brilliants and pure gold" and that Lincoln had "acted the clown." But if Alexander Woollcott was correct that at Gettysburg Lincoln was trying to reach a Southern as well as a Northern audience, the President must have regretted that not a single Confederate-controlled newspaper reported the actual words he spoke that day.[1]

Put in its proper context, the Gettysburg Address was Lincoln's most profound public statement that a democracy could persist only if equality was at its core. It took a century, however, before the country at large came to this understanding. In January 1863, Lincoln could not put moral force behind the Emancipation Proclamation, fearing that doing so would jeopardize its ability to withstand legal challenges. Ten months later, Lincoln publicly rectified that omission at Gettysburg. In quoting Thomas Jefferson's assertion in the Declaration of Independence that "all men are created equal" and adding his own pledge "that this nation, under God, shall have a new birth of freedom," Lincoln made clear that the Gettysburg Address centered on equality. In his final line, "that government of the people, by the people, for the people, shall not perish from the earth,"

Lincoln offered perhaps the finest ideal of democratic government in the history of mankind. Although those three lines are typically quoted separately, Lincoln's final sentence blended the two: "It is rather for us to be here dedicated to the great task remaining before us—that from these honored dead we take increased devotion to that cause for which they gave the last full measure of devotion—that we here highly resolve that these dead shall not have died in vain—that this nation, under God, shall have a new birth of freedom—and that government of the people, by the people, for the people, shall not perish from the earth." After the Emancipation Proclamation went into effect in January 1863, the Union army fought and died for Union *and* freedom. Lincoln never intended his promotion of democracy ("of the people, by the people, for the people") to stand apart from the earlier part of the sentence in which he called for "a new birth of freedom" or from the first lines of the speech where he rededicated the nation to the principle "that all men are created equal."

The diverse ways the Gettysburg Address has been interpreted in these three American cities—Gettysburg, New York, and Richmond—especially when compared to London, shows an explicit attempt to reunify in the aftermath of the war. One might suspect that as the nation slowly reunified, the regional interpretations of the Gettysburg Address would fade and be replaced by a single national view. In the larger context, historian David Blight argues, that is exactly what happened: "In American culture romance triumphed over reality, sentimental remembrance won over ideological memory."[2] Lincoln's assertion that equality of opportunity was an integral part of democracy proved polarizing in the century after the Civil War, and, thus, the dominant narrative was one of marginalizing that particular concept even while the speech received great accolades for a variety of other reasons. The divergent textbooks used in the North and South, the contrasting comments on the speech offered at the dedication of the Lincoln Memorial in 1922, the silence emanating from the South on the speech during World War II and the Cold War, and the outright dismissal of the Address by a number of Southerners during the Civil War Centennial in the 1960s—or their acceptance of only the portions dealing with democracy—all reveal that through 1963, the nation fundamentally disagreed as to whether the Gettysburg Address summarized the ideals of America or represented a diversion best forgotten.

Whereas Lincoln's vision remained a stumbling block for national unity into the 1950s, the Gettysburg Address, on the international stage,

195

drew many foreign nations closer to the United States. From China in 1911 to Bulgaria in 1944, Peru in 1945, and France in 1958, countries around the world modeled new governments and constitutions on the political philosophy Lincoln laid out at Gettysburg. That the reaction within the United States remained divergent but that parts of the country held an interpretation in common with a number of foreign nations further highlights the delicate nature of American unity and the constant care needed to maintain that cohesion.

Within the United States, a slow shift began in the late 1950s and early 1960s. With the increasing visibility and urgency of the Civil Rights Movement came a new dominant narrative that saw Lincoln at Gettysburg as arguing for the intertwining of democracy and equality. This message had been a minority counternarrative in earlier decades before rising in the early 1960s to become to the dominant interpretation of the speech. Martin Luther King Jr.'s Dream speech in 1963 that blended the Declaration of Independence, Emancipation Proclamation, and Gettysburg Address into a unified vision of America articulated this interpretation and helped turn the Gettysburg Address into what communications expert Richard Katula calls the "centerpiece of American racial discourse."[3] Lincoln, once viewed as the Great Emancipator, then Oracle of Nationalism, was becoming the first leader in the Civil Rights Revolution. Not everyone approved of the shift. By focusing on the aspects dealing with political theory ("government of the people, by the people, for the people"), white Southerners ignored the parts dealing with race and liberty ("all men are created equal," "a new birth of freedom"). As historian Pierre Nora comments, "Memory, being a phenomenon of emotion and magic, accommodates only those facts that suit it."[4]

The watershed came in 1963, and after that point, the federal legislation that would make Lincoln's call for equality of opportunity a legal reality came rather quickly: the Twenty-Fourth Amendment (1964), the Civil Rights Act of 1964, the Voting Rights Act of 1965, and, perhaps most important, the Equal Employment Opportunity Commission—established as part of the Civil Rights Act of 1964. While elements of racism remain in the United States, and markers such as income equality and the lack of African Americans in positions of business and civic leadership indicate there is still much progress to be made, these acts of the 1960s removed most of the barriers that legally prevented equality of opportunity. After a hundred years, America moved to enact Lincoln's vision.

Epilogue

The world will little note nor long remember what we say here.
—Abraham Lincoln, November 19, 1863

When Martin Luther King Jr. invoked the Gettysburg Address in his Dream speech, he appeared to release Lincoln's words from a century of labor and send them off into a productive retirement. King incorporated the ideals of the Gettysburg Address and elevated them even higher in the same way that Lincoln incorporated and sharpened the ideals of the Declaration of Independence a century earlier. In so doing, King transformed his Dream into the national vision, supplanting—momentarily, anyway—the Gettysburg Address. In the late 1980s, a National Endowment for the Humanities survey of high school seniors found that 88.1 percent could identify the source of "I have a dream," whereas it was 73.9 percent for the Gettysburg Address and 65.7 percent for Declaration of Independence. Like the Gettysburg Address, King's Dream is both malleable and undefinable, and as Eric Sundquist notes, "King has been recruited for causes that might have surprised him."[1] The two men share that in common.

In the Black Power era of the late 1960s and early 1970s, it was African Americans who denied that Lincoln was committed to equality of any kind. In a 1968 *Ebony* article "Was Abe Lincoln a White Supremacist?" Lerone Bennett Jr. contends, "[Lincoln] was a firm believer in white supremacy . . . [who] had profound doubts about the possibility of realizing the rhetoric of the Declaration of Independence and the Gettysburg Address on this soil."[2] Historian Scott Sandage argues, "Earlier, Lincoln had been the only symbol of interracial appeal on whom black protesters could lay claim; the martyrdom of King, Malcolm X, and others, the rise of Black Power, and the advent of black history programs gave protesters a constellation of contemporary black heroes."[3] For a time, some thought they no longer needed the Gettysburg Address.

Those at their wits' ends still turned to Lincoln. In the darkest hours of their presidencies, both Democrat Lyndon Baines Johnson and Republican Richard Nixon defended their policies while standing in front of the Lincoln Memorial, seeking a connection to Lincoln and his greatest speech. A few years later, another president who saw nothing but roadblocks in his path found the answer during a visit to the site of the nation's greatest battle and speech. On September 10, 1978, President Jimmy Carter, Egyptian President Anwar Sadat, and Israeli Prime Minister Menachem Begin were frustrated with the complete lack of progress they had made in negotiating a peace between the two Middle Eastern countries. The two Middle Eastern leaders had not seen each other in three days and at their last meeting had refused to speak. Carter halted the process that morning and took the men twenty miles north from Camp David to Gettysburg, hoping the metaphor of his nation's Civil War and its incredible costs would help break the logjam. In her 1984 memoirs, Rosalynn Carter noted that Sadat, a military man, "was very interested in our Civil War. He knew much of the history of the area we were going to visit and recalled the details of the battle." In contrast, "Begin, an admirer of Abraham Lincoln, recited the Gettysburg address to us as we neared the famous battle site." Perhaps there was something in Lincoln's words that had an impact on these men, for they agreed, a week later, to the framework for a peace agreement that would substantially improve relations between the two nations.[4]

At the local level, representatives from Pennsylvania were in negotiations to bring a copy of the Gettysburg Address back to its "hometown." Pennsylvanians had long lamented that not one of the five copies of the famous speech resided in Gettysburg, and, thus, in 1978, the Pennsylvania congressional delegation petitioned the Librarian of Congress, Daniel Boorstin, to allow one of that institution's two copies to be displayed in Gettysburg. Boorstin, himself the author of a magisterial history of the country, agreed and allowed one copy of the speech to reside in the Gettysburg National Military Park Visitor Center during the busiest months of the tourist season. One problem remained: insuring the speech for any damage that might be done while in transit and against possible theft. The insured value? Three million dollars. Whether that was too much, too little, or just right is difficult to judge. Luckily, the insurance evaluation was a moot point, as the speech was safely transported from the Library of Congress to Gettysburg during each tourist season for fifteen years before the deal came to an end in the early 1990s.[5] Sadly, due to the ongoing preservation efforts and the fragile nature of the five original manuscripts in Lincoln's hand, there are now many times when not a single copy is on public display anywhere in the nation.

While King's Dream supplanted Lincoln's Gettysburg Address for some Americans, internationally it is still the sixteenth president's words that people find most applicable. In 1981, Cuban leader Fidel Castro claimed, "Lincoln belongs to us," while China's Jiang Zemin frequently cites the Address. In Taiwan, a 1989 conference, "Lincoln and Democracy," began on November 12, Sun Yat-sen's birthday, and further sought to link the two men and their nations. In the foreword to the book that came out of the proceedings, Yu-Tang D. Lew, the president of the Lincoln Society in Taipei, stated that the Gettysburg Address's "famous formula for democracy, 'Government of the people, by the people, for the people' is the corner stone of the Constitution of the Republic of China."[6]

Ironically, those exposed to the ideals of the Gettysburg Address in foreign lands are not always treated equally. In India's western state of Gujarat, students taught in English are introduced to Abraham Lincoln by sixth grade, but those taught in Gujarati are given no formal readings on the American.[7] The same pattern held in China until recent years when more and more children are learning English and, thus, gain an early exposure to Abraham Lincoln.[8] This contrasts with the United States, where, historically, a standard elementary or middle school exercise is to memorize and recite the Gettysburg Address. That fewer students are doing so today represents a shift in educational philosophies regarding the value of memorization more than a declining interest in the speech.

It is a sign of the speech's secure place in the American pantheon that it can now be treated with playful irreverence without provoking serious protest. One such depiction comes from the 1989 Hollywood film *Bill & Ted's Excellent Adventure*. High school students Bill Preston and Ted Logan travel back in time, find Abraham Lincoln—and a host of other historical figures—and bring him to 1988 to assist with their history report. A decidedly not solemn Lincoln addresses the crowd in a high school gymnasium, beginning, "Four score and [looks at his pocket watch] seven minutes ago we, your forefathers, were brought forth upon a most excellent adventure conceived by our new friends, Bill and Ted.

These two great gentlemen are dedicated to a proposition which was true in my time, just as it's true today. Be excellent to each other. And ... PARTY ON, DUDES!" Lincoln possessed a tremendous sense of humor and enjoyed jokes, so perhaps he would have found this movie amusing rather than offensive.

In 2012, producer Tim Burton introduced moviegoers to Seth Grahame-Smith's *Abraham Lincoln: Vampire Hunter.* The movie drips with symbolism and blends the Battle and Address to suggest that at Gettysburg, Lincoln gave the nation what it needed to triumph over evil. Lincoln's mother tells her young son, "Until every man is free, we are all slaves," just hours before her death at the hands of a vampire. The vampires feast heavily on the enslaved population, and Lincoln comes to see the abolition of slavery as part of his ongoing war against the vampires. Realizing that he cannot personally defeat every vampire with his ax, Lincoln turns to words and ideas instead, entering the political arena and eventually ascending to the presidency. During the Civil War, the vampires align with the South and provide the forces that allow the Confederate army to emerge victorious during the first day at Gettysburg. Lincoln, however, quickly develops a plan to equip the Union army with silver bullets and bayonets, enabling them to slay the vampires. We see Lincoln in the Executive Mansion planning the route to Gettysburg, observing, "It is eighty miles to Gettysburg, eighty miles will decide whether this nation belongs to the living or the dead." Knowing that his train to Gettysburg will be watched, Lincoln instead sends the silver weapons via the Underground Railroad with former slaves who place the tools of their people's liberation in the hands of the Union army. In the penultimate scene, Lincoln gives his famous speech—surprisingly in a far more accurate interpretation than many other attempts to show this iconic moment. As Lincoln is about to depart for Ford's Theater, he rejects the offer to become a vampire and secure immortality, declaring, "Vampires aren't the only things that live forever." Indeed, here this wildly fantastical movie merges with history, for Lincoln's words do live on.

Steven Spielberg's *Lincoln*, also from 2012, offers another silver-screen take on the Gettysburg Address. Though the movie begins in early 1865 and takes as its subject Lincoln's behind-the-scenes work on the legislation that would become the Thirteenth Amendment, Spielberg could not resist the temptation to include the Gettysburg Address. The opening scene features Lincoln speaking with two African American soldiers. As the scene concludes, one recites much of the Gettysburg Address, illustrating the Gary Wills thesis that the Gettysburg Address "remade" America in 1863.

Three days after the movie's release in 2012, Spielberg spoke to a crowd estimated at nine thousand in Gettysburg's Soldiers' National Cemetery to commemorate the 149th anniversary of the speech. While Spielberg's remarks were both reverent and enjoyable, perhaps even more striking were some of the audience members. Near the edge, two African American reenactors in Union uniforms stood not far from a man portraying Confederate General Robert E. Lee. The scene reveals the place of the Gettysburg Address in our memory, for neither U.S. Colored Troops nor Lee were present on November 19, 1863, but that did not stop their modern-day heirs from seeking a connection with the great speech.

Pop culture has embraced the Gettysburg Address in more media than just the silver screen. In 2004, with the Boston Red Sox trailing the New York Yankees by a game in the American League Championship Series, *Sports Illustrated* writer Frank Deford penned "The Fenway Park Address." Deford called on Sox fans to "forgive all those brave BoSox who lost their noble reputations in certain cursed Series past" in order "that memories of the Babe, by the Bambino, for the Sultan of Swat, shall yet perish from The Hub." The Red Sox went on to win the series in dramatic fashion, then swept the St. Louis Cardinals in the World Series, overcoming four score and six years of history.[9] After invoking the Gettysburg Address, could it turn out any other way?

Like Deford, people have been rewriting the Gettysburg Address to suit their own purposes since at least 1865 when Domingo Sarmiento, an Argentinian statesman, published a biography of Lincoln that significantly altered the wording of the Gettysburg Address's final paragraph to "[Lincoln] concluded by saying that with this act *the nation was proclaiming at the top of its voice* that the fallen of the battle had not sacrificed their lives in vain, because, with God's guidance, the liberty bathed in their blood would be reborn, and that government of the people, by the people and for the people is not destined to perish from the face of the earth."[10] Most of today's incarnations tend to be little more than partisan attempts to point out the unsuitability of the political platforms of one's opponent, but their frequent appearances keep the memory of the Gettysburg Address before the public.

Other uses have been more sobering. On September 11, 2002, the first anniversary of the terrorist attacks on America, a crowd gathered at Ground Zero to read aloud the 2,801 names of those who perished in the attacks. Rather than offering an original contribution, New York Governor George Pataki simply recited the Gettysburg Address. Historian Gabor Boritt sees this as the ultimate expression of the power of the Gettysburg Address: "The ceremony is beamed around the globe. People who listen understand. Americans are saying, this is who we are." Historian David Blight has a different take: "Why couldn't Americans find any other poet of our own age to write and speak at the first anniversary of the September 11 attacks on New York? Did the Gettysburg Address really fit that commemorative moment, or was it simply too risky to leave such an occasion to the partisan whims of the speech writers serving such inarticulate leaders as George Pataki and George W. Bush?"[11] Either way, the result is the same: One of the few things Americans today agree upon is that Lincoln's words at Gettysburg are still suitable and of continuing relevance.

Indeed, those charged with fighting the war on terror found Lincoln a helpful ally just as their Cold War ancestors had a half century earlier. As historian Jay Sexton explains, "Confronted with rampant anti-Americanism following the invasion of Iraq in 2003, the Bush administration turned to America's most iconic and revered figure for help." Mirroring United States Information Agency activities from the 1950s and 1960s, the government sponsored "Lincoln Corners" in public libraries in Asia that provided funding for both books and lectures on Lincoln. Simultaneously, the Department of State put together both a new anthology of Lincoln writings and a travelling exhibit on his life.[12] Statesmen fighting for the hearts and minds of international audiences still find Lincoln and his greatest speech to be one of their primary weapons.

As the bicentennial of Lincoln's birth approached, the Gettysburg Address again came sharply into focus. The decade-long planning of that commemoration was nearly coincident with the rise of an African American from Illinois, a lawyer and public intellect turned politician named Barack Obama, who represented for many the final realization of Lincoln's vision and Martin Luther King Jr.'s "Dream." Obama courted the comparisons, announcing his candidacy not in Chicago but on the steps of the Old State Capitol in Lincoln's Springfield, was sworn in with Lincoln's Bible, keeps a copy of the Emancipation Proclamation in the Oval Office, and had a private screening of *Lincoln* with director Spielberg and screenwriter Tony Kushner. Perhaps most important, Obama regularly invokes the language and ideals of Abraham Lincoln.

When Senator Obama announced his presidential candidacy in Springfield in February 2007, he cited Lincoln as his inspiration: "The life of a tall, gangly, self-made Springfield lawyer tells us that a different future is possible." Obama, whose *Audacity of Hope* was then first on the *New York Times* bestseller list for nonfiction, continued, "He tell us there is power in words," and then paraphrased Lincoln, "Together, we can finish the work that needs to be done, and usher in a new birth of freedom on this Earth."[13] When, twenty-one months later, Obama became the first African American elected to the nation's highest post, he paraphrased the Gettysburg Address in his acceptance speech: "But above all, I will never forget who this victory truly belongs to—it belongs to you. . . . It grew strength from the young people who rejected the myth of their generation's apathy; who left their homes and their families for jobs that offered little pay and less sleep; from the not-so-young people who braved the bitter cold and scorching heat to knock on the doors of perfect strangers; from the millions of Americans who volunteered, and organized, and proved that more than two centuries later, a government of the people, by the people and for the people has not perished from this Earth. This is your victory."[14] Obama followed up by making "a new birth of freedom" the theme of his inauguration—an event preceded by a celebration on the steps of the Lincoln Memorial.

After a gunman opened fire during a public meeting near Tucson, Arizona, on January 8, 2011, killing six and wounding thirteen others—Congresswoman Gabrielle Giffords among them—it was again the Gettysburg Address to which Obama turned. The president noted that those who had come to the meeting that day "were fulfilling a central tenet of the democracy envisioned by our founders: representatives of the people answering questions to their constituents, so as to carry their concerns back to our nation's capital. Gabby called it 'Congress on Your Corner,' just an updated version of government of and by and for the people." In a phrase reminiscent of both Lincoln and John F. Kennedy, Obama continued, "Their actions, their selflessness poses a challenge to each of us. It raises the question of what, beyond prayers and expressions of concern, is required of us going forward. How can we honor the fallen? How can we be true to their memory?"[15] The Gettysburg Address is far from the only Lincoln speech that Obama references. The First and Second Inaugural Addresses are other favorites, as are some lines from more obscure speeches. Unlike so many speakers who use the Gettysburg Address as their go-to Lincoln reference anytime they want to invoke the nation's greatest president, Obama's deeper knowledge of Lincoln's many writings and speeches allows him to select ones that, in some cases, more aptly fit the circumstances.[16]

In accepting the Nobel Peace Prize in 2012 on behalf of the European Union, president of the European Council Herman Von Rompuy, in referring to the general economic woes of the EU and specifically to unemployment rates topping 25 percent in both Greece and Spain, commented, "If I can borrow the words of Abraham Lincoln, at the time of another continental test, what is being assessed today is whether that union, or any union so conceived and so dedicated, can long endure."[17] In the nineteenth century, the line most often quoted is "government of the people, by the people, for the people," and the mid-twentieth century saw increasing uses of "dedicated to the proposition that all men are created equal" and "a new birth of freedom." Von Rompuy's comment could signal that in the twenty-first century, people will find resonance in new lines of the speech. Regardless, the speech is ever present, ready to be called to duty at any moment, a moral yardstick with which to measure our progress both in this nation and the nations of the world.

Notes

Abbreviations

ALSC Abraham Lincoln Sesquicentennial Commission
CW *Collected Works of Abraham Lincoln*
GNMPL Gettysburg National Military Park Library

Introduction

1. "'Lincoln Is World-Wide Symbol of Freedom' Declares Secretary of State," *Gettysburg (PA) Times*, November 18, 1963, 1.
2. Curzon, *Modern Parliamentary Eloquence*, 73.
3. Simon, *Gettysburg*, 102; G. Garibaldi, M. Garibaldi, and N. Garibaldi, to Abraham Lincoln, August 6, 1863, in Holzer, *Dear Mr. Lincoln*, 130. Chapter 5 of the present work includes a discussion of the Italian commemoration of the speech during the Lincoln birth sesquicentennial of 1959.
4. "Constitution," *Journal Officiel de la Republique Français*, October 5, 1958, 1.
5. Simon, *Gettysburg*, 97–99.
6. Wills, *Lincoln at Gettysburg*, 145, 38; Boritt, *Gettysburg Gospel*, 3, 175. A search of the keywords "Gettysburg Address" in the *New York Times* database shows that for every decade from 1900 through 1969, the speech appeared in the newspaper at least once a week on average and reached a rate of every other day from 1930 through 1969. Looking before 1900 is problematic, as the speech was rarely referred to as the Gettysburg Address.
7. Blight, "Theft of Lincoln," 269–70; Donald, *Lincoln Reconsidered*, 18.
8. Boritt, *Gettysburg Gospel*, 161.
9. Nora, "General Introduction," 7.
10. Kenny, "Freedom and Unity," 164; De-min, "Standard," 230–33.

1. The Final Resting Place: The Creation and Dedication of the Soldiers' National Cemetery

1. Faust, *This Republic of Suffering*, 69, 247, 90.
2. David Wills to Andrew Curtin, July 24, 1863, in J. Bartlett, *Soldiers' National Cemetery*, 1–2.
3. Hofstadter, *American Political Tradition*, 132.
4. Lincoln, "Annual Message to Congress, December 1, 1862," in Lincoln, *CW*, 5:537.
5. Bradsby, *1886 History of Adams County*, 375–76.

6. Theodore Dimon to John F. Seymour, August 1, 1863, in *Report of the General Agent*, 60–61.

7. Georg, "'This Grand National Enterprise': The Origins of Gettysburg's Soldiers' National Cemetery & Gettysburg Battlefield Memorial Association," unpublished MS, 1982, 7, 15–17, GNMPL.

8. Ibid., 31–33.

9. *Revised Report*, 9, 147.

10. Ibid., 167.

11. Warren, *Lincoln's Gettysburg Declaration*, 93–94; Ayers, "Their Unfailing Friend," 1.

12. Massachusetts Historical Society, *Edward Everett*, 1.

13. Boritt, *Gettysburg Gospel*, 40–41.

14. Carr, *Lincoln at Gettysburg*, 22–23; Barton, *Lincoln at Gettysburg*, 48; Kunhardt, *New Birth of Freedom*, 36–37.

15. Three recent works note that in October the press reported Lincoln would attend the ceremonies: George, "World Will Little Note," 387; Boritt, *Gettysburg Gospel*, 38; and D. L. Wilson, *Lincoln's Sword*, 208.

16. Andrew Curtin to Abraham Lincoln, September 4, 1863, Abraham Lincoln Papers, Library of Congress.

17. Miers, *Lincoln Day by Day*, 3:204–13. Michael Burlingame also posits that Curtin may have used this August meeting to ask Lincoln to speak in Gettysburg. Burlingame, *Abraham Lincoln*, 2:569.

18. David Wills to Andrew Curtin, November 7, 1863, *Adams Sentinel* (Gettysburg, Pennsylvania), November 10, 1863; *Revised Report*, 8, 14–15.

19. Harvey Sweney to Andrew Sweney, November 29, 1863, GNMPL.

20. "Dedication of the National Cemetery at Gettysburg," *Indianapolis (IN) Daily Journal*, November 23, 1863.

21. Frothingham, *Edward Everett*, 414.

22. L. Warren, *Lincoln's Gettysburg Declaration*, 65–66.

23. Hay, *Inside Lincoln's White House*, 111–12.

24. J. Howard Wert, "Lincoln at Gettysburg," *Patriot* (Harrisburg, Pennsylvania), February 12, 1909.

25. Boritt, *Gettysburg Gospel*, 74. John Hay said that Lincoln stood in the doorway. Hay, *Inside Lincoln's White House*, 111–12. Junius Remensnyder recalled that Lincoln spoke from a balcony. Junius Remensnyder, "Lincoln's Delivery of the Gettysburg Address as It Impressed This School Boy Spectator," *Washington Post*, February 11, 1912, SM1. Gettysburg's three local papers and the Associated Press account by Joseph Gilbert do not mention a location for the speech. The editor of *Lincoln Day by Day* asserts that this speech occurred around 10:00 P.M. in response to a serenade by the 5th New York band. If that is correct, then the speech likely came from the window of the second-floor bedroom Lincoln occupied for the evening. However, it is not entirely clear that the speech came *before* Lincoln retreated to the bedroom. Miers, *Lincoln Day by Day*, 3:221.

26. "The National Necropolis," *New York Herald*, November 20, 1863.

27. "The Gettysburg Celebration," *Philadelphia (PA) Inquirer*, November 21, 1863; Boritt, *Gettysburg Gospel*, 67.

28. "Consecration of the Soldiers' National Cemetery," *Adams Sentinel* (Gettysburg, Pennsylvania), November 24, 1863.

29. Hay, *Inside Lincoln's White House*, 112.

30. Mearns, "Unknown at This Address," 122.

31. "National Necropolis," *New York Herald*, November 20, 1863. This is the version the Associated Press reported.

32. Jacobs, *Lincoln's Gettysburg World-Message*, 62.

33. Hay, *Inside Lincoln's White House*, 112.

34. *New York World*, November 21, 1863.

35. Hay, *Inside Lincoln's White House*, 112.

36. Neely, *Abraham Lincoln Encyclopedia*, 114–15; Carwardine, *Lincoln*, 272.

37. J. C. Andrews, "Pennsylvania Press," 24–25.

38. "Statement Given by Judge Wills to Charles M. McCurdy, about 1890," Vertical File Collection, Folder 10–18 "Eyewitney Accounts of the Gettysburg Address, November 19 1863," GNMPL. This statement was printed by McCurdy in his *Gettysburg*, who explains: "[Wills] came to me one day nearly more than thirty years ago and said that he had prepared a statement covering his recollections of the circumstances attending the preparation of Lincoln's Gettysburg Address, and that he wished to give me a copy because, as time passed, everything relating to the address would be of increasing interest and value." 33. It was also printed in Orton Carmichael's *Lincoln's Gettysburg Address* in 1917. On February 12, 1941, the *Gettysburg Times* printed the account with the explanation that it had been sent to Louisa A. W. Russell in March 1893 in response to a letter from her. It seems Wills sent the affidavit out in response to questions about Lincoln's stay at his home and the authorship of the Address.

39. D. L. Wilson, *Lincoln's Sword*, 211; Nicolay, "Lincoln's Gettysburg Address," 601; Lamon, *Life of Abraham Lincoln*, 2:471.

40. Jacobs, *Lincoln's Gettysburg World-Message*, 63.

41. L. A. Warren, *Lincoln's Gettysburg Declaration*, 74;

42. "Consecration of the Soldiers' National Cemetery," *Adams Sentinel* (Gettysburg, Pennsylvania), November 24, 1863.

43. Burlingame, *Abraham Lincoln*, 2:572.

44. "Dedication of National Cemetery," *Star and Banner* (Gettysburg, Pennsylvania), November 26, 1863; "Storrick Shook Lincoln's Hand Day of Speech," *Gettysburg (PA) Times*, November 20, 1938.

45. H. C. Holloway, "Lincoln at Gettysburg," *Compiler* (Gettysburg, Pennsylvania), November 21, 1914.

46. Skelly, *Boy's Experiences*, 26–27.

47. Harvey Sweney to Andrew Sweney, November 29, 1863, folder 10–18, "Eyewitness Accounts of the Gettysburg Address, November 19 1863," Vertical File Collection, GNMPL.

48. "Consecration of the Soldiers' National Cemetery," *Adams Sentinel* (Gettysburg, Pennsylvania), November 24, 1863.

49. Hay, *Inside Lincoln's White House*, 112; *Revised Report*, 180.

50. N. Brooks, "Personal Reminiscences of Abraham Lincoln," 565; N. Brooks, "Glimpses of Lincoln in War Time," 465; Boritt, *Gettysburg Gospel*, 82.

51. *Revised Report*, 182.

52. L. A. Warren, *Lincoln's Gettysburg Declaration*, 99.

53. Jacobs, *Memoirs*, 63.

54. Charles Baum, "President Lincoln's Speech," CW/VFM5, Gettysburg College Special Collections.

55. Harvey Sweney to Andrew Sweney, November 29, 1863, Vertical File Collection, Folder 10–18 "Eyewitness Accounts of the Gettysburg Address, November 19 1863," GNMPL.
56. Gilbert, "Lincoln in 1861," 134.
57. Lincoln, "Address Delivered at the Dedication of the Cemetery at Gettysburg," November 19, 1863, Newspaper Version, *CW*, 7:19–21.
58. Faust, *This Republic of Suffering*, 9, 17.
59. Gallagher, *Union War*, 36, 62; Lincoln, "Annual Message to Congress," December 1, 1862, *CW*, 5:537.
60. Wills, *Lincoln at Gettysburg*, 38.
61. Manning, *What This Cruel War Was Over*, 184.
62. Lincoln, "Temperance Address," February 22, 1842, *CW*, 1:279.
63. Nicolay quoted in Tarbell, *Early Life*, 166.
64. Lincoln, "Speech in Independence Hall," February 22, 1861, *CW*, 4:240.
65. Wills, *Lincoln at Gettysburg*, 145.
66. Dew, *Apostles of Disunion*, 75; Armitage, *Declaration of Independence*, 96.
67. Lincoln, "Honors to Henry Clay," July 6, 1852, *CW*, 2:130. D. L. Wilson, "Lincoln's Declaration," 166–81, summarizes Lincoln's evolving thoughts about the Declaration and the ways he incorporated that document into his attacks on slavery in the 1850s.
68. Lincoln, "Speech at Peoria, Illinois," October 16, 1854, *CW*, 2:266, 276.
69. Abraham Lincoln to Joshua Speed, August 24, 1855, *CW*, 2:323.
70. D. L. Wilson, "Lincoln's Declaration," 170.
71. Abraham Lincoln to James N. Brown, October 18, 1858, *CW*, 3:327.
72. Lincoln, "Speech at Chicago, Illinois," July 10, 1858, *CW*, 2:501.
73. Brann, "Reading of the Gettysburg Address," 24.
74. Lincoln, "Speech in Independence Hall," February 22, 1861, *CW*, 4:240.
75. Lincoln, "Speech at Springfield, Illinois," June 26, 1857, *CW*, 2:405–6.
76. Carwardine, *Lincoln*, 14.
77. Boritt, "Did He Dream," 4, 6, 8, 10, 13; Carwardine, *Lincoln*, 211; Magness and Page, *Colonization after Emancipation*, 10–11.
78. Abraham Lincoln to James C. Conkling, August 26, 1863, *CW*, 6:407, 409–10.
79. Paradis, *African Americans*, 40–42.
80. Abraham Lincoln to James Wadsworth, [January 1864], *CW*, 7:101; Abraham Lincoln to Michael Hahn, March 13, 1864, *CW*, 7:243.
81. Wills, *Lincoln at Gettysburg*, 38; Waldstreicher, *Slavery's Constitution*, 3.
82. Elmore, *Lincoln's Gettysburg Address*, 1, 14, 18–19, 80, 90, 106, 121, 181; Carwardine, *Lincoln*, 43.
83. See, for example, Lincoln, "Message to Congress in Special Session," July 4, 1861, *CW*, 4:426.
84. In the Associated Press transcript, the word is *governments*; in the currently preferred Bliss version of the speech, it is just *government*. *Governments* is used here as it is what readers in 1863 would have seen. Jacobs, *Lincoln's Gettysburg World-Message*, 114.
85. Biagini, "Principle of Humanity," 81.
86. Webster, "Second Reply to Hayne," *Great Speeches*, 257.
87. Parker, "Speech at the New England Antislavery Convention," *Collected Works*, 5:105; Burlingame, *Abraham Lincoln*, 2:570; *Illinois State Register* (Springfield), October 27, 1856; Elmore, *Lincoln's Gettysburg Address*, 123.

88. Angle, *"Here I Have Lived,"* 188; Lincoln, "'A House Divided': Speech at Springfield, Illinois," June 16, 1858, *CW*, 2:461; Matt. 12:25 (King James Bible); Parker,
"Sermon of the Dangers Which Threaten the Rights of Man in America," *Collected Works*, 6:132.

89. Lew, "Lincoln and Human Rights," 96.

90. Gilbert, "Lincoln in 1861," 134.

91. "Lincoln at Gettysburg: Recollections of Rev. H. C. Holloway, DD," *Gettysburg
(PA) Compiler*, November 21, 1914.

92. Baum, "President Lincoln's Speech."

93. Lincoln, "Address Delivered at the Dedication of the Cemetery at Gettysburg,"
November 19, 1863, *CW*, 7:19–21. Charles Hale, an official emissary from Massachusetts and the nephew of Edward Everett, also wrote down the speech as
Lincoln spoke. Unlike Gilbert, Hale did not correct his version against Lincoln's
manuscript, and as such, many argue, it is the closest version to what Lincoln
actually said.

94. "Lincoln and Burns Event," *Gettysburg (PA) Compiler*, November 28, 1914.

2. The Luckless Sallies of That Poor President Lincoln: Responses to the Gettysburg Address, 1863

1. Harris, *Blue & Gray*, 6.

2. Ibid., 6–8.

3. Ibid., 182.

4. J. C. Andrews, *South Reports*, 25.

5. Schwarzlose, *Newspapers*, xxv.

6. Harris, *Blue & Gray*, 15.

7. Reid, "Newspaper Responses," 51–53, 59.

8. McKay, *Civil War*, 13, 14, 33.

9. Ibid., 14, 20, 22; Goodman, *Sun and the Moon*, 87.

10. McKay, *Civil War*, 24, 51, 62, 159, 209, 216, 235.

11. J. C. Andrews, *North Reports*, 21; Whitman quoted in Goodman, *Sun and the
Moon*, 84; circulation rates from Campbell, *English Public Opinion*, 37.

12. "The Orations of Everett and Beecher," *New York Herald*, November 21, 1863.

13. Wills, *Lincoln at Gettysburg*, 38.

14. McKay, *Civil War*, 24.

15. "Edward Everett at Gettysburg," *New York Ledger*, December 19, 1863.

16. "The Consecration of the Gettysburg Cemetery," *Liberator* (Boston), November
27, 1863.

17. "The Messages—The Loyal and the Disloyal," *New York Dispatch*, December
13, 1863.

18. "A Fifth-Rate Lawyer," August 13, 1860; "The President's Message," December 8,
1862; September 12, 1864, all in *Gettysburg (PA) Compiler*. Much of my thinking
about Stahle and his view of Lincoln is informed by Kid Wongsrichanalai, "Mr.
Stahle's Lincoln."

19. George, "World Will Little Note," 395. That version also appears in the December
5, 1863, edition of *Frank Leslie's Illustrated Newspaper*.

20. Harvey Sweney to Andrew Sweney, November 29, 1863, GNMPL. Union victories in the fall of 1864 also had an impact on voting.

21. Wright, *Secession Movement*, 127.

22. "The Result in the County," November 12, 1860; "Adams County—Official," November 14, 1864; "The Counties the Rebels Invaded," November 9, 1863, all in *Gettysburg (PA) Compiler*.

23. Risley, "Confederate Press Association," 224–28.

24. John Graeme Jr., November 24, 1863, *Richmond (VA) Examiner*, *Richmond (VA) Sentinel*, and *Richmond (VA) Whig*. The *Richmond Dispatch* carried the same account except that it printed the year as 1864 instead of 1860. The only Richmond daily not to carry the account was the *Richmond Enquirer*.

25. It seems likely that "Exchange Bureau" refers to the Bureau of Exchange of Prisoners of War. During meetings to discuss the parole and exchange of prisoners, it was common to pass along newspapers.

26. Graeme is not the only person to have missed the part of the *New York Herald* containing Lincoln's Gettysburg Address. In an editorial for the *Philadelphia Sunday Bulletin* on November 17, 1963, Herman Blum said that the *New York Herald* "mentioned the address as the 'dedicatory remarks of the President,' without reporting what he said." The following year, Blum self-published his editorial as *The Beacon That Was Lit at Gettysburg*.

27. Tyler, "John Moncure Daniel," 3:153; Andrews, *South Reports*, 29–30; Bridges, *Pen of Fire*, 32, 100.

28. For an extended discussion on the ways Pericles influenced Lincoln, see Wills, *Lincoln at Gettysburg*, 41–62.

29. Evans, "Richmond Press," 25–26.

30. I. Bartlett, "Edward Everett Reconsidered," 453.

31. Evans, "Richmond Press," 17–18.

32. "The Inaugural," "From Washington," and "Telegraphic News," March 5, 1861; "The Presidential Inauguration," March 6, 1861; "Latest from the North," March 8, 1865, all in *Richmond (VA) Dispatch*.

33. "Old Abe's Last," *Virginian* (Lynchburg, Virginia), December 4, 1863.

34. J. C. Andrews, *South Reports*, 299–300.

35. Hearn, *When the Devil*, 100.

36. "Mr. Everett on 'State Sovereignty' and 'Reserved Rights,'" *New Orleans (LA) Daily True Delta*, December 4, 1863.

37. "Everett and Beecher Compared as Orators," *New Orleans (LA) Bee*, December 3, 1863.

38. "The Gettysburg Cemetery Consecration Ceremonies," *New Orleans (LA) Times*, December 2, 1863.

39. *Memphis (TN) Daily Bulletin*, November 26, 1863. The aforementioned *Memphis Appeal* was an itinerant paper at this point in the war, publishing outside of the city, and therefore not under Union influence.

40. Davis, *Papers*; J. Jones, *Rebel War Clerk's Diary*; Gorgas, *Civil War Diary*; Chesnut, *Mary Chesnut's Civil War*; McGuire, *Diary of a Southern Refugee*.

41. Dibner, *Atlantic Cable*, 36, 43, 78; "Latest Intelligence. America," *Times* (London), December 3, 1863.

42. William Francis Collopy examined four Irish papers for November and December 1863 but found no references to the Gettysburg Address, despite stories in each paper devoted to the war in America. The papers are *Clare Journal and Ennis Advertiser*, *Freeman's Journal and Daily Commercial Advertiser* (Dublin), *Galway Vindicator and Connaught Advertiser*, and *Limerick Reporter and Tipperary Vindicator*.

43. Campbell, *English Public Opinion*, 17, 50; on circulation numbers of *Uncle Tom's Cabin*, see Westwood, "Audience," 137.

44. Sexton, *Monroe Doctrine*, 138–39.

45. Lincoln, "First Inaugural Address," March 4, 1861, *CW*, 4:263. Lincoln used that line in his first debate with Stephen Douglas at Ottawa, Illinois, on August 28, 1858, and reiterated it in a speech at Columbus, Ohio, on September 16, 1859.

46. Blackett, *Divided Hearts*, 33.

47. Campbell, *English Public Opinion*, 21–22, 28, 41, 48.

48. Westwood, "Audience," 137.

49. Heckman, "British Press Reaction," 150–51; H. Jones, *Blue & Gray Diplomacy*, 29.

50. "The Civil War in America," *Times* (London), January 30, 1863. London's population in 1863 was just over three million.

51. Campbell, *English Public Opinion*, 14, 37.

52. Blackett, *Divided Hearts*, 16.

53. "America," *London Morning Post*, December 3, 1863. The formatting in the *Post* is slightly different than in the *Daily Telegraph*: "Mr. Lincoln, Mr. Seward, and the *corps diplomatique* were present at the dedication of the Gettysburg Cemetery. Edward Everett made an oration."

54. "The Civil War in America," *London Morning Post*, December 12, 1863.

55. Westwood, "Audience," 138, 140.

56. "The Civil War in America," *London Morning Post*, December 12, 1863.

57. "News of the Week," *Spectator*, November 28, 1863; "America," *Saturday Review of Politics, Literature, Science, and Art*, December 12, 1863. For an example of the *Bee-Hive's* coverage of pro-emancipation meetings, see "Negro Emancipation," *Bee-Hive*, November 28, 1863.

58. In his "Cornerstone" speech in 1861, Confederate Vice President Alexander Stephens had sought to disavow Thomas Jefferson's ideas in the Declaration, arguing that the concept of slavery as a necessary evil "rested upon the assumption of the equality of the races. This was an error." But one must remember that Stephens was not a Virginian, as Jefferson had been, and thus found it easier to disavow that man. Stephens, "Cornerstone Speech."

59. Baum, "President Lincoln's Speech."

3. A Prophet with a Vision: 1901–22

1. W. Wilson, "An Address at the Gettysburg Battlefield, July 4, 1913," *Papers*, 28:23–26.

2. "A Government of the People," *Baltimore (MD) Afro-American Ledger*, July 5, 1913, 4.

3. Gannon, *Won Cause*, 8.

4. Washington, *Up from Slavery*, 9.

5. Boritt, *Gettysburg Gospel*, 161, 171.

6. *Hartford (CT) Courant*, June 9, 1864; Boritt, *Gettysburg Gospel*, 138.

7. Boritt, *Gettysburg Gospel*, 150.

8. For examples of funeral orations employing the Gettysburg Address, see Carnahan, *Oration*, 24; P. Brooks, *Life and Death*, 24; McClintock, *Discourse Delivered*, 14; *Funeral Observances*, 28–29. Boritt contends that few of these speeches mention the Gettysburg Address, but this author's research reveals the opposite. In the current chapter, unless otherwise noted, all references to the speech use the Final Version or Bliss version, Lincoln, "Address Delivered at the Dedication of the Cemetery at Gettysburg," November 19, 1863, Final Text, *CW*, 7:22–23.

9. Sumner, "Promises of the Declaration of Independence," in *Charles Sumner*, 12:248, 271–72, original emphasis.

10. George Bacon's 1865 biography of Lincoln, published in London, reprinted a number of the columns run in English and French newspapers after Lincoln's death, including those from most of London's major papers, and yet, none referenced the Gettysburg Address. Bacon's biography quotes the entire Address but offers little commentary. *Life and Administration*, 75.

11. *Revised Report*, 153.

12. J. Bartlett, *Soldiers' National Cemetery*, 63, 66, 101.

13. "The Gettysburg Oration," *New York Times*, July 2, 1869, 4.

14. Nast, "Death at the Polls," 1.

15. Boritt, *Gettysburg Gospel*, 177.

16. On *Reynolds's Newspaper*, see Smith, "'Stuff Our Dreams Are Made Of,'" 126.

17. Lease, "Wall Street Owns the Country."

18. "Make Lincoln Rise from His Grave," *Atlanta (GA) Constitution*, April 17, 1896, 9.

19. Boritt, *Gettysburg Gospel*, 161.

20. Bryan, "Lincoln as an Orator," *Speeches*, 2:423.

21. Bankston and Caldas, *Public Education*, 43–45, 51, 55.

22. *Gettysburg Speech*; *Lincoln's Gettysburg Speech*; *Speeches by Lincoln*.

23. Robertson, "Historical Inaccuracies," 284.

24. J. W. Jones, *School History*, 8, 293.

25. A tremendous essay on the interpretation of Lincoln in these early textbooks is Goldfield, "Lincoln's Image."

26. "Text Books Used in the Public Schools of the City of Richmond, Session, 1904–1905," Broadside 1904:20, Broadside Collection, Virginia Historical Society.

27. Lee, *New School History*, preface (original emphasis).

28. Gannon, *Won Cause*, 147.

29. Michigan State Superintendent of Public Education, *Lincoln at Gettysburg*.

30. Hart, *School History of the United States*, 347–48.

31. Goldfield, "Lincoln's Image"; Latané, *History*, 381.

32. Warren, *Lincoln's Gettysburg Declaration*, 62.

33. M. R. S. Andrews, "Perfect Tribute," 17–20.

34. Ibid., 23.

35. Kristin Hoganson's *Fighting for American Manhood* is an excellent look at the late 1890s anxieties about the lack of manly leaders in the United States. An *Atlanta Constitution* editorial from April 1, 1898, "Wanted—A Man, an American," made the same point by comparing the current lack of effective leadership to that offered by Abraham Lincoln a generation earlier.

36. McMurtry, "Perfect Tribute," 28.

37. Charles Baum, "President Lincoln's Speech," CW/VFM5, Gettysburg College Library Special Collections.

38. Today, the film, also titled *The Perfect Tribute*, is nearly impossible to view. There is a copy at UCLA, but it is guarded carefully. As a part of the Lincoln birth bicentennial in 2009, the University of Illinois hosted a film festival and searched for a copy. The family of Charles Sale found one among his estate, a copy of which is now viewable at the Abraham Lincoln Presidential Library in Springfield, Illinois.

39. Hayner, *List of Materials*, 22.

40. Rutherford, *Measuring Rod*, 5.

41. Ibid., *South Must Have*, 1–2.

42. Ibid., 13, 30, 33, 49.

43. Janney, *Burying the Dead*, 6.

44. Gettysburg National Military Park Commission, *Annual Reports*, 190.

45. "Reunion on Gettysburg Battlefield," *Times* (London), July 1, 1913, 7.

46. "Gettysburg," *Times* (London), July 3, 1913, 9.

47. W. Wilson, *History of the American People*, 4:308–9; W. Wilson, "From the Diary of Colonel House," December 22, 1913, *Papers of Woodrow Wilson*, 29:55; W. Wilson, "After-Dinner Remarks," December 21, 1916, *Papers of Woodrow Wilson*, 40:121.

48. Weeks, *Gettysburg*, 106; "A Government of the People," *Baltimore (MD) Afro-American Ledger*, July 5, 1913, 4; *Philadelphia (PA) Age*, quoted in Kachun, *Festivals of Freedom*, 155; Gannon, *Won Cause*, 8, 179, 182–83.

49. 27 Cong. Rec. 1038–39 (January 16, 1895) ["National Military Park, Gettysburg, PA"].

50. Boritt, *Gettysburg Gospel*, 192–93.

51. Brown, *Public Art*, 37.

52. Savage, *Standing Soldiers*, 5, 7.

53. Curzon, *Modern Parliamentary Eloquence*, 72–73.

54. Ibid., 73–75.

55. Smith, "'Stuff Our Dreams Are Made Of,'" 127–28.

56. Charnwood, *Abraham Lincoln*, 362–63.

57. Monaghan, "Lincoln's Debt," 37.

58. Elias, *Abraham Lincoln*, 164–65.

59. Weeks, *Gettysburg*, 66–68, 71, 73.

60. Minnigh, *Gettysburg*, 56.

61. "59th Annual Institute," *Gettysburg (PA) Times*, November 17, 1913, 1–2.

62. *Star and Sentinel* (Gettysburg, Pennsylvania), November 19, 1913, 2. For a discussion of the literary partnership between Lincoln and Seward in authoring Lincoln's First Inaugural Address, see Donald, *Lincoln*, 282–84.

63. "Anniversary of Lincoln Oration at Gettysburg," *Gettysburg (PA) Times*, November 20, 1913, 1.

64. "Pay Tribute to Lincoln," *Star and Sentinel* (Gettysburg, Pennsylvania), November 26, 1913, 1.

65. Ibid., 4.

66. "Anniversary of Lincoln Oration at Gettysburg," *Gettysburg (PA) Times*, November 20, 1913, 1; Bradsby, *1886 History of Adams County*, 355.

67. "Pay Tribute to Lincoln," *Star and Sentinel* (Gettysburg, Pennsylvania), November 26, 1913, 4.

68. Boos, *Speech That Became Immortal*, 23.

69. "Pay Tribute to Lincoln," *Star and Sentinel* (Gettysburg, Pennsylvania), November 26, 1913, 4.

70. Ibid.

71. Lincoln, *Abraham Lincoln*, 34–35; John P. Nicholson, "Scrapbook Containing Correspondence & Related Items Regarding the Movement for Placing Bronze Tablets of the Gettysburg Address, 1909–1920," Abraham Lincoln Presidential Library, Springfield, Illinois. Both the Bliss and Everett copies are printed on adjoining pages. The version used for the current volume is located at the Abraham Lincoln Presidential Library, and an attached letter indicates that only a

limited number were printed and were intended for the use of senators on the occasion of the Lincoln birth centennial on February 12, 1909.

72. Boritt, *Gettysburg Gospel*, 287–90. For a convincing argument that the second copy was the version Lincoln read at Gettysburg, see Fortenbaugh, "Lincoln as Gettysburg Saw Him," 6.

73. Nicholson, "Scrapbook."

74. Gilbert, "Lincoln in 1861," 137.

75. "Seek Lincoln's Own Words," *New York Times*, February 21, 1913, 6.

76. Thomas, *Lincoln Memorial*, xxvii, 37, 65, 100.

77. Carr, *Lincoln at Gettysburg*, 59.

78. *Star and Sentinel* (Gettysburg, Pennsylvania), November 19, 1913.

79. Gilbert, "Lincoln in 1861," 135.

80. "Pay Tribute to Lincoln," *Star and Sentinel* (Gettysburg, Pennsylvania), November 26, 1913, 4.

81. "Anniversary of Lincoln Oration at Gettysburg," *Gettysburg (PA) Times*, November 20, 1913, 1.

82. Boos, *Speech*, n.p.

83. "Pay Tribute to Lincoln," *Star and Sentinel* (Gettysburg, Pennsylvania), November 26, 1913, 4; "Anniversary of Lincoln Oration at Gettysburg," *Gettysburg (PA) Times*, November 20, 1913, 1.

84. "Pay Tribute to Lincoln," *Star and Sentinel* (Gettysburg, Pennsylvania), November 26, 1913, 4.

85. Untitled, *Star and Sentinel* (Gettysburg, Pennsylvania), December 3, 1913, 1.

86. Weeks, *Gettysburg*, 94–97.

87. Schwartz, "Collective Memory and History," 476; G. W. Williams, *History of the Negro Race*, 2:274; Ira Berlin, "Soldier, Scholar, Statesman, Trickster," *New York Times*, November 17, 1985, http://www.nytimes.com/1985/11/17/books/sodlier-scholar-statesman-trickster.html, accessed December 7, 2012.

88. "Fiftieth Anniversary of Lincoln's Gettysburg Address," *Richmond (VA) Planet*, November 15, 1913, 4.

89. Schwartz, "Collective Memory and History," 476; DuBois, "Opinion," 103; Peterson, *Lincoln in American Memory*, 174–75; Sandage, "Marble House Divided," 149.

90. Schwartz, *Abraham Lincoln and the Forge of National Memory*, 212.

91. Thomas, *Lincoln Memorial*, 5, 13, 19, 22.

92. Ibid., 16, 26, 31, 33, 37, 89, 108.

93. Ibid., xix; Brown, *Public Art*, 158; Schwartz, *Abraham Lincoln in the Post-Heroic Era*, 52.

94. Schwartz, *Abraham Lincoln and the Forge of National Memory*, 222.

95. Thomas, *Lincoln Memorial*, 156; Holzer, *Lincoln Anthology*, 428.

96. Concklin, *Lincoln Memorial*, 78–81.

97. Holzer, *Lincoln Anthology*, 429, 432–33.

98. Ibid., 81.

99. Concklin, *Lincoln Memorial*, 78–81.

100. "Harding Dedicates Lincoln Memorial; Blue and Gray Join," *New York Times*, May 31, 1922, 3.

101. "Text of President's Address," *New York World*, May 31, 1922, 1.

102. "Segregation at the Lincoln Memorial Dedication," *Richmond (VA) Planet*, June 10, 1922, 1.

103. Mumford, *Sticks and Stones*, 141–42.
104. Baum, "President Lincoln's Speech."

4. For That Cause They Will Fight to the Death: Wartime Usages of the Gettysburg Address

1. "The Americans in France," *Times* (London), June 28, 1917, 2.
2. Nagler, "Abraham Lincoln's Image." Nagler based his information on a Worldcat search.
3. "Honor Memory of Lincoln's Speech," *Gettysburg (PA) Times*, November 20, 1914, 1.
4. "Exercises at Monument," *Gettysburg (PA) Times*, November 20, 1915, 1.
5. John White Johnston to Samuel Reck, May 10, 1918, "Gettysburg Address, Anniversaries," Vertical Files, Adams County Historical Society.
6. "Like Gettysburg Address," *Dallas (TX) Morning News*, January 10, 1915.
7. "From Arras to Gettysburg," *New York Times*, September 19, 1915, 14.
8. "Crisis, Says Butler Divides Americans," *New York Times*, February 26, 1916, 9.
9. "Congress Honors Memory of Lincoln," *New York Times*, February 13, 1917, 6.
10. Roosevelt, *Fear God*, 47.
11. Seager, *And Tyler Too*, 481–82, 490.
12. Tyler, *Encyclopedia of Virginia Biography*, 5:859–61.
13. Mary Todd Lincoln to Edward Lewis Baker Jr., January 16, 1880, in Turner and Turner, *Mary Todd Lincoln*, 694. Historian Catherine Clinton brought this letter to my attention during a conference at Gettysburg College in June 2009. She discusses the letter in *Mrs. Lincoln*.
14. "The Hohenzollerns and the Slave Power," *New York Times*, April 22, 1917, E2.
15. Tyler, "South and Germany," 2.
16. Ibid., 9–10.
17. Ibid., 11–12.
18. Monroe, "Lincoln the Dwarf," 38.
19. Lyon G. Tyler to William E. Barton, February 19, 1930, folder 6, box 10, Barton Papers.
20. William E. Barton to Lyon G. Tyler, February 22, 1930, folder 6, box 10, Barton Papers.
21. Everett, "Davis, Lincoln, and the Kaiser," 405–6. The Pepper quote also comes from Everett.
22. "Former Mrs. Cleveland Teaches Patriotism," *New York Times*, January 27, 1918, 38.
23. Woodrow Wilson to Ellen Axson, February 24, 1885, W. Wilson, *Papers of Woodrow Wilson*, 4:287.
24. Blakey, *Historians on the Homefront*, 1–3.
25. Schwartz, *Abraham Lincoln and the Forge of National Memory*, 227–28, 232, 242.
26. Ibid., 239.
27. Ibid., 236.
28. U.S. Bureau of the Census, *Fourteenth Census of the United States, 1920*.
29. "Father Abraham," *Stars and Stripes*, February 8, 1918, 4; "In France—Memorial Day, 1918," *Stars and Stripes*, May 24, 1918, 1.
30. "A Christmas Letter from the A.E.F. to America," *Stars and Stripes*, December 20, 1918, 4.

31. On the arguments that the United States needed a war in order to restore its manhood, see Hoganson, *Fighting for American Manhood*.
32. "A Great Example," *Times* (London), April 16, 1915, 9.
33. "Lincoln Statue Unveiled," *Times* (London), September 16, 1919, 5.
34. "The Lincoln Statue at Manchester," *Times* (London), May 6, 1919, 7.
35. Elihu Root, "Address in Parliament Square, London, Presenting Saint Gaudens's Statue of Lincoln to the British People, July 28, 1920," in Root, *Men and Policies*, 65.
36. Nagler, "National Unity and Liberty," 245; Nagler, "Abraham Lincoln's Image and Reception in Germany"; Emile Ludwig, "A New Lincoln: A World Figure," *New York Times*, February 9, 1930, SM1.
37. For a broader perspective on the uses of Abraham Lincoln during World War II, see Schwartz, "Memory as a Cultural System," and *Abraham Lincoln in the Post-Heroic Era*, 59–90.
38. "Shall Not Perish," *New York Times Magazine*, December 14, 1941, SM4.
39. R. P. Warren, *Legacy of the Civil War*, 79; "Applause at Gettysburg," 1; "Constitution Put on View," *New York Times*, October 2, 1944, 21.
40. "The Case of 'Social Justice,'" April 16, 1942, 20; "Text of Platform Draft Prepared by Wilkie," July 11, 1944, 10; "Mail-Bag Excerpts," February 15, 1942, E7; "Lincoln's Memory Is Revered by City," February 13, 1943, 7; all in *New York Times*.
41. Schwartz, "Memory as a Cultural System," 919; "Display Ad 13—No Title," *New York Times*, February 10, 1942, 5; "60,000,000 Americans Can't Be Wrong," *New York Times*, June 11, 1944, SM20.
42. Mondale and Patton, *School*, 113.
43. Bankston and Caldas, *Public Education*, 60.
44. Giordano, *Twentieth Century Textbook Wars*, 17.
45. Wesley, *NEA*, 60.
46. McGregor, *Living Democracy*, 1; Educational Policies Commission, *Our Democracy*, 9.
47. Cook, *Troubled Commemoration*, 21–22.
48. National Council for Social Studies, *Social Studies Mobilize for Victory*, 3, 6, 8, 11.
49. L. A. Warren, *Lincoln's Gettysburg Declaration*, 165–66; Boritt, *Gettysburg Gospel*, 289.
50. "The Press: Marshall Field at Work," *Time Magazine*, September 27, 1943, 44. The third, or Everett, copy of the Address, as outlined in chapter 3 of the current volume, was originally drafted by Lincoln in early 1864 in response to Edward Everett's request for a manuscript that could be bound with his own from that day and auctioned off at the New York Sanitary Fair. The details of the sale are murky, but, apparently, Carlos Pierce of Boston, a close friend of Everett, purchased the collection for $1,000. Pierce died in 1870, and in 1875, his widow sold it to the Keyes family, also of Boston. It is that copy Senator Henry W. Keyes of New Hampshire read aloud in Congress on Lincoln's birthday in 1920. In 1929, autograph dealer Thomas Madigan bought the copy for $100,000 and sold it a year later to Chicago banker James C. Ames for $150,000. From 1935 until 1944, the speech was exhibited at the Chicago Historical Society.
51. "Lincoln's Gettysburg Address Presentation—Remote from Springfield," radio script, March 24, 1944, Lincolniana Collection, Abraham Lincoln Presidential Library. CBS did not move into television until the 1950s.
52. Klein, *History*, 15, 22.

53. "Address Delivered at Gettysburg Memorial Day Exercises May 30, 1944," program, folder 10–32 "Memorial Day Exercises," Vertical Files, Gettysburg National Military Park Library. An account also ran in the *New York Times*, May 31, 1944, 10.

54. "Too Short to Be Taken Seriously," *Richmond (VA) News Leader*, February 9, 1944.

55. Schwartz, *Abraham Lincoln in the Post-Heroic Era*, 68.

56. Woollcott, *For Us the Living*, 9.

57. Smith, "'Stuff Our Dreams Are Made Of,'" 123.

58. Churchill, "Joint Session of Congress," December 26, 1941, in Churchill, *Churchill War Papers*, 1685; "Text of Churchill's Address Proclaiming Solidarity of Three Great Powers," *New York Times*, January 19, 1945, 12; "Churchill and Attlee Addresses in House of Commons on Britain and Her Role in Foreign Affairs," *New York Times*, August 17, 1945, 4; "Mr. Churchill's Broadcast," *Times* (London), August 26, 1941, 3.

59. "Windsor Visits Military Chiefs," *New York Times*, September 27, 1941, 9; "Vision of Lincoln Held Needed Now," *New York Times*, March 19, 1943, 22; Monaghan, "Lincoln's Debt to the British," 39.

60. Mitgang, "Friend of a Free Press," 241.

61. "Greece's Monarch Ends Dictatorship," *New York Times*, February 8, 1942, 31; Wills, *Lincoln at Gettysburg*.

62. "To Solve the German Problem—A Free State?" *New York Times*, August 15, 1943, SM6.

63. "Letters to the Times," *New York Times*, August 21, 1943, 10.

64. "Balkan Sentiment Seen Cool to Kings," *New York Times*, December 20, 1943, 4; "Bulgars Announce 3 Social Reforms," *New York Times*, September 22, 1944, 9.

65. Frank M. Garcia, "Brazil to Set Poll Day in 90 Days; To Pick President by Direct Vote," *New York Times*, March 1, 1945, 1; "All Parties Vote on Peru President," *New York Times*, June 10, 1945, 16.

66. Breeskin, *William H. Johnson*, 11, 12, 14, 16.

67. Powell, *Homecoming*, 135, 155–56.

68. "New Deal Friendship," *Chicago (IL) Defender*, July 31, 1943, 14; James Johnson, "Home Front Crackup Seen," *Chicago (IL) Defender*, August 7, 1943, 14.

69. Curzon, *Modern Parliamentary Eloquence*, 73.

70. The image of the "Double V" first appeared in the *Pittsburgh (PA) Courier* on February 7, 1942.

5. The Very Core of America's Creed: 1959–63

1. W. G. Williams, *Tragedy of American Diplomacy*, 127.

2. Von Eschen, "Who's the Real Ambassador?" 111, 115.

3. The Lincoln Group of the District of Columbia consisted of politicians, historians, and general Lincoln enthusiasts dedicated to studying and remembering the nation's sixteenth president. In the late 1950s, Iowa Representative Fred Schwengel was one of the most important members and introduced into Congress the legislation for the Abraham Lincoln Birth Sesquicentennial commemoration.

4. Belmonte, *Selling the American Way*, 98–99.

5. Osgood, *Total Cold War*, front cover, 11, 48–49.

6. Cull, *Cold War*, 2, 11, 22–23; Osgood, *Total Cold War*, 26.

7. Osgood, *Total Cold War*, 11.

8. Cull, *Cold War*, 91.

9. Belmonte, *Selling the American Way*, 59, 66, 81; Osgood, *Total Cold War*, 89.

10. Osgood, *Total Cold War*, 77, 7.

11. Dudziak, *Cold War*, 137.

12. Belmonte, *Selling the American Way*, 98–99.

13. Osgood, *Total Cold War*, 3, 50, 92.

14. ALSC, *Abraham Lincoln*, vii, xiv, 83; "State Activity," 2. Ralph Yarborough was quite liberal and was the only Southern senator to vote for every civil rights bill from 1957 to 1970. States with commissions included California, Connecticut, Idaho, Illinois, Indiana, Kansas, Kentucky, Louisiana, Massachusetts, Michigan, New Hampshire, New Jersey, New York, Ohio, Pennsylvania, Washington, West Virginia, and Wisconsin. Washington, D.C., and the territory of Guam also established commissions.

15. "President's Talk on Lincoln," *New York Times*, February 12, 1959, 22; "Lincoln Round the World," *Lincoln Sesquicentennial Intelligencer* 1, no. 2 (March 1959): 2–3.

16. ALSC, *Abraham Lincoln*, 49, 95, 170–71, 173; Edmund Wilson, *Patriotic Gore*, 115.

17. Cull, *United States Information Agency*, 101.

18. Petersen, *Gettysburg Addresses*, 88–93.

19. ALSC, *Abraham Lincoln*, 51.

20. Osgood, *Total Cold War*, 115, 117, 118, 121; Belmonte, *Selling the American Way*, 97.

21. Osgood, *Total Cold War*, 262.

22. Szasz, "1958/59 Comic Book," 857. The Abraham Lincoln Presidential Library has copies of all the above translations with the distribution numbers penciled on the inside front cover. James Cornelius, the Lincoln curator, brought these to my attention.

23. Kim, *Abraham Lincoln*, ix–xi.

24. Spaeth, "Meet Jiang Zemin."

25. ALSC, *Abraham Lincoln*, 50, 100, 107, 110, 116, 121.

26. Ibid., 5.

27. "Honduras," *Lincoln Sesquicentennial Intelligencer* 1, no. 3 (1959), 4.

28. Bowman, *Militarization*, 149.

29. Ibid., 49.

30. Ibid., 160–62; Drake, *Between Tyranny and Anarchy*, 32; W. G. Williams, *Tragedy*, 14.

31. Tim Weiner, "F. Mark Wyatt, 86, C.I.A. Officer, Is Dead," *New York Times*, July 6, 2006, http://www.nytimes.com/2006/07/06/us/06wyatt.html?_r=0, accessed May 20, 2013.

32. "Italy," *Lincoln Sesquicentennial Intelligencer* 1, no. 3 (1959), 5.

33. Osgood, *Total Cold War*, 77.

34. Grambs, *Abraham Lincoln*, 39–44.

35. Belmonte, *Selling the American Way*, 155.

36. The five states without commissions were Alaska, Hawaii, Idaho, Nevada, and North Dakota. U.S. Civil War Centennial Commission, *Civil War Centennial*, 51.

37. Virginia Civil War Commission, *Civil War Centennial*, 2.

38. U.S. Civil War Centennial Commission, *Civil War Centennial*, 3.

39. Cook, *Troubled Commemoration*, 27.

40. U.S. Civil War Centennial Commission, *Guide*, 5, 14; U.S. Civil War Centennial Commission, *Civil War Centennial*, 58; Virginia Civil War Commission, *Civil War Centennial*, 2.

41. *Symbol and the Sword*, 53; Oedel, *Massachusetts*, 4:25–27; Hayner, *List of Materials*, 21–22; Higginbotham, Hunter, and Kent, *Pennsylvania*, 19.

42. Maryland Civil War Centennial Commission, *Centennial Anniversary*, 46; Delaware Civil War Centennial Commission, *Final Report*, 6.

43. Proctor, *Florida Commemorates*, 2.

44. Cook, *Troubled Commemoration*, 204.

45. Sundquist, *King's Dream*, 64.

46. Simon, *Gettysburg*, ix, 1, 5.

47. Cook, *Troubled Commemoration*, 88–90. The other fairly comprehensive overview of this crisis is Ellis, *Steps in a Journey*.

48. Cook, *Troubled Commemoration*, 13; "Civil War Parley Bows to Kennedy," *New York Times*, March 26, 1961, 1.

49. Wiener, "Civil War," 240.

50. Fried, *Russians Are Coming*, 130.

51. Wiener, "Civil War," 238, 248.

52. Simon, *Gettysburg*, 5–6.

53. Cook, *Troubled Commemoration*, 131–43.

54. "Long-Time Civil War Buff of Danville Named Centennial Commission Director," *Danville (VA) Register*, December 5, 1961, 1.

55. Cook, *Troubled Commemoration*, 150–53.

56. Allan Nevins to James I. Robertson Jr., January 2, 1963, folder "Lincoln and the Gettysburg Address Correspondence," box 85, "Subject Correspondence," Nevins Papers.

57. Cook, *Troubled Commemoration*, 222.

58. James I. Robertson Jr. to Allan Nevins, February 2, 1968, folder "Civil War Centennial Commission," box 88, "Civil War Centennial Commission," Nevins Papers.

59. "Good Taste, Restraint Urged for Centennial Observance at Gettysburg by Shrine Speaker," *Gettysburg (PA) Times*, January 10, 1963, 1–2.

60. Neff, *Honoring*, 5.

61. "Good Taste, Restraint Urged For Centennial Observance at Gettysburg by Shrine Speaker," *Gettysburg (PA) Times*, January 10, 1963, 1–2.

62. James I. Robertson Jr. to Allan Nevins, January 11, 1963, folder "Permanent Folder," box 88, "Civil War Centennial Commission," Nevins Papers.

63. Simon, *Gettysburg*, 42–43.

64. James I. Robertson Jr. to Allan Nevins, February 20, 1963, folder "Miscellaneous Correspondence," box 88, "Civil War Centennial Commission," Nevins Papers.

65. Caro, *Passage of Power*, 255, 257.

66. Johnson, "Remarks at Gettysburg."

67. Simon, *Gettysburg*, 20–21.

68. "Negroes Liberty Held 'Unfinished,'" *New York Times*, June 30, 1963, 39. Hesburgh served on the commission from 1957 to 1972.

69. Edith Evans Asbury, "Eisenhower Cites Perils to Liberty," *Gettysburg (PA) Times*, July 1, 1963, 17.

70. Simon, *Gettysburg*, 76–77, 82.

71. Edith Evans Asbury, "Hughes Charges Moral Failure to Aid Negroes since Civil War," *New York Times*, July 2, 1963, 14.

72. Sundquist, *King's Dream*, 143.

73. Sandage, "Marble House Divided," 146–47.

74. Sundquist, *King's Dream*, 147.

75. Farmer quoted in Sandage, "Marble House Divided," 150.

76. K. D. Miller, "Voice Merging and Self-Making," 24.

77. Sandage, "Marble House Divided," 157.

78. Martin Luther King Jr., "Call for a Prayer Pilgrimage for Freedom," *Papers*, 4:153.

79. "Powhatan Has First School Integration," *Richmond (VA) News Leader*, August 29, 1963, 1.

80. Simon, *Gettysburg*, 42–43, 45–46.

81. "'Lincoln Is World-Wide Symbol of Freedom' Declares Secretary of State," *Gettysburg (PA) Times*, November 18, 1963, 1.

82. Simon, *Gettysburg*, 49.

83. Ibid., 103–5.

84. J. E. Chadwick to Milton Baker, November 23, 1963, "Civil War Centennial, Adams County," Vertical Files, Adams County Historical Society.

85. Simon, *Gettysburg*, 100–102.

86. "Official Program of the 100th Anniversary of Lincoln's Gettysburg Address, November 17–19, 1963," "Gettysburg Address, Anniversaries," Vertical Files, Adams County Historical Society.

87. Simon, *Gettysburg*, 49, 95-96.

88. Ibid.

89. "'Lincoln Is World-Wide Symbol,'" 1, 7.

90. Howard Hoffer, "Centennial Discord," *Gettysburgian* (Gettysburg, Pennsylvania), November 22, 1963, 2–3.

91. Blight, "Theft of Lincoln," 269.

92. "'Lincoln Is World-Wide Symbol,'" 7.

93. "War Justified in 'Address' Here in 1863, Speaker Says," *Gettysburg (PA) Times*, November 18, 1963, 1, 8. Gettysburg College has sponsored the annual Fortenbaugh lecture since 1962. Coinciding with the anniversary of Lincoln's Gettysburg Address, the lecture is named after Robert Fortenbaugh, professor of history at Gettysburg College from 1923 until his passing in 1959. "Fortenbaugh Lecture."

94. "If A. Lincoln Were Speaking Here Today," *Gettysburg (PA) Times*, November 19, 1963, 1, 8. On MacLeish, see Cull, *Cold War*, 24.

95. Nevins, *War for the Union*, 3:449–50.

96. Simon, *Gettysburg*, 105-6.

97. Ibid., 57, 106–11.

98. "Parade Moves in Same Route Taken in '63," *Gettysburg (PA) Times*, November 19, 1963, 1, 8.

99. Simon, *Gettysburg*, 57, 116–17.

100. Ibid., 118.

101. Ibid., 119–20.

102. Allan Nevins to Arthur Goodhart, November 21, 1963, folder "Lincoln and the Gettysburg Address Correspondence," box 85 "Subject Correspondence," Nevins Papers.

103. Nevins, *Lincoln and the Gettysburg Address*, preface, n.p.; Allan Nevins to James I. Robertson Jr., June 20, 1963, Allan Nevins to James I. Robertson, Jr., June 25, 1963, both in folder "Lincoln and the Gettysburg Address Correspondence," box 85, "Subject Correspondence," Nevins Papers.

104. "Amid One of the Worst Blizzards in Years," *100 Years After*, February 1964, 1. This was the monthly newsletter of the U.S. Civil War Centennial Commission.

105. Goodhart, "Lincoln and the Law," 39, 41, 48, 57, 69.

106. Dos Passos, "Lincoln," 18, 20, 33, 36–37; Lincoln, "Address to the New Jersey Senate," February 21, 1861, *CW*, 4:235.

107. Douglas, "Significance," 115.

108. Douglas, *In the Fullness*, 585.

109. Ibid., 6, 11.

110. ALSC, *Abraham Lincoln*, 182.

111. Reviews, folder "Lincoln and the Gettysburg Address Correspondence," box 85, "Subject Correspondence," Nevins Papers.

112. A work suggesting which texts were dominant for each era is Lerner, Nagai, and Rothman, *Molding the Good Citizen*, 159–61.

113. Canfield and Wilder, *Making of Modern America*, 316–17.

114. Muzzey, *History of Our Country*.

115. Wirth, *United States History*, 241.

116. Canfield and Wilder, *Making of Modern America*, 316–17.

117. Todd and Curti, *Rise of the American Nation* (1961), 397; Todd and Curti, *Rise of the American Nation* (1968), 566.

118. Bailey, *American Pageant* (1956), 438; Bailey, *American Pageant* (1979), 408.

119. Bragdon and McCutchen, *History of a Free People* (1954), ix; (1961), xii; (1964), xii.

120. Ibid. (1967), 60.

121. Dean, "'Who Controls,'" 322–25. For elementary schools, the book was Dingledine, Barksdale, and Nesbitt, *Virginia's History*; for middle schools, Simpkins, Hunnicutt, and Poole, *Virginia: History, Government, Geography*; and for high school, Hemphill, Schlegel, and Engelberg, *Cavalier Commonwealth*.

122. Dean, "'Who Controls,'" 328.

123. Simpkins, Hunnicutt, and Poole, *Virginia: History*, 401.

124. Dean, "'Who Controls,'" 329, 344, 348–49.

125. "Lincoln's Gettysburg Speech," *Illinois State Journal* (Springfield), November 17, 1879.

126. U.S. Civil War Centennial Commission, *Civil War Centennial*, 3.

Conclusion

1. Goodwin, *Team of Rivals*, 617; *Richmond (VA) Examiner*, November 28, 1863; Woollcott, *For Us the Living*, 9.

2. Blight, *Race and Reunion*, 4.

2. Bennett, "Was Lincoln a White-Supremacist?" 36.

3. Sandage, "Marble House Divided," 160.

4. Carter, *First Lady from Plains*, 253.

5. Daniel Flood to Daniel Boorstin, April 17, 1978, box B-26 "Gettysburg Address Exhibit," GNMPL; Louis B. Craig to Chet Harris, October 4, 1978, box B-27 "Gettysburg Address Exhibit," GNMPL.

6. N. Miller, "That Great and Gentle Soul," 206; Spaeth, "Meet Jiang Zemin"; Lew, *Universal Lincoln*, i.

7. Lal, "Defining a Legacy," 174.

8. De-min, "Standard," 231.

9. Deford, "Fenway Park Address."

10. Miller, "That Great and Gentle Soul," 208.

11. Timothy Williams, "Names of 2,801 Victims Read Aloud in Somber Ground Zero Ceremony," Associated Press, September 11, 2002; Boritt, *Gettysburg Gospel*, 206; Blight, "Theft of Lincoln," 270.

12. Sexton, "Projecting Lincoln," 288–89.

13. "Senator Obama's Announcement," *New York Times*, February 10, 2007, www.ny-times.com/2007/02/10/us/politics/110bama-text.html, accessed December 12, 2012.

14. "Obama's Victory Speech," *New York Times*, November 5, 2008, www.nytimes.com/2008/11/04/us/politics/04text-obama.html, accessed December 12, 2012.

15. "Obama's Speech in Tucson," *New York Times*, January 13, 2011, www.nytimes.com/interactive/2011/01/13/us/politics/20110113_OBAMA_ARIZONA.html, accessed December 12, 2012.

16. That is not to say that President Obama always gets his Lincoln references right. The history community has pounced on our current Illini president on more than one occasion when he has either misattributed a quote to Lincoln or manipulated Lincoln's words to his own end. One example comes from Obama's 2012 State of the Union address in which he said, "I'm a Democrat. But I believe what Republican Abraham Lincoln believed: That government should do for people only what they cannot do better by themselves, and no more." In fact, the Lincoln quote Obama is paraphrasing is, "The legitimate object of government, is to do for a community of people, whatever they need to have done, but can not do, at all, or can not, so well do, for themselves—in their separate, and individual capacities. In all that the people can individually do as well for themselves, government ought not to interfere." "Fragment on Government," [July 1, 1854?], *CW*, 2:220–21.

17. Andrew Higgins, "European Officials Accept Union's Nobel Peace Prize," *New York Times*, December 10, 2012, www.nytimes.com/2012/12/11/world/europe/european-union-officials-accept-nobel-peace-prize.html, accessed December 12, 2012.

Bibliography

Abraham Lincoln Presidential Library, Springfield, Illinois.

Abraham Lincoln Sesquicentennial Commission. *Abraham Lincoln Sesquicentennial, 1959–1960: Final Report of the Lincoln Sesquicentennial Commission*. Washington, DC: GPO, 1960.

Adams County Historical Society, Gettysburg, Pennsylvania.

Andrews, J. Cutler. *The North Reports the Civil War*. Pittsburgh: University of Pittsburgh Press, 1955.

———. "The Pennsylvania Press during the Civil War." *Pennsylvania History* 9 (January 1942): 22–36.

———. *The South Reports the Civil War*. Princeton: Princeton University Press, 1970.

Andrews, Mary Raymond Shipman. "The Perfect Tribute." *Scribner's Magazine*, July 1906, 17–24.

Angle, Paul. *"Here I Have Lived": A History of Lincoln's Springfield, 1821–1865*. Springfield, IL: Abraham Lincoln Association, 1935.

"Applause at Gettysburg." *Lincoln Lore*, 762, November 15, 1943, 1.

Armitage, David. *The Declaration of Independence: A Global History*. Cambridge, MA: Harvard University Press, 2007.

Ayers, Linda. "'Their Unfailing Friend': Edward Everett and the Mount Vernon Ladies' Association." Paper presented at the Annual George Washington Symposium, Mount Vernon, Virginia, November 8, 2003.

Bacon, G. W. *The Life and Administration of Abraham Lincoln*. London: S. Low, Son, and Marston, 1865.

Bailey, Thomas. *The American Pageant: A History of the Republic*. 1956. Rev. ed. Boston: Heath, 1979.

Bankston, Carl L., III, and Stephen J. Caldas. *Public Education: America's Civil Religion*. New York: Teachers College Press, 2009.

Bartlett, Irving H. "Edward Everett Reconsidered." *New England Quarterly* 69 (September 1996): 426–60.

Bartlett, John Russell. *The Soldiers' National Cemetery at Gettysburg: With the Proceedings at Its Consecration, at the Laying of the Corner-Stone of the Monument, and at Its Dedication*. Providence, RI: Board of Commissioners of the Soldiers' National Cemetery, 1874.

Barton, William E. *Lincoln at Gettysburg: What He Intended to Say; What He Said; What He Was Reported to Have Said; What He Wished He Had Said*. Indianapolis: Bobbs-Merrill, 1930. Reprint, New York: Peter Smith, 1950. Citations are to the 1950 edition.

———. Papers. Lincoln Collection, Special Collections Research Center, University of Chicago, Chicago.

Belmonte, Laura A. *Selling the American Way: U.S. Propaganda and the Cold War.* Philadelphia: University of Pennsylvania Press, 2008.

Bennett, Lerone, Jr. "Was Lincoln a White-Supremacist?" *Ebony,* February 1968, 35–42.

Biagini, Eugenio F. "'The Principle of Humanity': Lincoln in Germany and Italy, 1859–1865." In Carwardine and Sexton, *Global Lincoln,* 76–94.

Blackett, R. J. M. *Divided Hearts: Britain and the American Civil War.* Baton Rouge: Louisiana State University Press, 2000.

Blakey, George T. *Historians on the Homefront: American Propagandists for the Great War.* Lexington: University Press of Kentucky, 1970.

Blight, David. *American Oracle: The Civil War in the Civil Rights Era.* Cambridge, MA: Belknap Press, 2011.

———. *Race and Reunion: The Civil War in American Memory.* Cambridge, MA: Belknap Press, 2001.

———. "The Theft of Lincoln in Scholarship, Politics, and Public Memory." In *Our Lincoln: New Perspectives on Lincoln and His World,* edited by Eric Foner, 269–82. New York: Norton, 2008.

Blum, Herman. *The Beacon That Was Lit at Gettysburg: Words That Live and Grow.* Philadelphia: privately printed, 1964.

Bodnar, John. *Remaking America: Public Memory, Commemoration, and Patriotism in the Twentieth Century.* Princeton: Princeton University Press, 1992.

Boos, John. *A Speech That Became Immortal.* Albany, NY: privately printed, 1936.

Boritt, Gabor. "Did He Dream of a Lily-White America? The Voyage to Linconia." In *The Lincoln Enigma: The Changing Faces of An American Icon,* edited by Boritt, 1–19. New York: Oxford University Press, 2001.

———. *The Gettysburg Gospel: The Lincoln Speech That Nobody Knows.* New York: Simon and Schuster, 2006.

Bowman, Kirk. *Militarization, Democracy, and Development: The Perils of Praetorianism in Latin America.* University Park: Pennsylvania State University Press, 2002.

Bradsby, H. C. *1886 History of Adams County, Pennsylvania: Containing History of Their Counties, Their Townships, Towns, Villages, Schools, Churches, Industries, etc.; Portraits of Early Settlers and Prominent Men; Biographies.* Chicago: Warner, Beers, 1886.

Bragdon, Henry W., and Samuel P. McCutchen. *History of a Free People.* New York: Macmillan, 1954, 1961, 1964, 1967.

Brann, Eva. "A Reading of the Gettysburg Address." In *Abraham Lincoln, The Gettysburg Address, and American Constitutionalism,* edited by Leo Paul S. de Alvarez, 15–54. Irving, TX: University of Dallas Press, 1976.

Breeskin, Adelyn D. *William H. Johnson, 1901–1970.* Washington, DC: Smithsonian Institution Press, 1971.

Bridges, Peter. *Pen of Fire: John Moncure Daniel.* Kent, OH: Kent State University Press, 2002.

Brooks, Noah. "Glimpses of Lincoln in War Time." *Century Magazine,* January 1895, 457–67.

———. "Personal Reminiscences of Abraham Lincoln." *Scribner's Monthly,* February 1878, 561–69.

Brooks, Phillips. *The Life and Death of Abraham Lincoln: A Sermon Preached at the Church of the Holy Trinity, Philadelphia, Sunday Morning, April 23, 1865.* Philadelphia: H. B. Ashmead, 1865.

Brown, Thomas. *The Public Art of Civil War Commemoration: A Brief History with Documents*. Boston: Bedford/St. Martin's, 2004.

Brundage, W. Fitzhugh. *Where These Memories Grow: History, Memory, and Southern Identity*. Chapel Hill: University of North Carolina Press, 2000.

Bryan, William Jennings. *Speeches of William Jennings Bryan*. Vol. 2. New York: Funk and Wagnalls, 1911.

Burlingame, Michael. *Abraham Lincoln: A Life*. Baltimore: Johns Hopkins University Press, 2008.

Campbell, Duncan Andrew. *English Public Opinion and the American Civil War*. Royal Historical Society Studies in History. Woodbridge, UK: Boydell, 2003.

Canfield, Leon H., and Howard B. Wilder. *The Making of Modern America*. Boston: Houghton Mifflin, 1952, 1962.

Carmichael, Orton. *Lincoln's Gettysburg Address*. New York: Abingdon, 1917.

Carnahan, D. T. *Oration on the Death of Abraham Lincoln, Sixteenth President of the United States, Delivered before the Citizens of Gettysburg, Pa., June 1, 1865*. Gettysburg, PA: Aughinbaugh and Wible, 1865.

Caro, Robert A. *The Passage of Power: The Years of Lyndon Johnson*. New York: Alfred A. Knopf, 2012.

Carr, Clark E. *Lincoln at Gettysburg: An Address*. Chicago: A. C. McClurg, 1906.

Carter, Rosalynn. *First Lady from Plains*. Boston: Houghton Mifflin, 1984.

Carwardine, Richard. *Lincoln: A Life of Purpose and Power*. New York: Alfred A. Knopf, 2006.

Carwardine, Richard, and Jay Sexton. *The Global Lincoln*. New York: Oxford University Press, 2011.

Charnwood, Lord. *Abraham Lincoln*. New York: Henry Holt, 1916.

Chesnut, Mary. *Mary Chesnut's Civil War*. Edited by C. Vann Woodward. New Haven: Yale University Press, 1981.

Churchill, Winston. *The Churchill War Papers*. Edited by Martin Gilbert. 10 vols. New York: Norton, 1993–.

Clinton, Catherine. *Mrs. Lincoln: A Life*. New York: Harper, 2009.

Concklin, Edward F. *The Lincoln Memorial, Washington*. Washington, DC: GPO, 1927.

Cook, Robert J. *Troubled Commemoration: The American Civil War Centennial, 1961–1965*. Baton Rouge: Louisiana State University Press, 2007.

Cull, Nicholas. *The Cold War and the United States Information Agency: American Propaganda and Public Diplomacy, 1945–1989*. Cambridge: Cambridge University Press, 2008.

Curzon, Earl George. *Modern Parliamentary Eloquence*. London: Macmillan, 1914.

Davis, Jefferson. *The Papers of Jefferson Davis*. Edited by Haskell M. Monroe Jr. and James T. McIntosh. 12 vols. Baton Rouge: Louisiana State University Press, 1971–present.

Dean, Adam Wesley. "'Who Controls the Past Controls the Future': The Virginia History Textbook Controversy." *Virginia Magazine of History and Biography* 117, no. 4 (2009): 319–55.

Deford, Frank. "Fenway Park Address." *Sports Illustrated*, October 13, 2004. http://sportsillustrated.cnn.com/2004/writers/frank_deford/10/13/fenway.park.

Delaware Civil War Centennial Commission. *Final Report of the Civil War Centennial Commission of the State of Delaware*. Dover: Delaware Civil War Centennial Commission, 1966.

De-min, Tao. "'A Standard of Our Thought and Action': Lincoln's Perception in East Asia." In Carwardine and Sexton, *Global Lincoln*, 223–41.

Dew, Charles B. *Apostles of Disunion: Southern Secession Commissioners and the Causes of the Civil War.* Charlottesville: University of Virginia Press, 2001.

Dibner, Bern. *The Atlantic Cable.* Norwalk, CT: Burndy Library, 1959.

Dingledine, Raymond C., Jr., Lena Barksdale, and Marion Belt Nesbit. *Virginia's History.* New York: Charles Scribner's Sons, 1956.

District of Columbia Civil War Centennial Commission. *The Symbol and the Sword.* Washington, DC: District of Columbia Civil War Centennial Commission, 1962.

Donald, David Herbert. *Lincoln.* New York: Touchstone, 1995.

———. *Lincoln Reconsidered: Essays on the Civil War Era.* New York: Knopf, 1956.

Dos Passos, John. "Lincoln and His Almost Chosen People." In Nevins, *Lincoln and the Gettysburg Address*, 15–37.

Douglas, Paul H. *In the Fullness of Time: The Memoirs of Paul H. Douglas.* New York: Harcourt Brace Jovanovich, 1971.

———. "The Significance of the Gettysburg Address." In Nevins, *Lincoln and the Gettysburg Address*, 93–117.

Douglass, Frederick. *The Frederick Douglass Papers: Series One.* Edited by John W. Blassingame, with the assistance of C. Peter Ripley, Lawrence N. Powell, Fiona E. Spiers, and Clarence L. Mohr. New Haven: Yale University Press, 1979–92.

Drake, Paul W. *Between Tyranny and Anarchy: A History of Democracy Latin America, 1800–2006.* Stanford: Stanford University Press, 2009.

DuBois, W. E. B. "Opinion of W. E. B. DuBois: The World and Us," *Crisis* 24, no. 3 (1922): 103–7.

Dudziak, Mary L. *Cold War Civil Rights: Race and the Image of American Democracy.* Princeton: Princeton University Press, 2000.

Educational Policies Commission. *Our Democracy.* Washington, DC: National Education Association of the United States, 1941.

Elias, Edith L. *Abraham Lincoln.* London: George G. Harrap, 1916.

Ellis, L. Ethan. *Steps in a Journey toward Understanding: Activities of the New Jersey Civil War Centennial Commission in 1961 at Trenton, Charleston, and Salem Church.* Trenton: New Jersey Civil War Centennial Commission, 1963.

Elmore, A. E. *Lincoln's Gettysburg Address: Echoes of the Bible and the Book of Common Prayer.* Carbondale: Southern Illinois University Press, 2009.

Evans, Marvin. "The Richmond Press on the Eve of the Civil War." *John P. Branch Historical Papers of Randolph-Macon College* 1 (January 1951): 5–54.

Everett, Lloyd T. "Davis, Lincoln, and the Kaiser." *Confederate Veteran* 25 (September 1917): 405–8.

Faust, Drew. *This Republic of Suffering: Death and the American Civil War.* New York: Vintage, 2008.

"Fortenbaugh Lecture." Civil War Institute. *Gettysburg College*, 2013. http://www.gettysburg.edu/cwi/events/fortenbaugh.

Fortenbaugh, Robert. "Lincoln as Gettysburg Saw Him." *Pennsylvania History* 14 (January 1947): 1–12.

Fried, Richard M. *The Russians Are Coming! The Russians Are Coming! Pageantry and Patriotism in Cold-War America.* New York: Oxford University Press, 1998.

Frothingham, Paul Revere, ed. *Edward Everett: Orator and Statesman.* Boston: Houghton Mifflin, 1925.

Funeral Observances at New London, Connecticut, in Honor of Abraham Lincoln, Sixteenth President of the United States, Wednesday, April 19, 1865, Including the Public Addresses of Rev. G. B. Willcox, and Rev. Thomas P. Field, D.D. New London, CT: Star and Farnham, 1865.

Gallagher, Gary. *The Union War.* Cambridge, MA: Harvard University Press, 2011.

Gannon, Barbara. *The Won Cause: Black and White Comradeship in the Grand Army of the Republic.* Chapel Hill: University of North Carolina Press, 2011.

George, Joseph, Jr. "The World Will Little Note? The Philadelphia Press and the Gettysburg Address." *Pennsylvania Magazine of History and Biography* 114 (July 1990): 385–98.

Gettysburg College Special Collections, Gettysburg, Pennsylvania.

Gettysburg National Military Park Commission. *Annual Reports of the Gettysburg National Military Park Commission to the Secretary of War.* Washington, DC: GPO, 1913.

Gettysburg National Military Park Library, Gettysburg, Pennsylvania.

Gettysburg Speech and Other Papers by Abraham Lincoln and an Essay on Lincoln by James Russell Lowell, The. Riverside Literature Series 32. Boston: Houghton Mifflin, January 1888.

Gilbert, Joseph I. "Lincoln in 1861." *Proceedings of the National Shorthand Reporters' Association Annual Meeting* 19 (1917): 131–40.

Giordano, Gerard. *Twentieth Century Textbook Wars: A History of Advocacy and Opposition.* New York: Peter Lang, 2003.

Goldfield, David. "Lincoln's Image in the American Schoolbook." *American Studies Journal* 53 (2009). http://asjournal.zusas.uni-halle.de/166.html.

Goodhart, Arthur Lehman. "Lincoln and the Law." In Nevins, *Lincoln and the Gettysburg Address*, 38–71.

Goodman, Matthew. *The Sun and the Moon: The Remarkable True Account of Hoaxers, Showmen, Dueling Journalists, and Lunar Man-Bats in Nineteenth Century New York.* New York: Basic Books, 2008.

Goodwin, Doris Kearns. *Team of Rivals: The Political Genius of Abraham Lincoln.* New York: Simon and Schuster, 2005.

Gorgas, Josiah. *The Civil War Diary of General Josiah Gorgas.* Edited by Frank E. Vandiver. Tuscaloosa: University of Alabama Press, 1947.

Grambs, Jean D., ed. *Abraham Lincoln through the Eyes of High School Youth.* Washington, DC: Lincoln Sesquicentennial Commission, 1959.

Harris, Brayton. *Blue & Gray in Black & White: Newspapers in the Civil War.* Washington, DC: Brassey's, 1999.

Hart, Albert Bushnell. *School History of the United States.* New York: American Book, 1918.

Hay, John. *Inside Lincoln's White House: The Complete Civil War Diary of John Hay.* Edited by Michael Burlingame and John R. Turner Ettlinger. Carbondale: Southern Illinois University Press, 1999.

Hayner, C. Irene. *A List of Materials on the Civil War Recommended for Use in Schools of Michigan.* Lansing: Michigan Civil War Centennial Commission, 1964.

Hearn, Chester. *When the Devil Came Down to Dixie: Ben Butler in New Orleans.* Baton Rouge: Louisiana State University Press, 1997.

Heckman, Richard Allen. "British Press Reaction to the Emancipation Proclamation." *Lincoln Herald* 71 (Winter 1969): 150–53.

Hemphill, William Edwin, Marvin Wilson Schlegel, and Sadie Ethel Engelberg. *Cavalier Commonwealth: History and Government of Virginia*. New York: Mc-Graw-Hill, 1957.

Higginbotham, Sanford W., William A. Hunter, and Donald H. Kent. *Pennsylvania and the Civil War: A Handbook*. Harrisburg: Pennsylvania Historical and Museum Commission, 1961.

Hofstadter, Richard. *The American Political Tradition: And the Men Who Made It*. New York: Random House, 1948.

Hoganson, Kristin. *Fighting for American Manhood: How Gender Politics Provoked the Spanish-American and Philippine-American War*. New Haven: Yale University Press, 1998.

Holzer, Harold. *Dear Mr. Lincoln: Letters to the President*. Carbondale: Southern Illinois University Press, 2006.

———. *The Lincoln Anthology: Great Writers on His Life and Legacy from 1860 to Now*. New York: Library of America, 2009.

———. "'Thrilling Words' or 'Silly Remarks': What the Press Said about the Gettysburg Address." *Lincoln Herald* 90 (Winter 1998): 144–45.

Jacobs, Henry Eyster. *Lincoln's Gettysburg World-Message*. Philadelphia: United Lutheran, 1919.

———. *Memoirs of Henry Eyster Jacobs*. Edited by Henry E. Horn. Gettysburg, PA: Adams County Historical Society, 1974.

Janney, Caroline E. *Burying the Dead but Not the Past: Ladies' Memorial Associations & the Lost Cause*. Chapel Hill: University of North Carolina Press, 2008.

Johnson, Lyndon Baines. "Remarks at Gettysburg on Civil Rights, May 30, 1963." *Miller Center, University of Virginia*. http://millercenter.org/president/speeches/detail/3380.

Jones, Howard. *Blue & Gray Diplomacy: A History of Union and Confederate Foreign Relations*. Chapel Hill: University of North Carolina Press, 2010.

Jones, J. William. *School History of the United States*. Baltimore: R. H. Woodward, 1896.

Jones, John B. *A Rebel War Clerk's Diary at the Confederate States Capitol*. Philadelphia: J. B. Lippincott, 1866.

Kachun, Mitch. *Festivals of Freedom: Memory and Meaning in African American Emancipation Celebrations, 1808–1915*. Amherst: University of Massachusetts Press, 2003.

Katula, Richard. "The Gettysburg Address as the Centerpiece of American Racial Discourse." *Journal of Blacks in Higher Education* 28 (Summer 2000): 110–11.

Kenny, Kevin. "'Freedom and Unity': Lincoln in Irish Political Discourse." In Carwardine and Sexton, *Global Lincoln*, 155–71.

Kim, Donggill. *Abraham Lincoln: An Oriental Interpretation*. Seoul, Korea: Jungwoo-sa, 1983.

King, Martin Luther, Jr. *The Papers of Martin Luther King, Jr.* Edited by Clayborne Carson, Peter Holloran, Ralph Luker, and Penny A. Russell. 6 vols. Berkeley: University of California Press, 1992.

Klein, Frederic. *History of the Lincoln Fellowship of Pennsylvania: Organized in 1938 to Commemorate the Anniversary of Abraham Lincoln's Gettysburg Address, November 19, 1863*. Gettysburg, PA: Lincoln Fellowship, 1963.

Kunhardt, Philip B., Jr. *A New Birth of Freedom: Lincoln at Gettysburg*. Boston: Little, Brown, 1983.

Lal, Vinay. "Defining a Legacy: Lincoln in the National Imaginary of India." In Carwardine and Sexton, *Global Lincoln*, 172–88.

Lamon, Ward Hill. *Life of Abraham Lincoln*. Boston: J. R. Osgood, 1872.

Latané, John Holladay. *A History of the United States*. Boston: Allyn and Bacon, 1918.

Lease, Mary. "Wall Street Owns the Country." In Zinn and Arnove, *Voices of a People's History*, 226.

Lee, Susan Pendleton. *New School History of the United States*. Rev. ed. 1899; reprint, Richmond, VA: B. F. Johnson, 1900. Citations are to the 1900 edition.

Lerner, Robert, Althea K. Nagai, and Stanley Rothman. *Molding the Good Citizen: The Politics of High School History Texts*. Westport, CT: Praeger, 1995.

Lew, Yu-Tang D. "Lincoln and Human Rights." In Lew, *Universal Lincoln*, 87–110.

———, ed. *The Universal Lincoln*. Taipei: Chinese Culture University Press, 1995.

Lincoln, Abraham. *Abraham Lincoln: First and Second Inaugural Addresses; Message July 5, 1861; Proclamation, January 1, 1863; Gettysburg Address, November 19, 1863*. Washington, DC: GPO, 1909.

———. *The Collected Works of Abraham Lincoln*. Edited by Roy P. Basler. 9 vols. New Brunswick, NJ: Rutgers University Press, 1953–55.

———. *Lincoln's Gettysburg Speech*. Parker's Lessons in Literature. Taylorville, IL: Parker, 1889.

———. Papers. Library of Congress, Washington, DC.

———. *Speeches by Lincoln*. Little Classic Series. Chicago: A. Flanagan, 1906.

Magness, Phillip W., and Sebastian N. Page. *Colonization after Emancipation: Lincoln and the Movement for Black Resettlement*. Columbia: University of Missouri Press, 2011.

Manning, Chandra. *What This Cruel War Was Over: Soldiers, Slavery, and the Civil War*. New York: Alfred A. Knopf, 2007.

Maryland Civil War Centennial Commission. *The Centennial Anniversary of the Civil War: Maryland's Observances*. Hagerstown: Maryland Civil War Centennial Commission, 1964.

Massachusetts Historical Society. *Edward Everett at Gettysburg*. Boston: Massachusetts Historical Society, 1963.

McClintock, John. *Discourse Delivered on the Day of the Funeral of President Lincoln, Wednesday, April 19, 1865, in St. Paul's Church, New York*. New York: J. M. Bradstreet and Son, 1865.

McCurdy, Charles. *Gettysburg: A Memoir*. Pittsburgh: Reed and Whitting, 1929.

McGregor, A. Laura. *Living Democracy in Secondary Schools*. Washington, DC: U.S. Office of Education, 1941.

McGuire, Judith W. *Diary of a Southern Refugee during the War*. New York: E. J. Hale and Son, 1867.

McKay, Ernest A. *The Civil War and New York City*. Syracuse, NY: Syracuse University Press, 1990.

McMurtry, R. Gerald. "The Perfect Tribute." *Lincoln Herald* 45 (June 1943): 28–29.

Mearns, David. "Unknown at This Address." In Nevins, *Lincoln and the Gettysburg Address*, 118–33.

Michigan State Superintendent of Public Education. *Lincoln at Gettysburg*. Bulletin no. 55. Lansing, MI: Michigan Department of Public Instruction, 1915.

Miers, Earl Schenck, ed. *Lincoln Day by Day: A Chronology, 1809–1865*. Washington, DC: Lincoln Sesquicentennial Commission, 1960.

Miller, Keith D. "Voice Merging and Self-Making: The Epistemology of 'I Have a Dream.'" *Rhetoric Society Quarterly* 19 (Winter 1989): 23–31.

Miller, Nicola. "'That Great and Gentle Soul': Images of Lincoln in Latin America." In Carwardine and Sexton, *Global Lincoln*, 206–22.

Minnigh, Luther W. *Gettysburg: "What They Did Here . . ." Historical Guide Book.* Mount Holly Springs, PA: Mount Holly Stationery, 1892.

Mitgang, Herbert. "Friend of a Free Press." In Lew, *Universal Lincoln*, 231–41.

Monaghan, Jay. "Lincoln's Debt to the British." *Lincoln Herald* 47 (June 1945): 36–40.

Mondale, Sarah, and Sarah Patton. *School: The Story of American Public Education.* Boston: Beacon Press, 2001.

Monroe, Dan. "Lincoln the Dwarf: Lyon Gardiner Tyler's War on the Mythical Lincoln." *Journal of the Abraham Lincoln Association* 24 (Winter 2003): 32–42.

Mumford, Lewis. *Sticks and Stones: A Study of American Architecture.* New York: Boni and Liveright, 1924.

Muzzey, David Saville. *A History of Our Country.* Boston: Ginn, 1952.

Nagler, Jörg. "Abraham Lincoln's Image and Reception in Germany." Paper presented at Lincoln Bicentennial Conference, American University of Paris, Paris, France, October 18, 2009.

———. "National Unity and Liberty: Lincoln's Image and Reception in Germany, 1871–1989." In Carwardine and Sexton, *Global Lincoln*, 242–58.

Nast, Thomas. "Death at the Polls and Free from All 'Federal Interference.'" *Harper's Weekly*, October 18, 1879, 1.

National Council for Social Studies. *The Social Studies Mobilize for Victory: A Statement of Wartime Policy Adopted by the National Council for the Social Studies, November 28, 1942.* Washington, DC: National Council for Social Studies, 1942.

Neely, Mark E., Jr. *The Abraham Lincoln Encyclopedia.* New York: Da Capo, 1982.

Neff, John R. *Honoring the Civil War Dead: Commemoration and the Problem of Reconciliation.* Lawrence: University Press of Kansas, 2005.

Nevins, Allan, ed. *Lincoln and the Gettysburg Address: Commemorative Papers.* Urbana: University of Illinois Press, 1964.

———. Papers. Columbia University Rare Book and Manuscript Library, New York.

———. *The War for the Union: The Organized War 1863–1864.* Vol. 3. New York: Charles Scribner's Sons, 1971.

Nicolay, John G. "Lincoln's Gettysburg Address." *Century Magazine*, February 1894, 596–608.

Nora, Pierre. "General Introduction: Between History and Memory." In *Realms of Memory: Rethinking the French Past*, 1:1–20. Translated by Arthur Goldhammer. New York: Columbia University Press, 1996.

Oedel, Howard. *Massachusetts in the Civil War.* Vol. 4. *A Year of Dedications, 1863–1864.* Boston: Massachusetts Civil War Centennial Commission, 1964.

Osgood, Kenneth. *Total Cold War: Eisenhower's Secret Propaganda Battle at Home and Abroad.* Lawrence: University Press of Kansas, 2006.

Paradis, James M. *African Americans and the Gettysburg Campaign.* Plymouth, UK: Scarecrow Press, 2013.

Parker, Theodore. *The Collected Works of Theodore Parker.* Edited by Frances Power Cobbe. 12 vols. London: Trübner, 1863–65.

Pepper, George Wharton. "Abraham Lincoln and the Issues of the World War." *Saturday Evening Post*, May 5, 1917.

Petersen, Svend. *The Gettysburg Addresses: The Story of Two Orations*. New York: Frederick Ungar, 1963.

Peterson, Merrill. *Lincoln in American Memory*. New York: Oxford University Press, 1994.

Powell, Richard J. *Homecoming: The Art and Life of William H. Johnson*. Washington, DC: Smithsonian Institution Press, 1991.

Proctor, Samuel. *Florida Commemorates the Civil War Centennial, 1961–1965: A Manual for the Observance of the Civil War in the Counties and Cities of the State of Florida*. Coral Gables: Florida Civil War Centennial Commission, 1962.

Reid, Ronald F. "Newspaper Responses to the Gettysburg Addresses." *Quarterly Journal of Speech* 53 (February 1967): 50–60.

Report of the General Agent of the State of New York for the Relief of Sick, Wounded, Furloughed and Discharged Soldiers. Albany, NY: Comstock and Cassidy, 1864.

Revised Report of the Select Committee Relative to the Soldiers' National Cemetery Together with the House of Representatives and the Commonwealth of Pennsylvania. Harrisburg, PA: Singerly and Myers, 1865.

Risley, Ford. "The Confederate Press Association: Cooperative News Reporting on the War." *Civil War History* 47 (September 2001): 222–39.

Robertson, Fred. "Historical Inaccuracies." *Confederate Veteran* 15 (June 1907): 284.

Roosevelt, Theodore. *Fear God and Take Your Own Part*. New York: George H. Doran, 1916.

Root, Elihu. *Men and Policies; Addresses by Elihu Root*. Edited by Robert Bacon and James Brown Scott. Cambridge, MA: Harvard University Press, 1925.

Rutherford, Mildred Lewis. *A Measuring Rod to Test Text Books, and Reference Books in Schools, Colleges and Libraries*. Athens, GA: United Confederate Veterans, 1919.

———. *The South Must Have Her Rightful Place in History*. Athens, GA: privately printed, 1923.

Sandage, Scott A. "A Marble House Divided: The Lincoln Memorial, the Civil Rights Movement, and the Politics of Memory, 1939–1963." *Journal of American History* 80 (June 1993): 135–67.

Sandburg, Carl. *Abraham Lincoln: The War Years*. New York: Charles Scribner's Sons, 1936.

Savage, Kirk. *Standing Soldiers, Kneeling Slaves: Race, War, and Monument in Nineteenth-Century America*. Princeton: Princeton University Press, 1997.

Schwartz, Barry. *Abraham Lincoln and the Forge of National Memory*. Chicago: University of Chicago Press, 2000.

———. *Abraham Lincoln in the Post-Heroic Era: History and Memory in Late Twentieth-Century America*. Chicago: University of Chicago Press, 2008.

———. "Collective Memory and History: How Abraham Lincoln Became a Symbol of Racial Equality." *Sociological Quarterly* 38, no. 3 (1997): 469–96.

———. "Memory as a Cultural System: Abraham Lincoln in World War II." *American Sociological Review* 61 (October 1996): 908–27.

Schwarzlose, Richard A. *Newspapers: A Reference Guide*. New York: Greenwood Press, 1987.

Seager, Robert, II. *And Tyler Too: A Biography of John & Julia Gardiner Tyler*. New York: McGraw-Hill, 1963.

Sexton, Jay. *The Monroe Doctrine: Empire and Nation in Nineteenth Century America*. New York: Hill and Wang, 2011.

———. "Projecting Lincoln, Projecting America." In Carwardine and Sexton, *Global Lincoln*, 288–302.

Simon, Louis M., ed. *Gettysburg—1963: An Account of the Centennial Commemoration.* Harrisburg: Commonwealth of Pennsylvania, 1964.

Simpkins, Francis Butler, Spotswood Hunnicutt, and Sidman P. Poole. *Virginia: History, Government, Geography.* New York: Charles Scribner's Sons, 1957.

Skelly, Daniel. *A Boy's Experiences during the Battles of Gettysburg.* Gettysburg, PA: privately printed, 1932.

Smith, Adam I. P. "'The Stuff Our Dreams Are Made Of': Lincoln in the English Imagination." In Carwardine and Sexton, *Global Lincoln,* 123–38.

Spaeth, Anthony. "Meet Jiang Zemin." *Time,* June 24, 2001. http://www.time.com/time/magazine/article/0,9171,987239,00.html.

Stephens, Alexander H. "'Cornerstone Speech': March 21, 1861, Savannah, Georgia." *Teachingamericanhistory.org.* http://teachingamericanhistory.org/library/document/corner-stone-speech-excerpt/.

Sumner, Charles. *Charles Sumner His Complete Works.* 20 vols. Boston: Lee and Shepard, 1900.

Sundquist, Eric. *King's Dream.* New Haven: Yale University Press, 2009.

Szasz, Ferenc Morton. "The 1958/59 Comic Book Biographies of Abraham Lincoln." *Journal of Popular Culture* 43, no. 4 (2010): 842–59.

Tarbell, Ida M. *The Early Life of Abraham Lincoln.* London: S. S. McClure, 1896.

Thomas, Christopher A. *The Lincoln Memorial & American Life.* Princeton: Princeton University Press, 2002.

Todd, Lewis Paul, and Merle Curti, *Rise of the American Nation.* New York: Harcourt, Brace, 1961, 1968.

Turner, Justin G., and Linda Levitt Turner. *Mary Todd Lincoln: Her Life and Letters.* New York: Alfred A. Knopf, 1972.

Tyler, Lyon G. "John Moncure Daniel." In *Encyclopedia of Virginia Biography.* New York: Lewis Historical, 1915.

———. "The South and Germany." *William and Mary College Quarterly Historical Magazine* 26 (July 1917): 1–20.

U.S. Bureau of the Census. *Fourteenth Census of the United States, 1920.* Vol. 3: *Population.* Washington, DC: GPO, 1922.

U.S. Civil War Centennial Commission. *The Civil War Centennial: A Report to the Congress.* Washington, DC: GPO, 1968.

———. *Guide for the Observance of the Centennial of the Civil War.* Washington, DC: GPO, 1959.

Virginia Civil War Commission. *Civil War Centennial/1961–65. Final Report: 1965—Virginia Civil War Commission.* Richmond: Virginia Civil War Commission, 1965.

Virginia Historical Society, Richmond, Virginia.

Von Eschen, Penny M. "Who's the Real Ambassador? Exploding Cold War Racial Ideology." In *Cold War Constructions: The Political Culture of United States Imperialism, 1945–1966,* edited by Christian Appy, 110–31. Amherst: University of Massachusetts Press, 2000.

Waldstreicher, David. *Slavery's Constitution: From Revolution to Ratification.* New York: Hill and Wang, 2009.

Warren, Louis A. *Lincoln's Gettysburg Declaration: "A New Birth of Freedom."* Fort Wayne, IN: Lincoln National Life Foundation, 1964.

Warren, Robert Penn. *The Legacy of the Civil War: Meditations in the Centennial.* New York: Random House, 1961.

Washington, Booker T. *Up from Slavery*. Boston: Bedford/St. Martin's, 2003.

Webster, Daniel. *The Great Speeches and Orations of Daniel Webster*. Edited by Edwin Whipple. Boston: Little, Brown, 1889.

Weeks, Jim. *Gettysburg: Memory, Market, and an American Shrine*. Princeton: Princeton University Press, 2009.

Wesley, Edgar B. *NEA: The First Hundred Years, the Building of the Teaching Profession*. New York: Harper and Brothers, 1957.

Westwood, Howard C. "The Audience for the Gettysburg Address." *Lincoln Herald* 84 (Fall 1982): 136–40.

Wiener, Jon. "Civil War, Cold War, Civil Rights: The Civil War Centennial in Context, 1960–1965." In *The Memory of the Civil War in American Culture*, edited by Alice Fahs and Joan Waugh, 237–57. Chapel Hill: University of North Carolina Press, 2004.

Williams, George Washington. *History of the Negro Race in America from 1619 to 1880*. New York: G. P. Putnam's Sons, 1882.

Williams, William G. *The Tragedy of American Diplomacy*. Cleveland: World, 1959.

Wills, Gary. *Lincoln at Gettysburg: The Words That Remade America*. New York: Simon and Schuster, 1992.

Wilson, Douglas L. "Lincoln's Declaration." In *Lincoln before Washington: New Perspectives on the Illinois Years*, 166–81. Urbana: University of Illinois Press, 1997.

———. *Lincoln's Sword: The Presidency and the Power of Words*. New York: Alfred A. Knopf, 2007.

Wilson, Edmund. *Patriotic Gore: Studies in the Literature of the American Civil War*. New York: Oxford University Press, 1962.

Wilson, Woodrow. *History of the American People*. New York: Harper and Brothers, 1918.

———. *The Papers of Woodrow Wilson*. Edited by Arthur S. Link. 69 vols. Princeton: Princeton University Press, 1966–94.

Wirth, Fremont P. *United States History*. Rev. ed. New York: American Book, 1955.

Wongsrichanalai, Kid. "Mr. Stahle's Lincoln: The *Gettysburg Compiler*'s Reactions to the Presidency of Abraham Lincoln." Senior seminar paper, Gettysburg College, Gettysburg, Pennsylvania, November 28, 2001.

Woollcott, Alexander. *For Us the Living*. Radio City, NY: Linguaphone Institute, 1941.

Wright, William C. *The Secession Movement in the Middle Atlantic States*. Cranbury, NJ: Associated University Press, 1973.

Zinn, Howard, and Anthony Arnove. *Voices of a People's History of the United States*. New York: Seven Stories Press, 2004.

Index

Jared Peatman is a leadership-development trainer, using historic metaphors ranging from the Alamo to Gettysburg to the Cuban Missile Crisis. In 2009, he was named the Organization of American Historians and Abraham Lincoln Bicentennial Commission Doctoral Fellow, and in 2012, he received the Hay-Nicolay Dissertation Prize for the best work on Abraham Lincoln or the Civil War. He is an alumnus of Gettysburg College (BA), Virginia Tech (MA), and Texas A&M University (PhD).